Employability Skills for Healthcare Providers

By

Dr. Lisa Jenkins, PT, MPT, EdD

Dedication

Rooted in love for my profession, this textbook is dedicated to healthcare students, graduates, and educators for a better tomorrow.

Foreword

Surprisingly, research confirms that a great number of employers find that young graduates seeking jobs today lack the skills to be considered "employable". In the case of the medical field, while today's graduates may possess the basic technical prerequisites to get hired, all too often these job seekers are deficient in such basic skills as communication, the ability to work collaboratively as a team, proper attire, and the ability to "think on their feet."

After more than 24 years as a physical therapist, business owner, and now educator, Lisa Jenkins, has worked with hundreds of DPT students as they seek employment after graduation. She has witnessed their disappointment – and, quite frankly shock, as they are told they lack the basics of employability skills. "I have worked so hard in school; I have a graduate degree, why is it so hard to get a job?" Lisa has heard these sentiments from frustrated and disappointed former students too many times to count.

Where is the disconnect? Are today's universities falling short with relevant curriculum? Have young people today been isolated and protected from the harsh realities of the real-world experience? Have companies been unclear on their workforce wants and needs? Is social media to blame? The answer to these questions likely is "yes" to all and more.

With years of practical classroom experience and having received feedback from hundreds of physical therapy companies, Lisa decided to prove what she sensed: Today's PT graduates need to be taught the basics of employability skills.

With this goal, she devoted hundreds of hours of research on employability skills. The result of her efforts is the creation of this textbook: Employability Skills for Healthcare Providers. This easy-to-read book is for students and educators. The book's chapters build upon themselves. The research – the lack of employability skills as seen by employers – is laid bare. Employability skills are defined and taught. And, finally, the book creates the framework, or the critical steps, young graduates must take to get a job.

For educators, this book is a primer for how to insert employability skills into the classroom. Each of this textbook's 13 chapters includes with assignments and activities the instructor can use to ensure the lessons are taught and are being absorbed by students. Many of the exercises are interactive; some are introspective, and most require the students and their instructor to benefit by learning more about themselves as human beings.

This textbook is not "rocket science" and isn't intended to be. After all, communication is a rather basic need. However, proper communication is a skill that must be learned, practiced, evaluated, and adapted with changing times and experience. Just because we can speak a language, doesn't mean we are communicating. And just because I have a degree, it doesn't mean I can get a job. So,says the research – clearly and unequivocally.

Lisa Jenkins is ultimately qualified to author this textbook. She currently is an assistant professor of physical therapy at the University of St. Augustine for Health Sciences, in Miami, Florida. Prior to joining the university's faculty more than seven years ago, she owned and operated her own business that focused on providing Continuing Education Credits (CEUs) to physical, occupational, and speech therapists with an emphasis on insurance documentation and federal reimbursement to rehabilitation companies. She has 24 years of experience as a practicing physical therapist, both as a company employee and business owner. She has her Educational Doctorate degree and Master of Physical Therapy degree from the University of St. Augustine for Health Sciences, in St. Augustine, Florida. She also has a Bachelor of Business Administration and Marketing from Stetson University, in DeLand, Florida. She is a certified clinical instructor and has held previous certifications in Healthcare Compliance and as a Brain Injury Specialist.

David Byron is a former journalist, lead spokesperson for large local government, and manager of a department with seven divisions, more than 500 employees, and a budget of $75 million. He is a certified public relations counselor and a communicator with 48 years of written, oral and personnel experience.

Prologue

Hi, my name is Katie. I am a student in the Doctor of Physical Therapy program. I am in my second year and will head to the clinic soon to participate in my clinical experiences. I feel nervous about my clinical experiences. I had a part-job during my undergraduate education, helping other students access library resources. I also volunteered during two 5K races to raise money for breast cancer awareness. But, other than these experiences, I have never worked a "real job." I am scared that my clinical instructor will ask me questions I do not know how to answer. I would die if that happened to me before a patient. Oh, who am I kidding? I am not just nervous; I am scared. I hate it when I get scared, I start to sweat, and I just freeze up. Oh, no, what if I freeze up? Help!

While Katie is a fictional character, she represents a large portion of the students in healthcare education. Most of these students have gone from undergraduate to graduate studies. Many of them have not held a "real job." Another factor influencing this group of students is that they grew up using technology. Today's students are accustomed to communicating via technology and social media. They have been filled with excessive amounts of feedback over routine events. For example, Katie posts a picture of a fancy coffee drink she purchased en route to class, and before she arrives on campus, thirty-two of her closest friends have complimented Katie for drinking a fancy coffee. Is it good for Katie to receive this sort of feedback? Or has it conditioned her brain to a false reality?

Epigraph

"I don't care what you ate for breakfast.
I am concerned with your ability to provide competent, patient-centered care."

Introduction

Did you know that 44.7% of Doctor of Physical Therapy (DPT) students during their clinical experiences displayed deficits in their employability skills, especially communication? Deficiencies with employability skills are not isolated to physical therapy students. Issues have been reported with all healthcare students. Unfortunately, 89% of U.S. executives reported difficulty recruiting graduates with competent employability skills. This news is disheartening whether you are a healthcare student, graduate, or educator. How did we get so off track, and what can we do about it?

It seems that too much time has been allocated to mastering technical skills, and not enough time has been allotted to teaching employability or soft skills. Structured according to Bloom's revised taxonomy, this textbook explores the optimal format for teaching and learning employability skills. The activities are purposefully designed to enhance development and to achieve competence with employability skills.

As a core faculty member and Associate Director of Clinical Education in a Doctor of Physical Therapy program, I have seen these deficits first-hand. Accordingly, I have invested tremendous time in remediating these skills when students fall short during their clinical experiences. Having recognized the severity of the problem, I felt compelled to find a better solution to the employability skill crisis.

Acknowledgment

This author would like to thank the University of St. Augustine for Health Sciences, Educational Doctorate program. I would not have been propelled to this project without participating in this program. This textbook started as a quantitative research study. After many revisions, Drs. Crocker and Hidalgo explained that I was getting ahead of myself. My brain was actively pursuing a solution instead of testing my hypothesis. Dr. Aguilar helped me to find another vision for my dissertation. It was at that point that my research study became a textbook.

Writing a textbook has been a very enjoyable process. This writing style has allowed me to express myself in a manner that better represents my professional personality. Feedback from Drs. McCraney and Aguilar were both informative and encouraging. They challenged me to think at a higher cognitive level, which resulted in a better product. I would also like to acknowledge my father, David Byron, for his edits and suggestions. Our conversations brought a new level of objectivity to my writing. I appreciate the opportunity to step outside my comfort zone and grow.

Author Biography

Lisa Jenkins, Physical Therapist, has held previous certifications as a Certified Brain Injury Specialist (CBIS) and in Healthcare Compliance (CHC). She is recognized as an expert in her field as evidenced by being published in several industry-specific publications, including Topics in Geriatric Rehabilitation, Advance for Occupational Therapy Practitioners, The Journal on Active Aging, The New York Times, Rehab Management, Advance for Physical Therapists and PT Assistants, and Advance for Directors in Rehabilitation.

As a certified Clinical Instructor, Lisa has focused on educating others and sharing information in various settings through public speaking engagements, hands-on/modeling, educationally based in-services, and formal state board-approved education programs on a national level for over 24 years.

Lisa practiced clinically in skilled nursing facilities, home health, schools, and the outpatient setting. She has worked at regional and national levels, providing education and training to various healthcare providers. She also founded and ran her seven-year business focused on provider education, primarily on documentation, billing, and ethical practice.

Today, Lisa teaches in the Doctor of Physical Therapy program for the University of St. Augustine for Health Sciences on the Miami campus. In addition to being a core faculty, Lisa is also an Associate Director of Clinical Education. She is responsible for placing and overseeing the students during their clinical experiences. Accordingly, Lisa is well-versed regarding students' competency with employability skills and the perceptions of those working in the clinical environment. As such, this topic is of extreme importance to Lisa.

Table of Contents

Chapter 1: What Are Employability Skills?

Introduction

Good for you! You were accepted into a healthcare program. You have studied hardto learn all sorts of wonderful things. Great job. You are now ready to enter the workforce and become a productive member of society. Or are you?

Figure 1

Young Graduate

Note. This picture depicts a young graduate excited about her recent accomplishment. The image was obtained from Microsoft Word, 2023.

In today's rapidly changing and competitive job market, having the right qualifications and experience is no longer enough to secure employment. Employers are increasingly seeking candidates with a range of employability skills that go beyond technical expertise and qualifications. Employability skills are the knowledge and skills required to retain a job, and they are essential for individuals to remain employable throughout their careers. These skills, formerly called soft skills, encompass various elements of emotional intelligence, communication, self-awareness, cultural competency, and compassion, which are crucial for delivering high-quality, patient-centered care. In this book, we will delve into the world of employability skills, their importance, and how you can develop and enhance these skills to increase your chances of success in the job market.

Terminal Learning Objectives

By the end of this chapter, the reader will be able to identify the three categories of employability skills and understand why they are important.

Enabling Learning Objectives

By the end of this chapter, the reader will be able to:

- Describe what employability skills are.
- Summarize the reasons why employability skills are important.

Instructor Notes

- *You will notice that the headers in this textbook are in the form of a question. Students should be prompted to make a note of the question and to write the answer to that question in their own words to ensure they master the concepts.*

What Are Employability Skills?

Employability skills are the knowledge and skills required to retain a job. This includes being competent in establishing relationships, communication, and teamwork, as well as being proficient in the skills of the trade. Employability skills encompass manyelements of emotional intelligence, communication, and self-awareness. They also include cultural competency and compassion to deliver high-quality, patient-centered care (Trotter, & Dunnivan-Mitchell, 2019). The definition of employability has evolved slightly over the years. It is not just a person's ability to find and keep a job but also to achieve employment continuity and career growth—more emphasis is placed on the importance of personal resources for employability (Martini et al., 2018).

Employability skills should be considered sustainable to be competitive in any industry (Sisodia & Agarwal, 2017). Employability skills include applied knowledge, effective relationships, and workplace skills. The literature includes several componentsof employability skills, but they all encompass the same general concepts.

> "People are always blaming their circumstances for what they are, the people who get on in the world are the people who get up and look for the circumstances that they want and if they can't find them, make them."
>
> —George Bernard Shaw

Figure 2

Employability Skills Framework with Sub-competencies Depicted

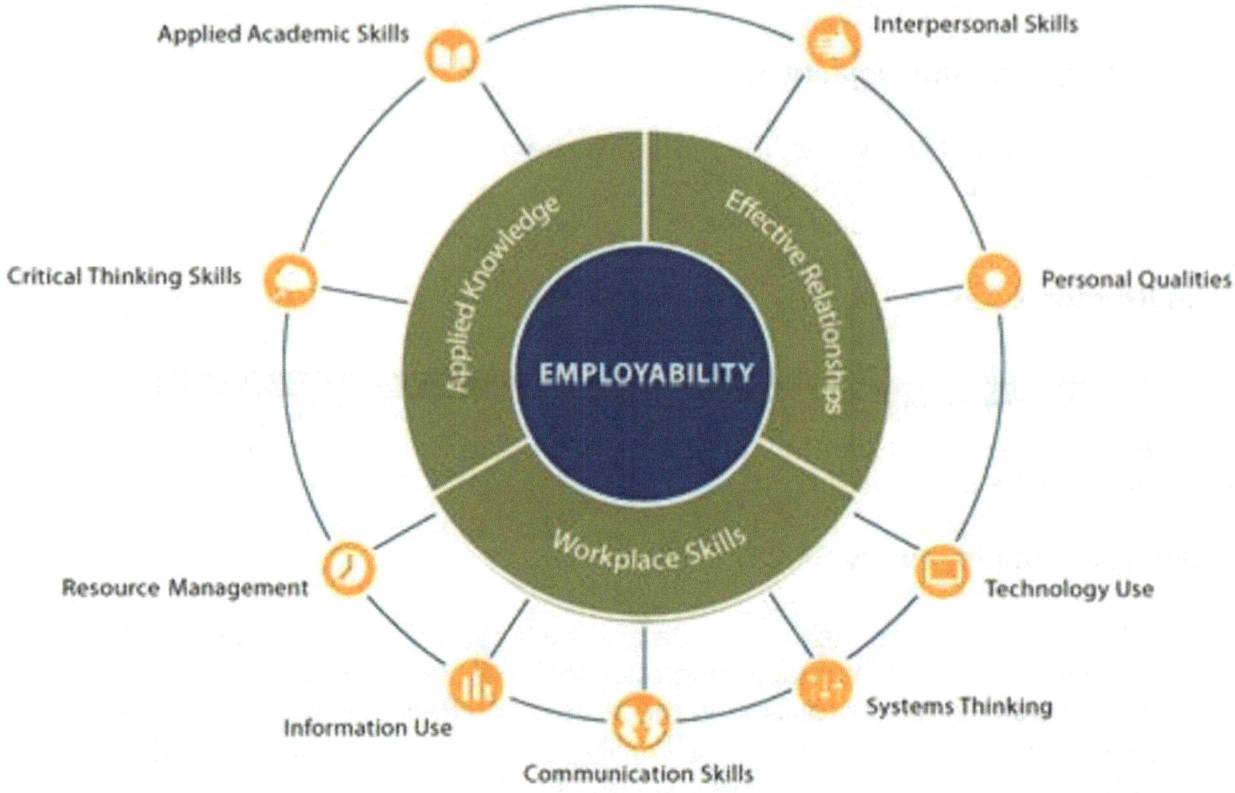

Note: This image provides a visual representation of the competencies associatedwith employability skills. The sub-competencies are depicted as the spokes of a wheel,functioning in unison for employability. Permission was obtained to use this image on March 29, 2023, from https://cte.ed.gov/initiatives/employability-skills-framework.

Effective communication is the most desirable employability skill in healthcare (Sisodia & Agarwal, 2017). In today's dynamic world, employees must be able to communicate constructively and cordially to develop and maintain working relationships.Employees communicate via multiple formats, such as oral and written communication. Effective communication requires active listening and nonverbal communication, especially during healthcare encounters.

"To effectively communicate, we must realize that we are all different in the way we perceive the world and use this understanding as a guide to our communication with others."
—Tony Robbins

Figure 3

Healthcare Provider Communicating via the Computer

Note: This image shows a healthcare provider communicating with others. Thisimage was obtained from Microsoft Word, 2023.

Effective communication is integral for building good relationships within and outside an organization. Communication plays a huge role in the climate of a workplace.If communication is hostile and without regard for others, it creates a sense of fear and uncertainty. If communication is open and honest, it fosters teamwork and collaboration.When employees feel their opinions matter and are welcomed and accepted, employees flourish and excel in their roles. Therefore, communication directly impacts acompany's accomplishments and turnover (Sisodia & Agarwal, 2017).

Instructor Notes

- *For synchronous teaching in a face-to-face format, play the telephone game. Whisper a sentence into a student's ear and have them pass it along to another student, who will then pass it along to another student. When the final student hears the sentence, have them repeat the sentence/phrase to the class and assess the accuracy of the message. Discuss the factors that influenced how themessage was conveyed and received.*
- *Share the following message on the screen for synchronous teaching in a virtualformat. "Take a student's attitude, never be too big to ask questions, never knowtoo much to learn something new." -Augustine Og Mandino. Then ask for students to share their interpretation of what it*

means. The point is to understandhow much interpretation of the correct message depends on the receiver's frameof reference or perspective.

Professionalism is commonly used to describe an employee's interpersonal and personal qualities. Unfortunately, professionalism is a comprehensive and subjectiveterm. It refers to the ability to adapt easily to a diverse working environment.
Professionalism requires a person to be flexible and sociable while maintaining the values and ethics of the organization (Sisodia & Agarwal, 2017). Personal and interpersonal skills enable a person to be aware of the needs of others in addition to their strengths, weaknesses, and biases. An employee who displays a 'can do' attitude,punctuality, and accountability is considered professional. A 'can do' attitude is positivemindset that helps a person accomplish whatever they set their mind to achieve.
Employers seek employees who are culturally aware and sensitive. They should possess loyalty and good conflict-resolution skills.

Instructor Notes

- *For synchronous teaching, ask students to come up with one word to define professionalism. Students will likely struggle with this because the definition is sosubjective. Ask the follow up question, "What are the reasons you feel that way?"The point is to realize that everyone has a slightly different perspective and that our lived experiences form our perspectives.*

Figure 4

Healthcare Providers Working as a Team to Care for a Patient

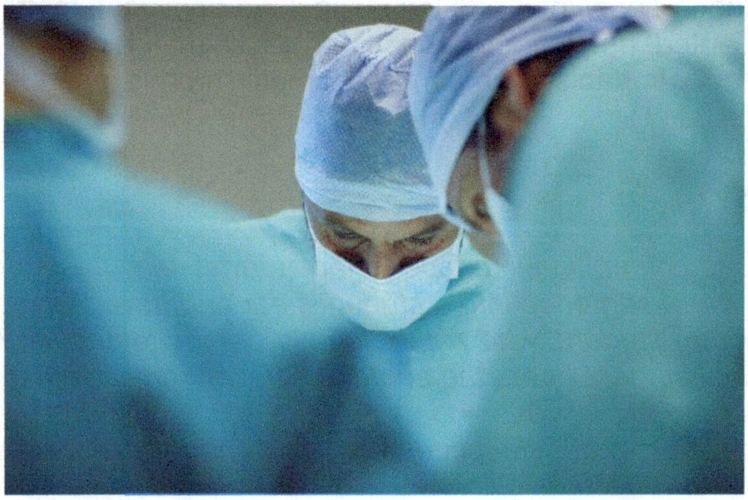

Note: This image is intended to demonstrate how all members of the team are imperative for a successful patient encounter. This image was obtained from MicrosoftWord, 2023.

Another employability skill especially important in healthcare is collaborating effectively as a team. The skills necessary to be an effective team member includebeing mentally flexible and having strong interpersonal and communication skills (Sisodia & Agarwal, 2017). In addition, being an effective team member requires aperson to know each member's role and contributions to the team. Teamwork alsodepends on mutual respect for each person's unique perspective.

Interpersonal skills are imperative for cultivating relationships (Sisodia & Agarwal, 2017). Interpersonal skills function either as an asset to an organization or a liability. When employees engage in active listening and professional communication, interpersonal skills become an asset and helps that organization to stand out above theothers. On the other hand, when a customer detects chaos, inconsistent message, or rude behavior, interpersonal skills become a liability to an organization. Competent interpersonal skills are conveyed through following policies, displaying empathy, and a willingness to work collectively toward a common goal.

Ten Tips for Forming Connections (Wooll, 2022, June 1)

- Be your authentic self.
- Respect people's boundaries.
- Stay focused on the present.
- Move past the surface level.
- Share the conversation.
- Be genuine with your admiration.
- Be a good listener.
- Schedule your time.
- Maintain eye contact.
- Offer a smile.

Instructor Notes

- *For synchronous teaching, have students write a discussion post ranking the tipsin order of importance. Then, ask them to explain why they feel the way they do.*
- *For synchronous teaching, have a class discussion. First, ask students to rank the ten tips in order of greatest importance. Then, students with differing opinionsshould explain why they feel the way they do.*
- *For synchronous or asynchronous teaching, have students select one of the tentips and write an essay explaining the meaning of the tip and providing three different examples of how to engage that tip in the healthcare setting. A grading rubric for the essay is provided in Appendix A.*

Critical thinking is an employability skill that helps an organization to remain competitive. Environments and industries evolve continuously. Organizations that evolve with the environment and industry can predict problems and create innovative solutions. Critical thinking requires analyzing concepts, developing creative approaches,and planning implementation. From an organizational perspective, solving problems is dependent upon resource management. The more knowledgeable a person has about their organization, the better they can efficiently allocate resources to maximize productivity. This also requires planning on multiple levels to ensure goal attainment (Sisodia & Agarwal, 2017).

A person's competence with employability skills requires self-awareness, self- motivation, and self-management. Without these qualities, a person lacks social awareness, and the social skills needed to respond competently. A way to improvethese qualities is by seeking and accepting feedback from others.

Why Are Employability Skills Important?

A survey of U.S. executives revealed that 92% of them deemed employability skills as equally or more important than technical skills. Furthermore, 89% reported difficulty recruiting graduates with these skills (Mainga et al., 2022). A study by the Association ofAmerican Colleges and Universities employers confirmed this claim 91% said employability skills are more important than the applicant's degree.

It's interesting to note that employers do not have a way to assess an individual's employability skills before hiring them. This is because higher education does not formally teach or assess employability skills. In addition, employability is a complex topic with no universally recognized measures (Reid et al., 2021). This means employers are not provided with a direct indication of a graduate's workplace-readiness skills (Thompson & Soccio, 2022). This makes it challenging for employers to determinewho to hire.

How do we deal with such a vague but an important topic? As a multi-dimensional,competency-based construct, employability skills are developed through higher education and workplace learning (Römgens et al., 2020). These skills are acquired through activities and pedagogies that support personal and professional growth.

Another aspect of employability that contributes to its complexity is the extremelydynamic modern working environment. Flexibility and agility are essential to be a productive team member (Mahajan et al., 2022). Transferability is essential to ensurethat employees can fulfill multiple roles within the organizational culture. The skills employers desire most in their employees are teamwork, communication, and decision-making. Employability is more than just the 'possession' of a set of skills.

Instructor Notes

- *For synchronous or asynchronous teaching, have students rank their competency with employability skills, as listed in the U.S. Department of Education's Employability Skills Framework. Ask for a personal reflection on thethree subcategories that explain why they rated themselves the way they did. This should be revisited at the end of the course to compare whether their self-reflection skills have improved. (See Appendix B)*

What are the Key Concepts from this Chapter?

- 92% of U.S. executives deemed employability skills as equally or more importantthan technical skills.
- 89% of U.S. executives reported difficulty recruiting graduates with these skills.
- Employability skills include applied knowledge, effective relationship, andworkplace skills.
- Effective communication is the most desirable employability skill in the healthcareindustry.
- Employability is not just a person's capability to find and keep a job, but it alsoincludes the ability to achieve employment continuity and career growth.

Summary Figure 5

Group of Professionals

Note: This image is intended to demonstrate how all members of the team are imperative for a successful patient encounter. This image was obtained from MicrosoftWord, 2023.

Employability skills enhance a person's ability to secure and retain a job. In addition,employability skills help a person advance in their career and adapt easily to changes intheir working environment and the industry (Anisimova & McNeilly, 2021). Employability skills are critical for achieving and maintaining employment in today's competitive job market. The concept of employability is multi-dimensional and competency-based, involving personal and professional growth. While there is no universally recognized measure for employability, the skills employers desire most in their employees are thoserelated to teamwork, communication, and decision-making.

However, employability is more than just possessing a set of skills. It requires individuals to be flexible, adaptable, and able to transfer their skills to different roles within an organizational culture. Ultimately, developing and enhancing employability skills is essential for individuals to remain employable throughout their careers and toachieve their career goals.

In the next chapter, we will discuss the trends influencing the working environmentspecific to healthcare. Just as different occupations require different technical abilities,the relative importance of employability skills varies per industry. In healthcare, a provider's competence with employability skills can determine the outcome of a life- threatening situation.

References

Anisimova, A.G. & McNeilly, E. (2021). Ways to develop employability skills in teaching translation to final-year students*. Professional Discourse & Communication, 3(*1),75–84. https://doi.org/10.24833/2687-0126-2021-3-1-75-84

Mahajan, R., Gupta, P. & Misra, R. (2022). Employability skills framework: A tripartiteapproach. *Education and Training.* https:doi.org/10.1108/ET-12-2020-00367

Mainga, W., Daniel, R. M., & Alamil, L. (2022). Perceptions of employability skills of undergraduate business students in a developing country: An exploratory study.*Higher Learning Research Communications*, *12*(1), 28–63.

Martini, M., Cavenago, D., & Mariani, L. (2018). When the outcome is employability: leading indicators for the governance of labour market services. *Public Organization Review*, *18*(4), 507–524. https://doi.org/10.1007/s11115-017-0393-3

Reid, A., Richards, A., & Willox, D. (2021). Connecting experiences to employabilitythrough a meaning-making approach to learning. *Journal of Teaching and Learning for Graduate Employability*, *12*(2), 99–113.

Römgens, I., Scoupe, R., & Beausaert, S. (2020). Unraveling the concept of employability, bringing together research on employability in higher educationand the workplace. *Studies in Higher Education*, *45*(12), 2588-2603, DOI: 10.1080/03075079.2019.1623770

Sisodia, S., & Agarwal, N. (2017). Employability skills essential for healthcare industry.

Procedia Computer Science, 122, 431–438. https://doi.org/10.1016/j.procs.2017.11.390
Thompson, J. & Soccio, P. (2022). 'This is what gets people hired!': Academic perspectives on employability skills in architecture and the potential impact of COVID-19. *Journal of Teaching and Learning for Graduate Employability*, *13*(1).https://doi.org/10.21153/jtlge2022vol13no1art1555
Trotter S., & Dunnivan-Mitchell S., (2019). Simulation enhances soft skills among inter-professionals participating in an international service-learning experience to a resource-limited country. *MedEdPublish*, *8*(1), 24, https://doi.org/10.15694/mep.2019.000024.1
Wooll, M. (2022, June 1). Make the connection: 10 effective ways to connect with people. Better up. https://www.betterup.com/blog/how-to-connect-with-people

Chapter 2: Employability Skills and Healthcare

Introduction

Now that we have a basic understanding of employability skills, we need to understand the healthcare industry. It is important to understand the trends in healthcare and the factors that dictate the pulse of the industry. Many factors have influenced the provision of healthcare services.

Terminal Learning Objectives

By the end of this chapter, the reader will better understand the trends that have impacted the healthcare industry, and the role employability skills have in healthcare.

Enabling Learning Objectives

By the end of this chapter, the reader will be able to:

- Explain the trends influencing healthcare.
- Outline the impacts that the COVID-19 pandemic had on healthcare delivery.
- Finally, describe the role of employability skills in healthcare.

Instructor Notes

- *You will notice the headers in this textbook are in the form of a question. Students should be prompted to make a note of the question and write the answer to that question in their own words to ensure they master the concepts.*

What Are the Trends Impacting Healthcare?

The healthcare arena has evolved with the onset of the 21st century. Three landmark events have prompted this evolution. The first event was the World Healthcare Organization's (WHO) introduction of patient-centered care (WHO, 2007). The second was the Institute of Medicine's (IOM's) publication of Crossing the Quality Chasm in 2001, reinforcing the shift toward patient-centered (IOM, 2021). The third event was the WHO's proposal to move toward a competency-based system (WHO, 2022). Other factors influencing the current state of healthcare include the push for increased transparency and consumerism, increased emphasis on the social determinants of health, and the COVID-19 pandemic.

> "It is not the strongest of the species that survives, nor the most intelligent, but the one most responsive to change."
> Charles Darwin

Figure 6

Electrocardiogram

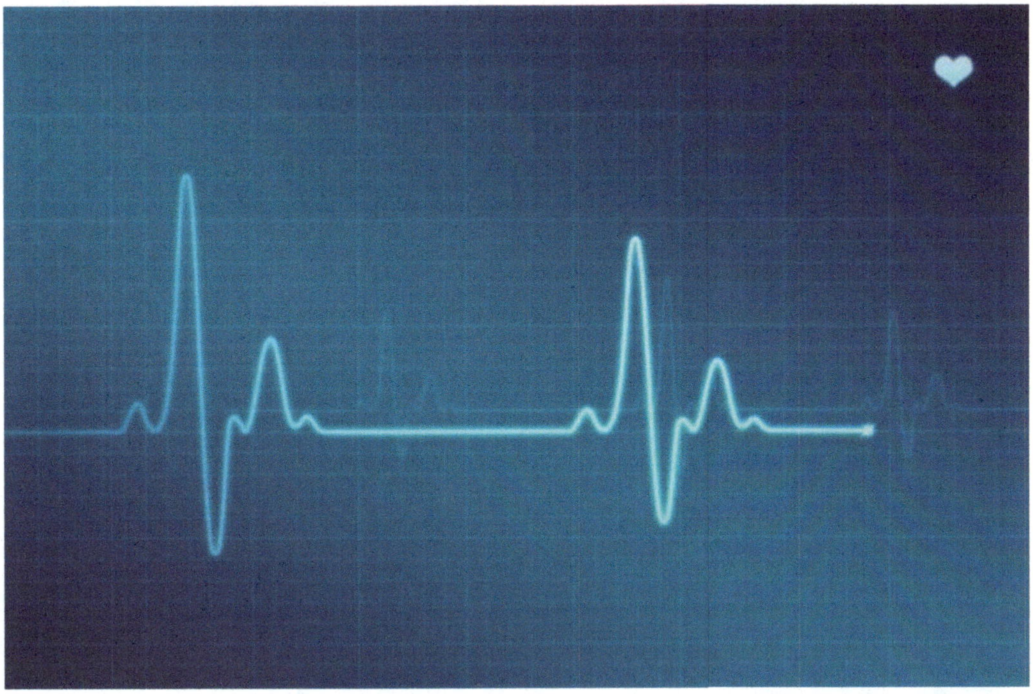

Note: The electrocardiogram (ECG) represents an example of technology use in healthcare. The image was obtained from Microsoft Word, 2023.

Before the 21st century, healthcare revolved around the doctor. The doctor served as the gatekeeper to patient care. Today, healthcare focuses on a patient-centered approach. Patient-centered care requires clear communication and teamwork (IOM, 2021). The WHO explained that patient-centered care is based on understanding the psychosocial dimensions of the patient and includes creating a supportive environment with consideration of culture and individual patient needs (WHO, 2007). Effective communication serves as a foundation for the interpersonal relationship between the patient and the clinicians. It helps to promote respect and dignity while empowering self-care by the patient (Afriyie, 2020). This is especially relevant because patients consider healthcare encounters to be uncomfortable, usually due to the fear of the unknown.

Healthcare education has evolved in response to the shift to patient-centered care. There have been dramatic technological advances, increased cultural diversity, and more complex working environments in which students must be prepared (Metgud & D'Silva, 2021). This evolutionary shift has triggered an increase in the educational requirements to become a degreed professional. According to Metgud and D'Silva (2021), the incorporation of additional coursework that emphasizes didactic content and psychomotor skills can result in reduced emphasis on teaching strategies designed to improve employability skills and increase effective communication. These changes have increased students' stress, which leads to decreased work performance and impaired communication in human interactions (Ciulea et al., 2021).

What Does it Mean to Provide Patient-Centered Care?

Figure 7

Young Healthcare Provider Caring for an Elderly Patient

Note: The healthcare provider is providing patient-centered care. The image was obtained from Microsoft Word, 2023.

Patient-centered care means the patient is the center of healthcare, and the physician and other providers work collaboratively for the patient's benefit (IOM, 2021). The shift toward patient-centered care requires healthcare providers to understand and incorporate the psychosocial dimensions of the patient. This includes establishing an environment inclusive of the culture and the individual's unique values (WHO, 2007).

Patient-centered care requires clinicians to exercise employability skills such as effective communication and efficient use of time and resources to make clinical decisions and resolve conflicts for the patient's benefit (Falco & Monaghan, 2018). This includes considering the social determinants of health, which represent the patient's culture, socioeconomic status, and educational level. These skills are taught in higher education through simulated patient-care encounters (Falco & Monaghan, 2018). Healthcare students are routinely given patient case scenarios requiring them to assess and treat various conditions within a specific amount of time and available resources. These simulations include a combination of hands-on interventions and simulated communication with the patient and other healthcare providers. Clinicians who are trained and convey mindful and empathetic communication can effectively deliver collaborative, patient-centered care, and ultimately improve patient safety and treatment outcomes.

Instructor Notes

- *For synchronous or asynchronous teaching, provide students with the list in Appendix C. Instruct students to rewrite the phrase listed in the first column in the second column using patient-centered language.*

Patient-centered care depends on how healthcare providers communicate and understand each other's roles in the healthcare delivery process (Luetmer, 2018). To provide patient-centered care, healthcare providers must communicate effectively, work collaboratively, and use resources efficiently for the patient's benefit (Falco & Monaghan, 2018). Healthcare providers must understand how each discipline complements one another. Effective collaboration requires clear, concise communication and teamwork (WHO, 2007).

For example, a group of providers working as a collaborative, interdisciplinary team, communicate with one another regarding the patient's needs and which team member is providing what service. Effective interdisciplinary teams hold one another accountable for their actions and the outcomes of the interventions. The patient is considered an active participant of the team, responsible for decisions regarding their care.

Figure 8

Interdisciplinary Team of Healthcare Providers Coordinating Their Patient Care Efforts

Note: These professionals are practicing interdisciplinary healthcare by communicating their efforts regarding patient care. The image was obtained from Microsoft Word, 2023.

Communication can facilitate or inhibit patient care. If performed mindfully, communication can foster the development of an interpersonal relationship between the patient and the clinician and the clinician and other healthcare providers. This is because mindful communication focuses on being attentive, aware, and careful with the message delivery. Using patient-centered language helps to promote respect and dignity of the patient and empowers the patient to manage their health conditions

(Afriyie, 2020). The healthcare provider should display active listening and reflective responses with humility when collecting pertinent information from the patient (Nemec et al., 2017).

What Is a Competency-Based System?

The trend of moving toward a competency-based system was proposed by the WHO (Gonzalo et al., 2022; WHO, 2022). The benefit of using a competency-based framework is that it promotes a standardization approach to meet the needs of patients (Gonzalo et al., 2022). Huang et al. (2022) explained that competency-based frameworks incorporate emotions and clinical reasoning to benefit the patient and the community being served. In addition, using an evidence-based system allows clinicians to identify their competency gaps for continuous improvement.

Figure 9

Young Healthcare Provider Looking Confident in her Knowledge

Note: This young healthcare provider is confident in her knowledge and abilities. The image was obtained from Microsoft Word, 2023.

Competency is defined as the ability to integrate and apply knowledge, skills, and attitudes to clinical performance within a specific context (WHO, 2022). Competency-based education is an inclusive approach to providing holistic healthcare. This prepares healthcare providers to deliver quality services collaboratively. This is important because healthcare continuously evolves, and providers must be resilient and adaptable. In addition, competency-based education promotes patient-centered care with collaborative decision-making and evidence-based practice (WHO, 2022). Thus, healthcare educational programs must include a curriculum based on competency, enhancing intricate abilities, and instruction on interprofessional collaboration. This contributes to the enrichment and development of employability skills.

The concept of competence is often considered in the debate on employability skills. This is because competence is defined as the "quality of being able and fit", making it a reliable predictor of employability. Competence is a composite of individual attributes and skills specific to the work context. Competence means successfully applying the acquired knowledge and skills to achieve meaningful and effective outcomes (Suleman, 2018).

Competency with employability skills is required to manage conflict and show empathy through effective communication. Research indicates an increasing need for skill development related to emotional intelligence. Medically precise, comprehensive care is dependent upon an emotionally supportive atmosphere. This environment promotes an inclusive space to develop the caregiver-patient relationship. Accordingly, deficiency in developing employability skills among healthcare students significantly diminishes the possibility of achieving a "caring environment" (Dimitrov & Vazova, 2020).

Developing standardization in competency frameworks is a significant step toward closing the educational gap and better aligning education with the needs of patients, communities, and health systems (Gonzalo et al., 2022). Trede et al. (2015) explained that competency-based assessments are fair and consistent. This is because they list the elements of practice and isolated competencies required for employment, which allows them to be objective and technical. Other key aspects of competency-based assessment practices include establishing a shared understanding of assessment criteria and providing feedback regularly (Stewart et al., 2016).

Instructor Notes

- *For synchronous and asynchronous discussions, have students express their opinions about whether they feel competency-based systems are like standardized tests (e.g., graduate entrance exam [GRE]). Then, they should compare the advantages of competency-based systems and standardized tests.*

What Are the Signs and Impacts of Increased Transparency and Consumerism in Healthcare?

The rising costs of consumer products and services show no signs of slowing. By necessity, consumers have become much more engaged in their healthcare services to ensure they are getting the best value for their money (Vogenberg & Santilli, 2019). Due to this, there is an increasing demand for transparency, such as why a specific treatment is indicated and why another is not. As a result, providers must manage their services to ensure consumers receive the highest-quality, cost-efficient services.

Instructor Notes

- *For synchronous teaching, divide the class into small groups. Challenge the student groups to see which group can produce the most ideas to incorporate increased transparency into patient care interventions.*

What Actions Would You Take to Demonstrate an Increased Emphasis on the Social Determinants of Health?

Figure 10

Healthcare Provider Customizing a Healthcare Resource for a Patient

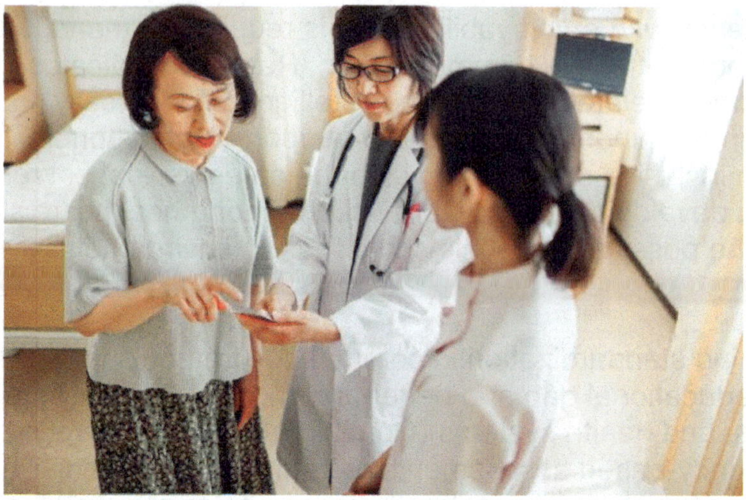

Note: This healthcare provider is empowering her patient with knowledge regarding how to obtain relevant medical information. The image was obtained from Microsoft Word, 2023.

Providers also need to emphasize where the healthcare experience occurs and the importance of social determinants of health (Vogenberg & Santilli, 2019). According to the Centers for Disease Control and Prevention (CDC; 2022, December 8), social determinants of health are where a person lives, their educational level, and their economic stability. Social determinants of health also include access to healthcare services and the individual's role in society. These factors are essential because they are the primary sources of health inequities.

Instructor Notes

- *For synchronous and asynchronous teaching, have students make a list of the social determinants of health. Then students should explain how each social determinant of health could impact a patient's behavior and actions. This could be a written assignment or class discussion.*

What Impacts Did the COVID-19 Pandemic Have on Healthcare?

In addition to the shift toward patient-centered care, the COVID-19 pandemic has influenced healthcare services. The pandemic affected all aspects of healthcare. It placed enormous demands on healthcare, which resulted in suspending or furloughing elective surgeries, releasing nonessential workers, and shortages of resources (COVID-19, 2022). The COVID-19 pandemic also changed how healthcare was delivered. Many providers began or increased their use of telemedicine.

The COVID-19 pandemic highlighted the need for several changes in healthcare. At the top of the list, the COVID-19 pandemic stressed the need for improved efficiency, responsiveness, and leadership transparency. An example of transparency is providing patients with an Explanation of Benefits (EOB). The EOB provides a breakdown of the services provided, how much the insurance company was billed, how much the insurance company paid the provider, and how much money the patient is potentially responsible to pay. COVID-19 also emphasized the need for enhanced communication, collaboration, and establishing clear pandemic guidelines based on evidence and science. The COVID-19 pandemic created the need for the global healthcare community to recognize the significance of the time and resource management or planning and preparation for healthcare crises to guarantee the fair distribution of vaccines. Plus, a more significant investment in the healthcare workforce must be made globally.

Figure 11

COVID-19 Vaccine

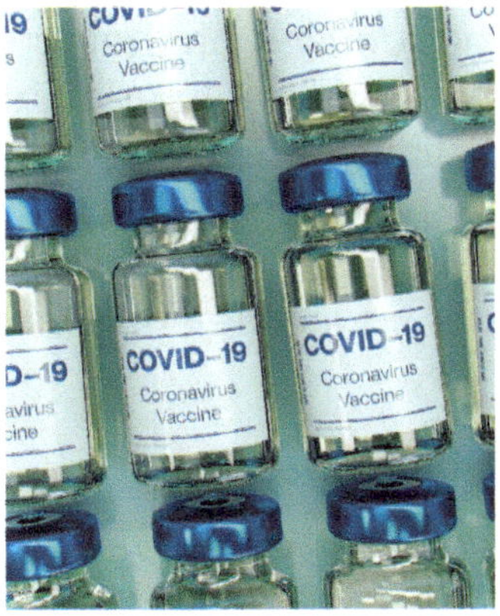

Note: Vials of the COVID-19 vaccine. This image by Daniel Schludi was obtained from Unsplash.com, 2023.

Roy et al. (2021) explained how the pandemic caused healthcare for non-COVID-19 conditions to decrease across high- and low-income countries. This will undoubtedly impact health outcomes, particularly for chronic diseases. Therefore, research should be focused on system improvement and the promotion of health equity. This calls upon public health professionals to address the disparity in healthcare services.

Palacios-Ceña et al. (2021) explored the impact of the COVID-19 pandemic on physical therapists (PTs). Initially, rehabilitation services were suspended during the first wave of the pandemic. Some of this was to prevent the further spread of the virus, and some of this was to create new beds for sick patients by using the rehabilitation spaces within hospitals. As a result, PTs were reassigned to other units within the hospital. The pandemic also created a new population of post-COVID patients for PTs to treat. PTs also used telemedicine to supplement or substitute for face-to-face therapy services. In addition, some PTs were furloughed in response to the pandemic. Collectively, these changes have permanently impacted the field of physical therapy.

Instructor Notes

- *For synchronous or asynchronous teaching, have students write an essay or produce a Vlog describing the impacts the COVID-19 pandemic had on the delivery of healthcare services. Students should be instructed to provide three specific examples of the impacts COVID-19 had on the delivery of healthcare services. Students should be instructed to cite at least three peer-reviewed journals, within the past five years to support their examples. A grading rubric for this essay or Vlog is included in Appendix D.*

How Are Employability Skills Different in Various Healthcare Professions Compared with Other Industries?

While employability skills are required for employment in all industries, the skillset required to succeed in healthcare is slightly different. The category of applied knowledge includes academic and critical thinking skills. The academic skills required to work in healthcare include the study of anatomy, physiology, and biology. Once the core knowledge is mastered, student learning focuses on their specialization (e.g., physicians, dental hygienists, physical therapists). In addition, education for healthcare professions includes both didactic and clinical education components. The didactic portion includes learning about content knowledge and hands-on psychomotor skills, such as taking blood pressure. The clinical education portion occurs in the clinical setting, as students engage with patients under the supervision of a licensed provider.

Figure 12

Child Having her Blood-Pressure Measured

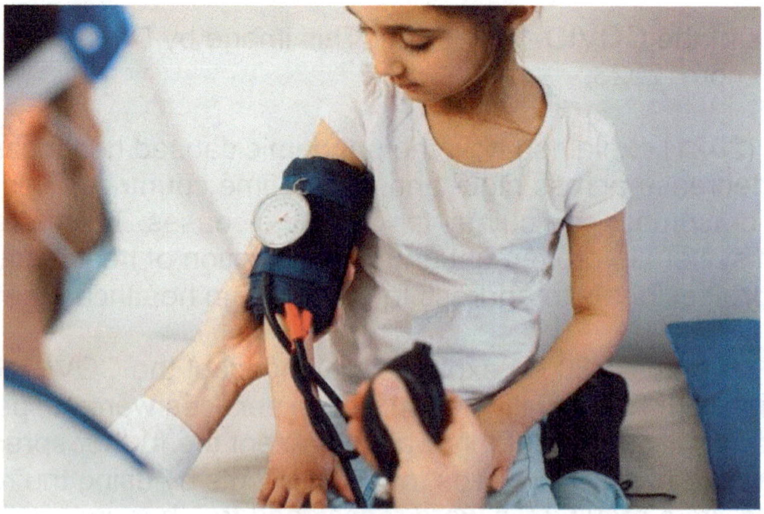

Note: This healthcare provider is measuring the little girl's blood pressure. The provider must use critical thinking to make decisions regarding her blood pressure. This image was obtained from Microsoft Word, 2023.

The other component of the applied knowledge category is critical thinking. This involves the analysis of facts, observations, and evidence to form a judgment. Critical thinking requires a healthy amount of skepticism for unbiased data analysis. In healthcare, critical thinking is often thought of as clinical reasoning. Critical thinking and clinical reasoning are similar. Both begin with observation. Once the basic problem has been identified, it must be analyzed. Following analysis, the next step is to make inferences about the data. In healthcare, an example could be running additional tests and measures to rule in or rule out a specific condition, which could be the root cause of the problem. After the healthcare provider has accepted or rejected a diagnosis, the next step is communication with the patient and the patient's healthcare providers. Once a diagnosis is identified, treatment is provided to the patient.

Effective relationships include interpersonal skills and personal qualities. In healthcare, these skills are especially important. It is incumbent upon the healthcare provider to actively listen to the patient and to convey empathy and caring. Personal qualities are the characteristics or attributes that make up a person's personality. Previously, a healthcare provider's interpersonal skills and personal qualities were often encased in the term 'bedside manner'. Patients would describe a provider as having a good bedside manner if the provider made the patient feel heard and cared for. The opposite is also true, if a provider disregards information the patient deems relevant, then the patient will not comfortably be seeking care from that provider in the future.

Figure 13

Healthcare Provider Rendering Personalized Care

Note: This female provider is conveying empathy and concern for her patient, demonstrating a good bedside manner. This image was obtained from Microsoft Word, 2023.

The last classification is workplace skills which include communication, systems thinking, resource management, and information and the use of technology. As healthcare involves interdependent systems, these skills are crucial for success. For example, the body can be broken into systems (e.g., the cardiovascular or nervous system). Healthcare entities also can be described as a collection of systems. For example, a large metropolitan city might have a hospital system with several locations. These might include hospitals of varying sizes and several outpatient facilities in the surrounding metropolitan area.

Information and technology vary by industry. In healthcare, the technology varies tremendously according to the services provided at each location. Technology includes everything from a patient portal to the most advanced X-ray machine. Healthcare providers often depend on technology to perform diagnostic tests and render treatment. Healthcare providers use the information for patient care. Patient information is shared as needed to maintain patient confidentiality.

Figure 14

Healthcare Providers Using Technology to Inform Clinical Decision-Making

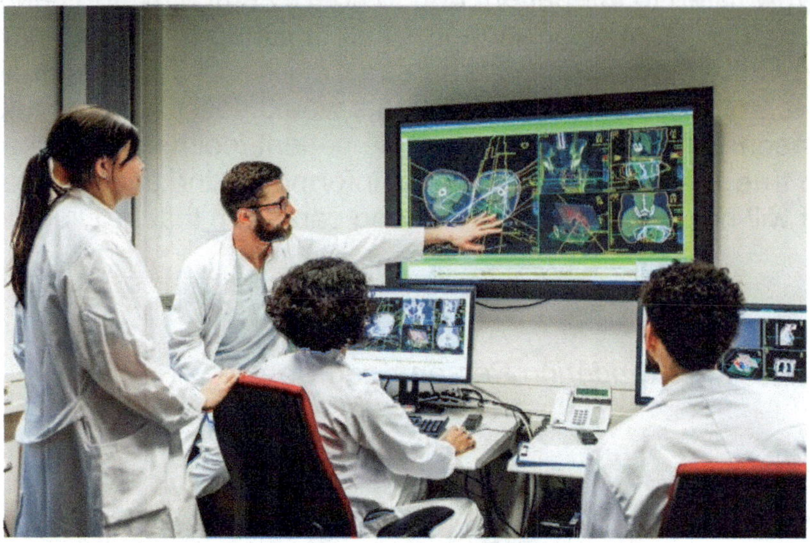

Note: These healthcare providers are using technology to make clinical decisions. This image was obtained from Microsoft Word, 2023.

Resource management for healthcare is the correct treatment intervention being provided to the right patient, in the right way, at the right time. All companies must manage their resources, or they lose customers or money. In healthcare, resource management can quickly become a high-stakes situation. What if a nurse were to provide the right medication to the wrong patient? This could be a deadly mistake.

Communication is the employability skill that has the most significant impact on healthcare is communication. Healthcare providers communicate with patients and other providers. Sometimes the communication is simple, and sometimes it is not. If a provider is unable to communicate with the patient effectively, it is highly unlikely the patient will follow through with the professional's recommendations. Effective communication is imperative to provide patient-centered care. Healthcare teams require a collaborative approach to patient care, which cannot happen without efficient and thorough communication.

Figure 15

Healthcare Provider Communicating with a Patient

Note: This healthcare provider is using communication to help bring a smile to her patient's face. This image was obtained from Microsoft Word, 2023.

What Are the Key Concepts from this Chapter?

- Patient-centered care requires healthcare providers to understand the patient's psychosocial dimensions and includes creating a supportive environment with consideration of culture and the patient's individual needs.
- Competency-based frameworks promote a standardization approach to meet the needs of patients.
- Patients have become more economically aware consumers and much more engaged in their healthcare services to ensure they get the best value. This is known as an increased demand for transparency.
- Social determinants of health are factors such as where a person lives, their educational level, their economic stability, and their access to healthcare services.
- The COVID-19 pandemic:
    - Placed enormous demands on healthcare.
    - Caused healthcare for non-COVID-19 conditions to decrease universally and highlighted healthcare disparities.
    - Spurred the passage of legislation for telemedicine.
    - Caused the reallocation of healthcare providers into new, non-traditional roles.
- Healthcare providers require well-defined employability skills to provide safe and effective services.

Summary

In this chapter, we explored the trends in healthcare: patient-centered care, the push toward a competency-based system, the need for increased transparency, and the emphasis on social determinants of health. We also discussed the vast implications of the COVID-19 pandemic. This chapter also focused on how employability skills differ in healthcare compared with other industries. In many respects, competency with employability skills is even more important for healthcare than other industries to ensure competent and safe patient care.

Now that we have a better understanding of the healthcare industry and the role employability skills play in the provision of healthcare services, we need to delve deeper into the meaning of these elusive skills. We will begin by discussing an overview of the US Department of Education's Employability Framework.

References

Afriyie, D. (2020). Effective communication between nurses and patients: An evolutionary concept analysis. *British Journal of Community Nursing*, *25*(9), 438–445. https://doi.org/10.12968/bjcn.2020.25.9.438

Centers for Disease Control and Prevention. (2022, December 8). *Social determinants of health at CDC*. https://www.cdc.gov/about/sdoh/index.html

Ciulea, L. E., Ban, A. R., Papp, E. G., & Szabo-Csifo, B. (2021). The importance of soft skills in fitness-specific activities. *Romanian Journal of Physical Therapy*, *27*(47), 25–33.

COVID-19: The economic impact of a pandemic on the healthcare delivery system in the United States. (2022). *Nursing Forum*, *57*(2), 323–327. https://doi.org/10.1111/nuf.12677

Dimitrov, Y., & Vazova, T. (2020). Developing capabilities from the scope of emotional intelligence as part of the soft skills needed in the long-term care sector: Presentation of pilot study and training methodology. *Journal of Primary Care & Community Health*, 11, 2150132720906275. https://doi.org/10.1177/2150132720906275

Falco, K., & Monaghan, H. M. (2018). Soft skills: The foundation for effective SPHM program leadership: A national survey. *International Journal of Safe Patient Handling & Mobility (SPHM)*, *8*(2), 76–90.

Gonzalo, J. D., Wolpaw, D. R., Cooney, R., Mazotti, L., Reilly, J. B., & Wolpaw, T. (2022). Evolving the systems-based practice competency in graduate medical education to meet patient needs in the 21st-century health care system. *Academic Medicine*, *97*(5), 655. https://doi.org/10.1097/ACM.0000000000004598

Huang, X., Li, Z., Wang, J., Cao, E., Zhuang, G., Xiao, F., Zheng, C., Zhang, X., Chen, M., Gao, L., Guo, P., Lin, P., Zheng, S., & Xin, G. (2022). A KSA system for competency-based assessment of clinicians' professional development in China and quality gap analysis. *Medical Education Online*, *27*(1). https://doi.org/10.1080/10872981.2022.2037401

Institute of Medicine (US) Committee on Quality of Health Care in America. (2001). Crossing the quality chasm: A new health system for the 21st century. *National Academies Press (US).*

Luetmer, M.T., Cloud, B.A., Youdas, J.W., Pawlina, W. & Lackman, N. (2018). Simulating the multi-disciplinary care team approach: Enhancing student understanding of anatomy through an ultrasound-anchored interprofessional session. *Anatomical Sciences Education*, 11, 94-99. doi https://doi-org.prx-usa.lirn.net/10.1002/ase.1731

Metgud, S., & D'Silva, P. (2021). Soft skills in physical therapy profession: Need of the hour. *Indian Journal of Physical Therapy and Research*, *3*(2), 69.

Nemec, P. B., Spagnolo, A. C., & Soydan, A. S. (2017). Can you hear me now? Teaching listening skills. *Psychiatric Rehabilitation Journal*, *40*(4), 415–417. https://doi.org/10.1037/prj0000287

Roy, C. M., Bollman, E. B., Carson, L. M., Northrop, A. J., Jackson, E. F., & Moresky, R. T. (2021). Assessing the indirect effects of COVID-19 on healthcare delivery, utilization, and health outcomes: A scoping review. *European Journal of Public Health*, *31*(3), 634–640. https://doi.org/10.1093/eurpub/ckab047

Stewart, J., Shanmugam, S., & Seenan, C. (2016). Developing 21st century graduate attributes: Incorporating novel teaching strategies in a physiotherapy curriculum. *European Journal of Physiotherapy*, *18*(3), 194–199.

Suleman, F. (2018). The employability skills of higher education graduates: Insights into conceptual frameworks and methodological options. *Higher Education*, *76*(2), 263+. https://link.gale.com/apps/doc/A547791419/EAIM?u=lirn55718&sid=bookmark-EAIM&xid=0e7c2bc4

Trede, F., Mischo-Kelling, M., Gasser, E. M., & Pulcini, S. (2015). Assessment experiences in the workplace: A comparative study between clinical educators' and their students' perceptions. *Assessment & Evaluation in Higher Education*, *40*(7), 1002–1016.

Trede, F., Mischo-Kelling, M., Gasser, E. M., & Pulcini, S. (2015). Assessment experiences in the workplace: A comparative study between clinical educators' and their students' perceptions. *Assessment & Evaluation in Higher Education*, *40*(7), 1002–1016.

Vogenberg, F. R., & Santilli, J. (2019). Industry trends. Key trends in healthcare for 2020 and beyond. *American Health & Drug Benefits*, *12*(7), 348–350.

Chapter 3: United States Employability Skills Framework Overview

Introduction

The U.S. Department of Education (n.d.) has developed an Employability Skills Framework. This framework is broken into three categories with nine components. The three categories consist of allied knowledge, effective relationships, and workplace skills. These categories will be broken down in more detail in the subsequent chapters.

The University of Queensland (UC) developed an employability framework based on experiential learning. The UC framework is based on four stages. This framework was selected for comparison because it is based on experiential learning.

Terminal Learning Objectives

By the end of this chapter, the reader will gain insight into the U.S. Department of Education's Employability Framework and how it compares to the University of Queensland's Employability Framework.

Enabling Learning Objectives

By the end of this chapter, the reader will be able to:

- Summarize the three categories of employability skills defined by the U.S. Department of Education.
- Compare the U.S. Department of Education's Employability Framework with the University of Queensland's Employability Framework.
- Explain the relationship between employability skills and the provision of healthcare services

Instructor Notes

- *You will notice the headers in this textbook are in the form of a question. Students should be prompted to note the question and write the answer to that question in their own words to ensure they master the concepts.*

What Comprises the U.S. Department of Education's Employability Skills Framework?

The Employability Skills Framework, developed by the U.S. Department of Education, includes applied knowledge, effective relationships, and workplace skills. This framework outlines the necessary skills to gain employment within all industries and business sectors. Employability skills enable a person to participate effectively in the workplace.

Figure 16

Employability Skills Framework by the U.S. Department of Education

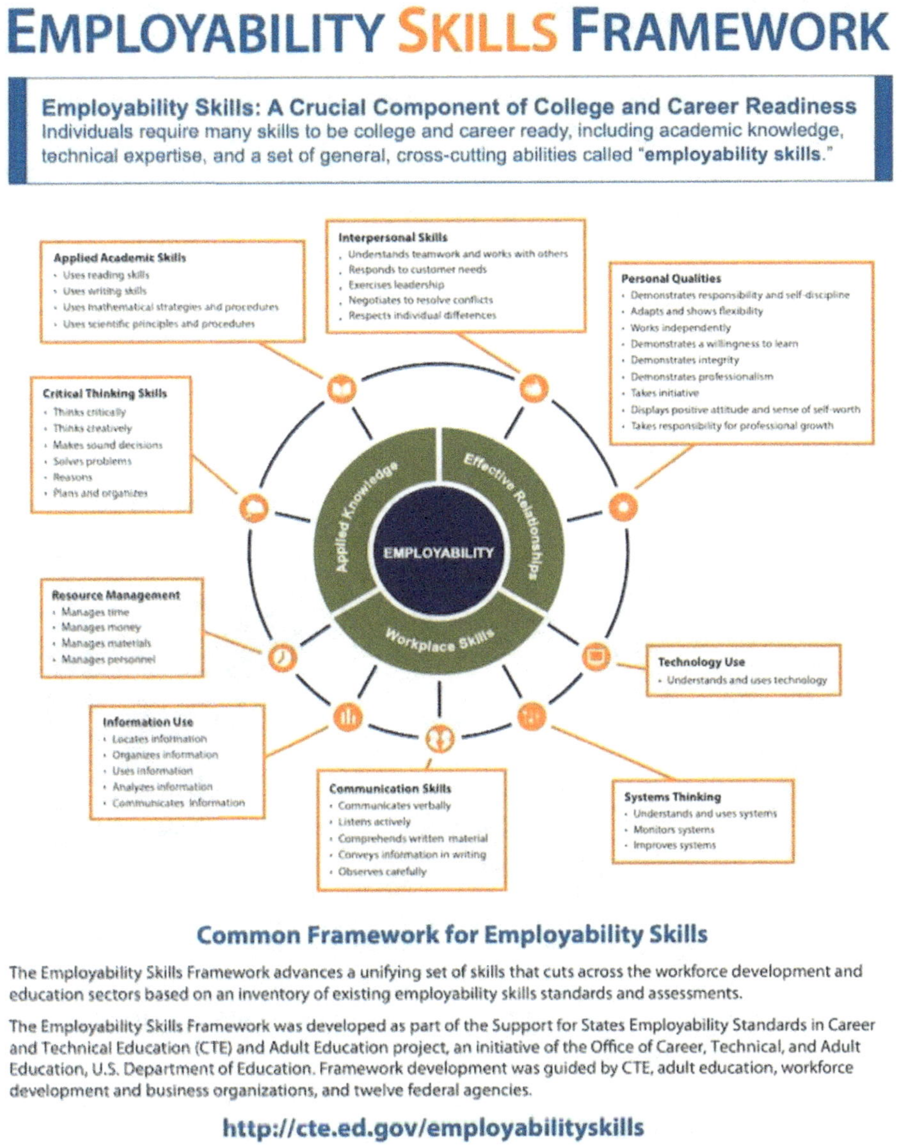

Note: This image is a visual of the competencies associated with employability skills. The sub-competencies are the spokes of a wheel, functioning in unison for employability. Permission was obtained to use this image on March 29, 2023, from https://cte.ed.gov/initiatives/employability-skills-framework.

Why Did the U.S. Department of Education Create an Employability Skills Framework?

In the past, employers would analyze the applicant pool in search of the most talented candidate. Today, employers realize they have a role in developing those talents. In 2012, the Employability Skills Framework was created through a collaborative effort between industry leaders and educators. The goal was to establish an inclusive set of employability skills necessary for success in all workforce sectors (PCRN, 2023, April 15). The establishment of an inclusive list of employability skills helps employers, educators, and graduates to have clear expectations about the working environment.

What Are Applied Knowledge Skills?

The applied knowledge category includes applied academic skills and critical thinking skills. Applied academic skills include reading and writing, scientific procedures and principles, and math strategies and procedures. Critical thinking is thinking creatively and critically to make sound decisions. Critical thinking requires weighing rationale, planning, and organizing to solve problems (U.S. Department of Education, n.d.).

Figure 17

Adult Student in the Library

Note: This adult student is smiling about obtaining knowledge in the library. This image was obtained from Microsoft Word, 2023.

What Are Effective Relationship Skills?

Effective relationships include interpersonal skills and personal qualities. Interpersonal skills are understanding teamwork and working well with others. Teamwork is when a group of colleagues work collaboratively to accomplish a common goal. This involves responding to customer needs, demonstrating leadership, respecting the individual qualities of others, and negotiating for conflict resolution. (U.S. Department of Education, n.d.).

The quality of teamwork directly impacts the effectiveness of patient care. When teams work well together, they use open communication and work collaboratively to accomplish their goals. Conversely, when teams do not work well, they lack trust and respect for one another. Communication is more closed, and there is a reduced sense of purpose and value (Godby Vail et al., 2023).

What Comprises Workplace Skills?

The workplace skills category is comprised of five components. First, communication encompasses verbal and written communication. Communication relies on active listening, spoken and written word comprehension, and careful observation. Second, resource management includes the management of time, money, resources, and personnel. Third, information use involves locating, organizing, using, analyzing, and communicating the information acquired. Fourth, systems thinking involves understanding and operating systems, such as team collaboration. This also includes monitoring and improving systems. The fifth component is technology use, which means understanding and using technology (U.S. Department of Education, n.d.). Finally, communication is consistently identified as the most integral of employability skills (Fogel & Lamash, 2021).

Figure 18

Healthcare Professionals at Work

Note: These healthcare professionals converse in the work environment. This image was obtained from Unsplash.com, 2023.

How Does the U.S. Department of Education's Employability Framework Compare to the University of Queensland (U.C.) Employability Skills Framework?

The U.S. Department of Education's Employability Skills Framework is not the only one in existence. For example, the University of Queensland (U.C.) Employability Skills Framework describes employability as a learning process where students find meaning in their experiences (U.C., 2023, March 19). Once students understand the value of the experience, they need to articulate it and apply it to the work environment.

The U.C. Framework has four pillars: awareness, experiences, learning, and transfer. Awareness is the comprehension and development of knowledge and skills and the personal attributes that guide workplace performance. Experiences are the curricular, co-curricular, and extracurricular activities used to develop employability skills. Learning is the reflective process where the individual finds value in learning. Finally, the transfer effectively applies communication and employability skills to the work environment (U.C., 2023, March 19).

The most significant difference between the U.S. Department of Education's and the U.C. framework is that the U.C. framework more closely resembles Kolb's Experiential Learning Theory (Reid et al., 2021). Kolb's Theory of Experiential Learning describes the four-stage cycle of learning through experience. For that reason, the U.C. framework aligns nicely with healthcare education. In addition, as we will discuss later in this text, healthcare education incorporates experiential learning throughout the program to enable students the opportunity to practice their hands-on skills in a low-stakes environment.

Figure 19

Adult Students Working Through a Problem

Note: This group of young, adult students are working through a problem. This image was obtained from Microsoft Word, 2023.

Why Is a Framework Necessary?

Using a framework for describing employability skills is akin to using a roadmap to find one's way. A framework provides a detailed description of the criteria that drives decisions. It also forms a rating system to evaluate the outcomes (Suman et al., 2020).

Applying the analogy of using a roadmap, suppose you want to travel somewhere. The detailed criteria might involve listing the names of the roads you might travel to get there. In addition, it will provide the order in which you must travel each road to arrive at your destination. If the path you selected has excessive traffic, your evaluation of your path might not be as positive as it would have been with less traffic. The employability frameworks describe the individual criteria or employability skills required to secure an occupation. As you pursue the path of achieving employment, the skills required to secure a position are the same criteria that will be used to measure your performance once employed.

Instructor Notes

- *For synchronous or asynchronous teaching, the Group Project Employability Skills Rubric in Appendix E can be a supplemental grading rubric to use during group projects. This will enable students to assess each other's competency with employability skills.*

What Are the Key Concepts from this Chapter?

- The Employability Skills Framework, developed by the U.S. Department of Education, is divided into three categories: applied knowledge, effective relationships, and workplace skills.
- The applied knowledge category includes:
    - Applied academic skills
    - Critical thinking skills
- The effective relationships category includes:
    - Interpersonal skills
    - Personal qualities
- The workplace skills category includes:
    - Communication
    - Resource management
    - Information use
    - Systems thinking
    - Technology use
- The U.C. Framework is comprised of:
    - Awareness
    - Experiences
    - Learning
    - Transfer

Summary

In this chapter, we introduced the Employability Skills Framework of the U.S. Department of Education. This was compared to the Employability Skills Framework from the University of Queensland in Australia. The U.S. framework includes applied knowledge, effective relationships, and workplace skills. These categories will be broken down in subsequent chapters.

References

Fogel, Y., & Larnash, L. (2021). Role perception of occupational therapists in education systems: Self-efficacy and employability skills. *Occupational Therapy International*, 1–7. https://doi.org/10.1155/2021/5531224

Godby Vail, S., Dierst-Davies, R., Kogut, D., Degiorgi Winslow, L., Kolb, D., Weckenman, A., Almeida, S., King, H. B., Chessen, E., Strickland, M., Logan, E., Gliner, M., Koeppl, P., & Marshall-Aiyelawo, K. (2023). Teamwork is associated with reduced hospital staff burnout at military treatment facilities: Findings from the 2019 Department of Defense Patient Safety Culture Survey. T*he Joint Commission Journal on Quality and Patient Safety*, *49*(2), 79–88. https://doi.org/10.1016/j.jcjq.2022.11.004

Perkins Collaborative Resource Network (PCRN). (Accessed 2023, April 15). Building Employability skills – For school – Jobs – Life [Video]. PCRN. https://cte.ed.gov/initiatives/employability-skills-framework#

Reid, A., Richards, A., & Willox, D. (2021). Connecting experiences to employability through a meaning-making approach to learning. *Journal of Teaching and Learning for Graduate Employability*, *12*(2), 99–113.

Suman, N., Marinic, M., & Kuhta, M. (2020). A methodological framework for sustainable office building renovation using green building rating systems and cost-benefit analysis. *Sustainability*, *12*(15). https://doi.org/10.3390/su12156156

The University of Queensland (U.C.). *Employability framework*. Accessed: March 1, 2023. https://employability.uq.edu.au/about/employability-framework

U.S. Department of Education. (n.d.) *Employability skills*. Perkins Collaborative Resource Network. https://cte.ed.gov/initiatives/employability-skills-framework

Chapter 4: Applied Knowledge Skills

Introduction

Thus far, we have introduced the U.S. Department of Education's Employability Framework and compared it to the University of Queensland's Employability Framework. This chapter provides greater detail of the criteria and skills that comprise the applied knowledge category.

Terminal Learning Objectives

By the end of this chapter, the reader will better understand the individual criteria or skills that comprise the category of applied knowledge skills.

Enabling Learning Objectives

By the end of this chapter, the reader will be able to:

- Describe what comprises the applied knowledge category.
- Define applied academic skills.
- Demonstrate an example of an applied academic skill.
- Describe critical thinking skills.
- Explain the requirements for developing critical thinking skills.
- Define the difference between critical thinking and clinical reasoning skills.

Instructor Notes

- *You will notice the headers in this textbook are in the form of a question. Students should be prompted to state the question and where to locate it to ensure they master the concepts.*

What Comprises the Employability Category of Applied Knowledge?

The U.S. Department of Education's Employability Skills Framework is broken into three categories. These include Applied Knowledge, Effective Relationships, and Workplace Skills. In addition, applied knowledge is further broken into applied academic and critical thinking skills.

> "Knowledge is like money: to be of value it must circulate, and in circulating it can increase in quantity and, hopefully, in value."
>
> – Louis L'Amour

Figure 20

Hierarchical Depiction of Applied Knowledge Skills

Applied Knowledge

Applied Academic Skills

- Uses reading skills
- Uses writing skills
- Uses mathematical strategies and procedures
- Uses scientific principles and procedures

Critical Thinking Skills

- Thinks critically
- Thinks creatively
- Makes sound decisions
- Solves problems
- Reasons
- Plans and organizes

Note: This is a hierarchical depiction of applied knowledge skills. The image is adapted from the U.S. Department of Education's Employability Skills Framework. Permission was obtained to use the original image on March 29, 2023, from https://cte.ed.gov/initiatives/employability-skills-framework.

> "The ability to read, write, and analyze; the confidence to stand up and demand justice and equality; the qualifications and connections to get your foot in the door and take your seat at the table — all of that starts with education."
>
> —Michelle Obama

What Are Applied Academic Skills?

Academic skills are a compilation of the knowledge, and hands-on, technical skills acquired through formalized higher education. Healthcare education focuses on the anatomy and physiology of the human body. There are specialized tracks (e.g., nursing, physical therapy, dental hygienists) within healthcare education that differentiate the healthcare team's professions.

Based on their specialized track, healthcare students learn how to use their hands-on, technical skills to provide a skilled treatment intervention to the patient. The acquired content knowledge should inform the identification of which hands-on procedure is most appropriate. Applied academic skills refer to the way a healthcare student uses the knowledge and skills they have acquired to treat the patient. Well-developed critical thinking skills enhance this process.

Figure 21

Healthcare Student Practicing her Technical Skills

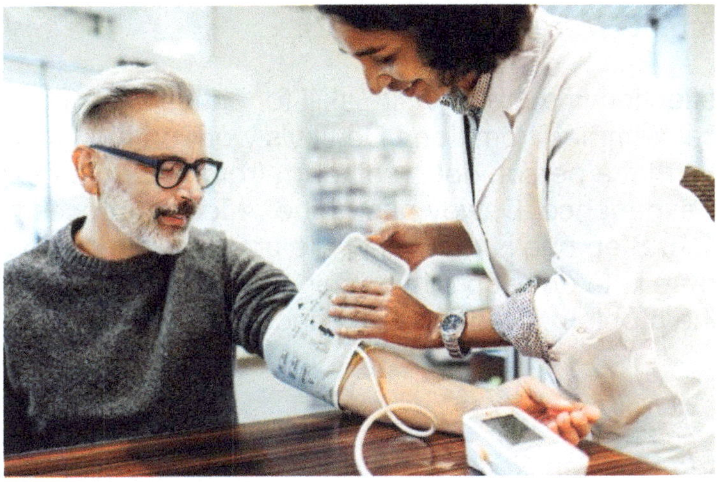

Note: This healthcare student is practicing her technical skills by taking the patient's blood pressure. This image was obtained from Microsoft Word, 2023.

How Would you Describe Critical Thinking Skills?

Critical thinking is the analysis of information for decision-making (Berg et al., 2023). It is comprised of a set of cognitive skills, including inference, assumption, deduction, interpretation, and evaluation. In addition, critical thinking is purposeful judgment guided by self-regulation, interpretation, and analysis (Céu Mendes Pinto Marques et al., 2022).

Figure 22

Healthcare Provider Performing Critical Thinking

Note: This healthcare provider is performing critical thinking. This image was obtained from Microsoft Word, 2023.

Experience facilitates the advancement of critical thinking and self-reflection. It expedites the connections between academic concepts and clinical practice. Critical thinking fosters the development of trust, creativity, and intellectual conscientiousness. As critical thinking evolves, a person builds intuitive capacity and deeper self-reflection (do Céu Mendes Pinto Marques et al., 2022).

Basic self-reflection is a prerequisite skill for critical thinking. The concept of reflective practice stemmed from John Dewey's work on thought development in 1933. Dewey's theory is that a person does not learn from having an experience, but rather reflecting on the experience. Dewey based the reflective process on the five-stage scientific approach. Step one is to identify the problem. Step two is to define the problem. Step three is to develop a hypothesis. Step four is the analysis and assessment of the problem. Step five is testing the solution (Richard et al., 2019).

Figure 23

Person Performing Self-Reflection

Note: This person is self-reflecting. This image was obtained from Microsoft Word, 2023.

Lafortune amended the definition of self-reflection because the original definition considered "reflective practice" as a process that begins with any experience with the subject matter. The amended definition suggests that reflective practice must go beyond the impression level. The reflective practice must incorporate a more critical, metacognitive, and ethical order (Richard et al., 2019).

Instructor Notes

- *For synchronous or asynchronous teaching, students should be instructed to pick three self-reflection questions included in Appendix F. Students should write an essay or produce a Vlog answering the three self-reflection questions. A rubric for this assignment is included in Appendix G.*

Critical thinking is a combination of high-level thinking and reflection. The highest level of reflection is the analysis of how assumptions, values, and beliefs impact decision-making. The use of guided reflections with probing questions enhances the development of critical thinking. (Berg et al., 2023).

Critical thinking and clinical reasoning are often thought of as interchangeable terms. However, they are not. Critical thinking requires a person to evaluate their thinking process, which exposes the assumptions, biases, and beliefs that influence clinical reasoning. Clinical reasoning is the process a healthcare provider uses to collect diagnostic data and narrative information from the patient to make a judgment on how to intervene therapeutically. Therefore, critical thinking is a prerequisite skill for clinical reasoning (Sullivan, 2022).

Figure 24

Healthcare Provider Explaining her Clinical Reasoning

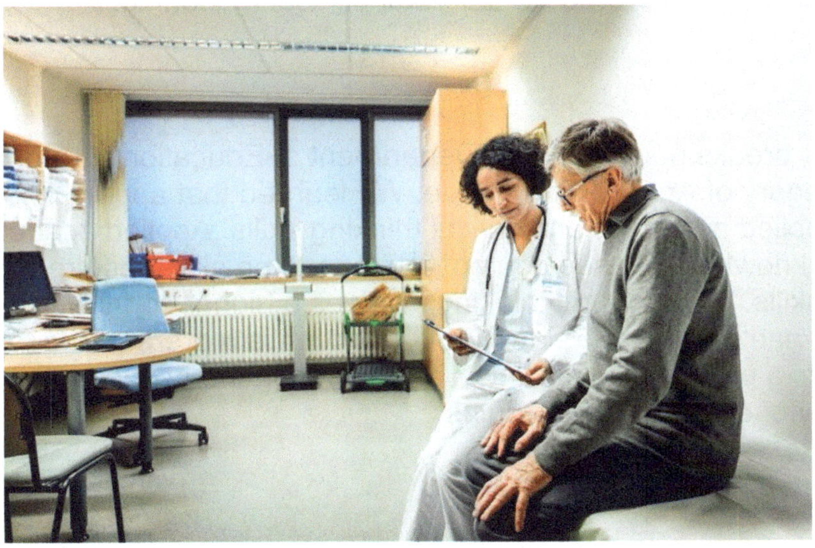

Note: This healthcare provider is explaining her clinical reasoning to a patient. This image was obtained from Microsoft Word, 2023.

In this regard, clinical reasoning is filtered through the clinician's personal experiences, beliefs, and biases. These biases can significantly impact health disparities. They are often unconscious reactions to social determinants of health. Due to this, clinical reasoning is more subjective than relying upon an empirical pattern recognition process. Clinical reasoning is dependent upon the therapeutic relationship between the clinician and the patient (Sullivan, 2022). For this reason, clinical reasoning is a collaborative process between the clinician and the patient. The clinician is responsible for gauging the patient's ability to make health-related behavioral changes.

What Are the Key Concepts from this Chapter?

- The U.S. Department of Education's Employability Skills Framework is broken into three categories: Applied Knowledge, Effective Relationships, and Workplace Skills.
- Applied knowledge is further broken into applied academic and critical thinking skills.
- Academic skills are a compilation of the knowledge, and hands-on, technical skills acquired through formalized higher education.
- Critical thinking is the analysis of information for decision-making.
- Critical thinking is a set of cognitive skills to include inference, assumption, deduction, interpretation, and evaluation.
- Self-reflection is a prerequisite skill for critical thinking.
- Critical thinking is a combination of high-level thinking and reflection.
- Clinical reasoning is the process a healthcare provider uses to collect diagnosticdata and narrative information from the patient to make a judgment on how to intervene therapeutically.
- Critical thinking is a prerequisite skill for clinical reasoning.

Summary

This chapter breaks down the U.S. Department of Education's Employability Skills Framework category of Applied Knowledge. We learned that applied knowledge is comprised of applied academic and critical thinking skills. Applied academic skills encompass the knowledge-based content and hands-on skills required to perform technical work skills. While critical thinking involves a higher cognitive process for the analysis of data and making decisions. Self-reflection is a prerequisite for critical thinking, which is a prerequisite of clinical reasoning. In the next chapter, we will delve into the category of effective relationships.

References

Berg, C., Philipp, R., & Taff, S. D. (2023). Scoping review of critical thinking literature in healthcare education. *Occupational Therapy in Health Care*, *37*(1), 18–39.

do Céu Mendes Pinto Marques, M., José Lopes, M., Domingues Cabral Magalhães, M. D., & Mota Sousa, L. M. (2022). Development of critical thinking in nursing students. *Revista Baiana de Enfermagem*, 36, 1–10. https://doi.org/10.18471/rbe.v36.42849

Richard, A., Gagnon, M., & Careau, E. (2019). Using reflective practice in interprofessional education and practice: A realist review of its characteristics and effectiveness. *Journal Of Interprofessional Care*, *33*(5), 424–436. https://doi.org/10.1080/13561820.2018.1551867

Sullivan, A., Beltran, C., Ranchoff, B., Hayes, M., Atkins, K., Tibbles, C., Cohen, A., Cohen, D. Huang, G. & Schwartzstein, R. (2022). Enhancing clinical teaching in critical thinking, high-value care, and health care equity. *Journal of Continuing Education in the Health Professions*, *42*(3), 164-173. doi:10.1097/CEH.0000000000000441.

Chapter 5: Effective Relationship Skills

Introduction

You might define effective relationships as the personal connections with your friends, family, and significant others. While this is not incorrect, it is not an all-encompassing definition. A person's ability to form effective relationships with others plays a vital role in all our daily interactions. This chapter explores the criteria and qualities that comprise effective relationships.

Figure 25

Young Adults Who Share an Effective Relationship

Note: These adults share an effective relationship. This image was obtained from Microsoft Word, 2023.

Terminal Learning Objectives

By the end of this chapter, the reader will better understand the individual criteria or skills that comprise effective relationship skills.

Enabling Learning Objectives

By the end of this chapter, the reader will be able to:

- Describe what comprises the category of effective relationships.
- Define interpersonal skills.
- Provide examples of various interpersonal skills.
- Explain what personal qualities are.
- Provide examples of different personal qualities.

Instructor Notes

- *You will notice the headers in this textbook are in the form of a question. Students should be prompted to state the question and where to locate it to ensure they master the concepts.*

What Comprises the Employability Category of Applied Knowledge?

The second category of the U.S. Department of Education's Employability Skills Framework is Effective Relationships. This is divided into interpersonal skills and personal qualities.

Figure 26

Hierarchical Depiction of Effective Relationship Skills

Effective Relationships

Interpersonal Skills

- Understands teamwork andworks with others
- Responds to customer needs
- Exercises leadership
- Negotiates to resolve conflicts
- Respects individual differences

Personal Qualities

- Demonstrates responsibility and self-discipline
- Adapts and showsflexibility
- Works independently
- Demonstrates a willingness to learn
- Demonstrates integrity
- Demonstrates professionalism
- Takes initiative
- Displays a positive attitude and sense of self-worth
- Takes responsibility for professional growth

Note: This is a hierarchical depiction of effective relationship skills. This image was adapted from the U.S. Department of Education's Employability Skills Framework. Permission was obtained to use the original image on March 29, 2023, fromhttps://cte.ed.gov/initiatives/employability-skills-framework.

What Are Interpersonal Skills?

Interpersonal skills include qualities such as empathy, respectfulness, and openness (Wolfer et al., 2021). Interpersonal relationships are an integral component of the competent delivery of health care. This is because well-educated and emotionally intelligent healthcare providers communicate more effectively and work more collaboratively to improve patient outcomes. In addition, interpersonal skills are unique to each individual since they are expressed in relation to a person's surrounding environment (Efrat, 2022).

Many employers believe interpersonal skills should be taught in higher education. However, these conceptual skills are more challenging to teach than concrete concepts and skills (Sharma, 2021). Students believe simulated learning experiences work best for improving confidence, clinical application, and interpersonal skills (Busch & Ma, 2023).

It is interesting to note the degree to which the situation influences interpersonal skills. This is referred to as "situated cognition", which posits that the context in which an event occurs affects the interpretation of the event. This interpretation can influence the event's outcomes (Lucas et al., 2023). From a formalized educational perspective, students need to be well-versed in the social and cultural contexts that influence a situation. Awareness of the potential social and cultural influences prepares healthcare students to navigate a situation more effectively.

Figure 27

Culturally Diverse Group of People

Note: These people are displaying awareness of the social and cultural influences of the situation. This image was obtained from Microsoft Word, 2023.

Awareness of social and cultural concepts is the first skill required for interpersonal skills. The second skill is controlling one's emotional response to a situation. This is referred to as emotional intelligence. A person can perceive the social and cultural influences of a situation, understand the other person's perspective, manage their own emotions about the situation, and act according to the other person's needs (Cox, 2018).

Emotional intelligence requires perceiving, understanding, and managing emotions (Pienimaa, 2023). Emotional intelligence consists of four dimensions: self-awareness, self-management, social awareness, and relationship management. Self-awareness is a person's ability to identify their emotions. Self-management is a person's ability to reason with their emotions for problem-solving. Social awareness is the ability to understand other people's emotions. Finally, relationship management is a person's ability to manage their emotions and those of others in the spirit of teamwork (Cox, 2018).

> "The world is your mirror, and your mind is a magnet. What you perceive in this world is largely a reflection of your own attitudes and beliefs. Life will give you what you attract with your thoughts. Think, act and talk negatively and your world will be negative. Think and act and talk with enthusiasm and you will attract positive results."
>
> —Michael LeBoeuf

Self-awareness and self-management skills typically develop before social awareness. An accurate self-assessment is a precursor to the expression of social competence. Accurate self-assessment facilitates critical thinking and clinical judgment. All are hallmarks of professional, collaborative practice (Cox, 2018).

Conflict resolution is an interpersonal skill that can be uncomfortable. Most people do not like engaging in conflict because it evokes many unpleasant feelings. Successful conflict resolution requires a person to seek to understand the reason for the dispute. Then a person must employ tactics to neutralize the disagreement. After that, the goal is to find a win-win solution. This is accomplished through collaboration, compromising, and occasionally withdrawing. Unfortunately, there is no universal way to resolve conflicts. The most important first step is to recognize that conflict is present. A common reason conflicts escalate is that adversaries don't realize they're in a conflict. The second stage is to halt the situation before it accelerates into a dispute. Finally, everyone must be able to express their viewpoint (Braverman, 2021).

Figure 28

Two Penguins Involved in Conflict

Note: These penguins are involved in conflict. This image was obtained from Microsoft Word, 2023.

What Comprises Personal Qualities?

Personal qualities are a person's morals, values, virtues, and beliefs. They are a person's unique characteristics or attributes, such as being helpful or sincere. A person's core beliefs and values inform their professional identity, which is comprised of their theoretical orientation and service-delivery style. Personal skills are a person's abilities, such as the ability to speak a second language. A clinician's personal qualities contribute to the development of a therapeutic relationship, which influences patient outcomes (Verner et al., 2021).

Individuation is the dynamic process in which clinicians and practitioners seek to achieve coherence between their personal qualities and professional identity (Verner et al., 2021). It is the process of trying to see how an individual 'fits' into their work environment. Understanding that people and environments are constantly changing can be especially challenging. Logically, the greater the self-awareness, the easier it is for a clinician to achieve congruence between their personal qualities and professional identity within the evolving environment.

Figure 29

Healthcare Provider Holding a Patient's Hand

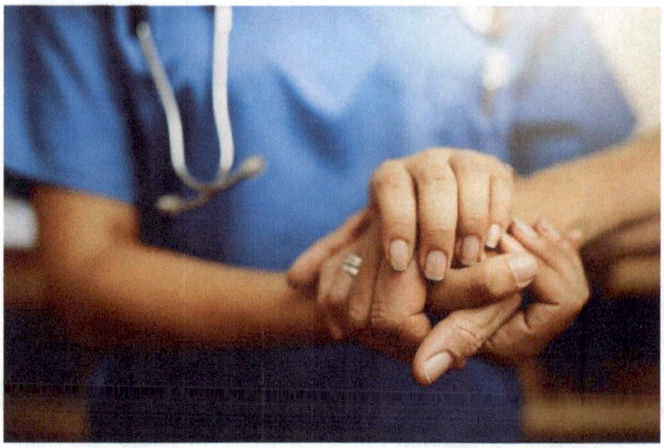

Note: This healthcare provider is holding a patient's hand to express care and empathy. This image was obtained from Microsoft Word, 2023.

New clinicians and healthcare students struggle to understand what these personal qualities 'look like' in clinical practice. Students, especially, are often still developing their personal qualities and/or understanding how their attributes influence their clinical practice. As a result, healthcare students and new clinicians feel a lack of congruence and cohesion between their personal and professional identities, which prevents individuation. This can raise concerns about how their deficiencies negatively impact patient outcomes (Verner et al., 2021).

What Are the Key Concepts from this Chapter?

- The category of Effective Relationships is divided into interpersonal skills and personal qualities.
- Interpersonal skills encompass qualities such as empathy, respectfulness, and openness.
- Interpersonal skills are unique to an individual as they are expressed in relation to a person's surrounding environment.
- "Situated cognition" posits that the context in which an event occurs affects the interpretation of the event.
- Emotional intelligence is the ability to perceive the social and cultural influences of a situation; to understand the other person's perspective; to manage their own emotions about the situation, and to act according to the other person's needs.
- Conflict resolution is seeking an understanding of the reason for the dispute.
- A common reason conflicts escalate is that adversaries don't realize they're in a conflict.
- Personal qualities are a person's morals, values, virtues, and beliefs. They are a person's unique characteristics or attributes.
- Individuation is the dynamic process in which clinicians and practitioners seek to achieve coherence between their personal qualities and professional identity.

Summary

This chapter discussed the U.S. Department of Education's Employability Skills Framework category of Effective Relationships. The chapter explored the concepts related to interpersonal skills and how interpersonal skills can impact the quality of patient care. Emotional intelligence is an essential aspect of interpersonal skills in health care. To convey emotional intelligence, a person must have self-awareness, self-management, social awareness, and the ability to manage their relationships.

Other factors that influence a person's ability to form effective relationships are the person's individual qualities, unique characteristics or attributes that come from a person's morals, values, virtues, and beliefs. The personal qualities displayed by the clinician contribute to the development of a therapeutic relationship, which influences patient outcomes. The next chapter delves into the category of workplace skills.

References

Braverman, A. (2021). Conflict resolution. *Nursing Management (Springhouse)*, *52*(9), 30-34. doi: 10.1097/01.NUMA.0000771740.79361.1c.

Busch, C. M., & Ma, T. (2023). Speech-language pathology graduate students' perception of satisfaction, confidence, and interpersonal skill development during simulated experiences amid COVID-19. *Perspectives of the ASHA Special Interest Groups*, *8*(1), 134–150. https://doi.org/10.1044/2022_PERSP-22-00073

Cox, K. M. (2018). Use of emotional intelligence to enhance advanced practice registered nursing competencies. *Journal of Nursing Education*, *57*(11), 648–654. https://doi.org/10.3928/01484834-20181022-04

Efrat, A. (2022). Reviews of literature regarding interpersonal skills and the workplace over the years 2011-2021. *Network Intelligence Studies*, *X*(19 (1/2022)), 53–63.

Lucas, G. M., Mell, J., Boberg, J., Zenone, F., de Visser, E. J., Tossell, C., & Seech, T. (2023). Customizing virtual interpersonal skills training applications may not improve trainee performance. *Scientific Reports*, *13*(1), 78. https://doi.org/10.1038/s41598-022-27154-2

Pienimaa, A., Talman, K., Vierula, J., Laakkonen, E., & Haavisto, E. (2023). Development and psychometric evaluation of the Emotional Intelligence Test (EMI-T) for social care and healthcare student selection. *Journal of Advanced Nursing*, *79*(2), 850–863. https://doi.org/10.1111/jan.15557

Sharma, S. (2021). Medical profession and soft skills. *Journal of Ayurveda*, *15*(3), 153.

Verner, D., Chandler, C., & Clarke, P. (2021). Exploring the contribution of personal qualities to the personal and professional development of trainee sport psychology practitioners within the individuation process. *Physical Culture & Sport. Studies & Research, 92*(1), 43–54.

Wolfer, C., Vîslă, A., Held, J., Hilpert, P., & Flückiger, C. (2021). Assessing interpersonal skills-A comparison of trainee therapists' and students' interpersonal skills assessed with two established assessments for interpersonal skills. *Clinical Psychology & Psychotherapy*, *28*(1), 226–232. https://doi.org/10.1002/cpp.2487

Chapter 6: Workplace Skills

Introduction

Workplace skills permeate all aspects of an organization. They define the company's workplace culture and its performance. For example, suppose you go out to dinner. If the restaurant is dirty, they burn your food, or the service is terrible, these things make a poor impression on you. If these things happen consistently, that restaurant will lose customers, which negatively affect performance and profitability. This is because workplace skills are critical to a company's success.

Figure 30

Customers Enjoying Their Lunch Break

Note: These restaurant patrons are enjoying their lunch break. This image was obtained from Microsoft Word, 2023.

Terminal Learning Objectives

By the end of this chapter, the reader will better understand the individual criteria or skills that comprise the category of workplace skills.

Enabling Learning Objectives

By the end of this chapter, the reader will be able to:

- Describe what comprises the category of workplace skills.
- Define technology use.
- Provide examples of technology use.
- Define information use.
- Provide examples of information use.
- Explain what systems thinking means.
- Provide examples using systems thinking in healthcare.
- Explain what resource management means.

- Provide examples of resource management in healthcare.
- Describe what communication skills are.
- Differentiate between different forms of communication skills.

Instructor Notes

- *You will notice the headers in this textbook are in the form of a question. Students should be prompted to state the question and where to locate it to ensure they master the concepts.*

What Comprises the Employability Category of Workplace Skills?

Workplace Skills is the final category of the U.S. Department of Education's Employability Skills Framework. This is divided into technology use, information use, systems thinking, resource management, and communication skills.

Figure 31

A Hierarchical Depiction of Workplace Skills

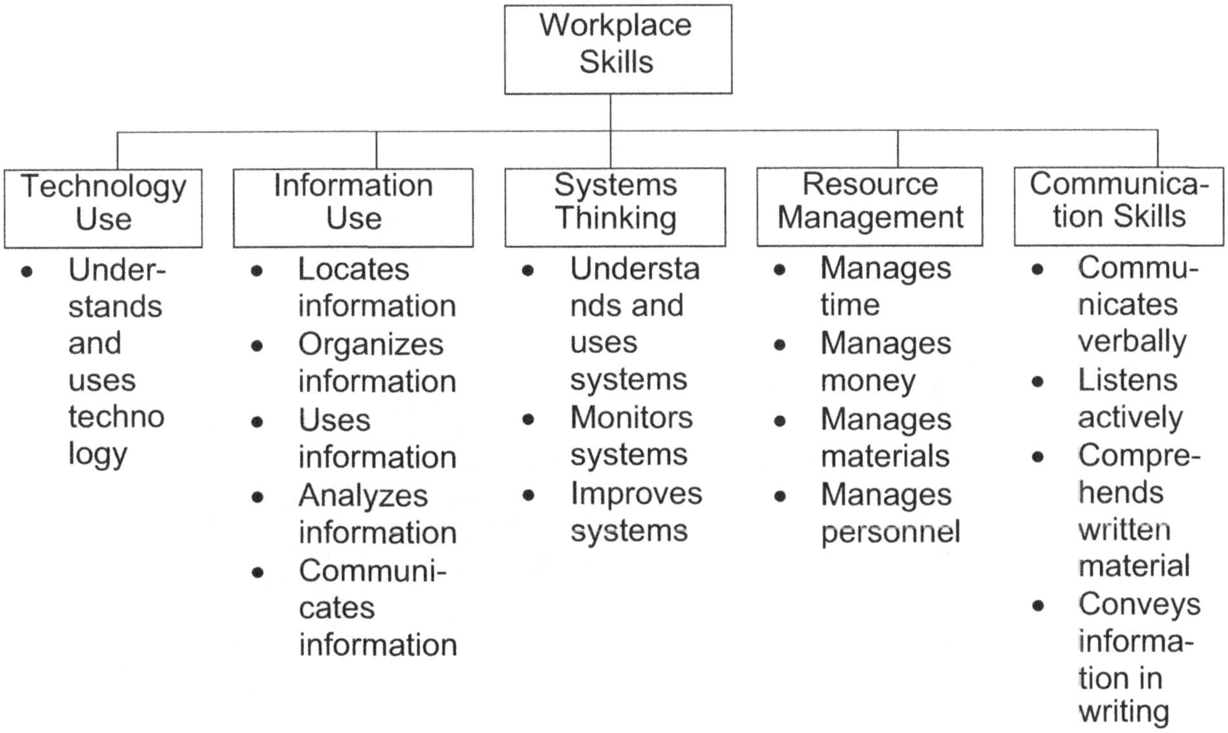

Note: This is a hierarchical depiction of workplace skills. This image was adapted from the U.S. Department of Education's Employability Skills Framework. Permission was obtained to use the original image on March 29, 2023, from https://cte.ed.gov/initiatives/employability-skills-framework.

What Does Technology Use Mean?

Technology has advanced tremendously, and now permeates much of our modern world. The field of healthcare is no exception. Technological advances have dramatically changed our access to health information and the fluidity of interpersonal communications to obtain medical information. We live in a 'wired lifestyle' or 'mobile culture.' Wireless technologies allow us to transmit data and services through mobile devices and personal computers. Telecommunications and multimedia technologies are used to create, store, retrieve and transmit data in real time (del Río-Lanza et al., 2020).

There are many ways in which technology use has vastly improved healthcare. The greatest benefit is the improved accessibility to healthcare services. It also helps us to understand the patient's preferences toward their healthcare. In addition, technology use promotes value-based healthcare, such as cost containment (del Río-Lanza et al., 2020). The benefits and uses of technology have advanced dramatically due to the COVID-19 pandemic. Digital technologies have become the mainstay in much of life. In a time when life seemed abruptly placed on pause, technology bridged the gap and became our connection to one another. In many aspects, our lives will never fully return to a pre-pandemic state.

Figure 32

Healthcare Provider Using Digital Technology

Note: This healthcare provider uses digital technology to accomplish her work. This image was obtained from Microsoft Word, 2023.

The introduction of wearable technology is another major advancement in healthcare. Applications such as these help patients manage their lifestyle choices. For example, patients can use technology to help monitor and track their diet, weight, and movement. The success of these applications mainly depends on their ease of use, the consistency of data entry, and the time demands for use (Phillips et al., 2019).

Wearable technology has the potential to transform the way patients understand and manage their health. Wearable technology has enhanced how patients understand and manage their conditions. The downside is that sometimes users fail to use them due to time constraints. For this reason, wearable devices that collect and correspond data continuously without user involvement are more successful (Phillips et al., 2019).

Figure 33

This Person Checks Her Wearable Technology

Note: This female is checking her wearable technology. This image was obtained from Microsoft Word, 2023.

One barrier to technology use is its lack of personalization. Despite the obvious value of technology, users desire a more human connection. Personalized feedback aids in understanding and accountability. This challenge has sparked several adaptive learning initiatives, such as the use of artificial intelligence. Technologies like this integrate user data analytics with customers' behaviors to for individualized feedback (Phillips et al., 2019).

What Does Information Use Mean?

Information use refers to the process of understanding what information sources people choose and how they apply them to their lives and individual situations. Information is the data that people acquire through all five senses to understand the world around them. One factor impacting information use is the degree of attention. Information use is often dependent on selective attention. This refers to the fact that people pay attention to information relatively passively until it becomes more useful and meaningful (Encyclopedia of Communication and Information, February 22, 2023).

People seek information when they are trying to understand a situation. There are several types of information: factual, conceptual, procedural, emotional, behavioral, attitudinal, and motivational. Information can be used instrumentally, such as learning to do something tangible. Information can be used cognitively to generate ideas or in an emotional manner to share feelings and support for others (Encyclopedia of Communication and Information, February 22, 2023).

Figure 34

This X-Ray Will Inform Clinical Decision-Making

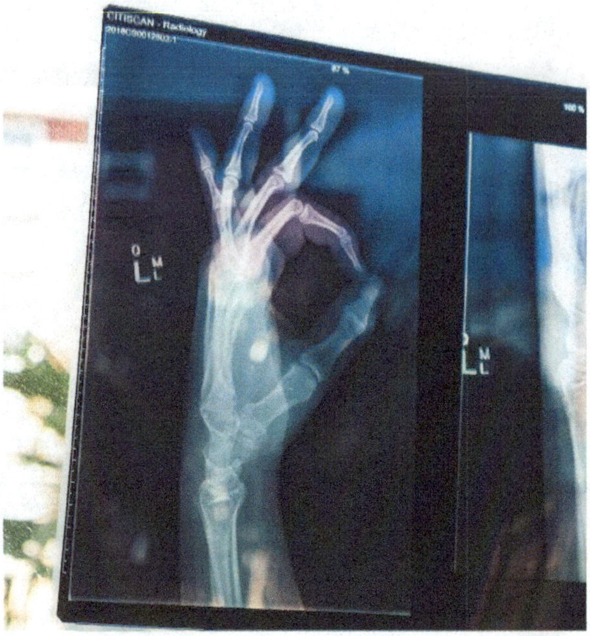

Note: This x-ray graph represents information to be used to inform decision-making at work. This image by Owen Beard was obtained from Unsplash.com, 2023.

Sharing information often depends on psychological, contextual, and social variables. The psychological variables are an individual's personality characteristics. Contextual variables are the nuances of the environment that affect information exchange, such as the comfort of the environment. Finally, social variables include social expectations and norms (Encyclopedia of Communication and Information, February 22, 2023).

The context in which people ask questions can directly impact information-related problems. This is sometimes referred to as the information use environment. Four factors comprise the information use environment: the people, the criteria used to evaluate the information related to a problem, where a person seeks knowledge, and how the person resolves problems (Encyclopedia of Communication and Information, February 22, 2023). In addition, from a non-work perspective, information use has social dimensions which overlay the information.

Sometimes people fail to use information. This is usually because they are unaware, they have access to the information. Sometimes people do not know what information is needed or available. Deficient communication, technical skills, or lack of trust in the source may contribute to poor information use. People are less inclined to retrieve information when it is very complex and must be collected from multiple sources.

Furthermore, information use depends on a person's information literacy. This is the ability to use information effectively. Information literacy requires the ability to reason, communicate effectively, and think critically and creatively. In addition, information use is associated with self-efficacy or the belief that one can accomplish a task. If people do not believe they can access the information successfully, they are less inclined to seek it. Finally, safe information use requires a person to have an ethical stance, integrity, and trust. Without those qualities, information is likely to be used for personal gain and not for the benefit of others (Encyclopedia of Communication and Information, February 22, 2023).

Figure 35

Healthcare Provider Demonstrating Information Literacy

Note: This healthcare provider is demonstrating information literacy. This image was obtained from Microsoft Word, 2023.

How Would You Describe System Thinking?

Systems thinking is analyzing how systems work from a holistic perspective. It requires recognizing, understanding, and integrating the parts into a functioning system. Systems thinking focuses on understanding how the components are interconnected and how behaviors interact synergistically (Hwang & Park, 2017).

Figure 36

Employee Overseeing a Team of People with Unique Tasks, Working Together as Part of a Larger System

Note: This employee is overseeing a team of people with unique tasks, working together as part of a larger system. This image was obtained from Microsoft Word, 2023.

Healthcare providers who are well-versed in systems thinking understand how complex care systems work collaboratively to identify systems problems and develop changes to make healthcare delivery safer for the patient (Hwang & Park, 2017). For this reason, complex healthcare systems emphasize learning how to collect data, compile it, and recognize connections. Once data is collected from multiple sources, it must be synthesized and analyzed for trends (Clark & Hoffman, 2019).

A rapidly changing healthcare environment makes it difficult for students to develop systems thinking proficiency without sufficient clinical experience. Due to this, education on system thinking needs to be multifaceted. System thinking development helps healthcare students see more than just themselves within the healthcare environment. Students better equipped to understand their role as part of a system can provide higher quality collaborative care (Clark & Hoffman, 2019).

To What Does Resource Management Refer?

Resource management is the practice of allocating resources for the greatest organizational value. It requires planning, scheduling, allocation, and transparency. The greater the transparency, the easier it is to assess all the strengths and weaknesses of resources. Transparency facilitates the effective allocation of resources. In many ways, the allocation of resources has the greatest impact on organizational value. Good resource management puts the right resource in the right place at the right time (Hansen, 2022, May 31).

Figure 37

People Making Decisions Regarding Resource Allocation

Note: These people are making decisions about resource allocation. This image was obtained from Microsoft Word, 2023.

What Are Communication Skills?

Effective communication is among the top four most important employability skills that employers seek (Mainga et al., 2022). Communication is a complex exchange of information that is influenced by multiple factors. These include the participants' relationship, personal understanding and perception of one another, and the situation. Other communication factors include mood, time, space, culture, facial expressions, and gestures. In addition, effective communication has been proven to improve patient satisfaction and adherence to care. These leads to improved quality of care and positive treatment outcomes (Afriyie, 2020).

Effective healthcare communication is accomplished when the provider and patient achieve mutual agreement and satisfaction regarding patient care. Successful communication in healthcare yields improved clinical reasoning by the clinician and enhanced compliance with treatment interventions on the part of the patient. Collaborative communication promotes patient-centered care, optimal treatment outcomes, and improved satisfaction (Afriyie, 2020).

Figure 38

Healthcare Provider Demonstrating Effective Communication

Note: This healthcare provider is demonstrating effective communication. This image was obtained from Microsoft Word, 2023.

There are several characteristics associated with effective communication. These include building a foundation for interpersonal relationships, promoting respect and dignity, achieving harmony, empowering self-care in the patient, patient-centered care, and clinical reasoning. To achieve effective communication, a person needs to possess certain personality traits. For example, people who are more introverted are often less likely to communicate as effectively as compared to those who are more extroverted (Afriyie, 2020). Likewise, a person with low self-esteem is usually less inclined to communicate. People with low self-esteem are often more sensitive to environmental cues and may feel more anxiety or fear regarding communication. Awareness of one's personality type and how others react to it can reduce workplace conflicts (Terry, 2020).

Patient-centered communication helps to establish a shared understanding of the problem and its treatment. It is accomplished by eliciting and respecting the patient's perspective, using open-ended questions, and avoiding medical jargon. The provider allows the patient sufficient time and must consider the options. It is essential to pay attention to the nonverbal behaviors. Using open body language and displaying a positive affect and attentiveness are most helpful for conveying empathy and establishing rapport. These are particularly important when providing patient education. Patients with a deeper understanding of their condition are more likely to comply with treatment interventions and convey their symptoms (Suojanen et al., 2018).

Cultural diversity is another factor that influences communication. Cultural diversity reflects a person's and their parent's country of birth, ancestry, languages spoken, religious affiliation, customs, and belief systems (Brooks et al., 2019). With so many influences, communication embracing cultural diversity can be challenging.

The best way to overcome cultural barriers is to understand your own cultural beliefs, values, attitudes, and those of others. It is best to use open communication to describe patient. It is crucial to respect the patient's choices, even if they differ from your own or what you believe is the best treatment approach for the patient (Brooks et al., 2019). Cultural competence is enhanced by self-awareness, active observation, andlistening. It's also important to observe how patients interact with their families and watch nonverbal behaviors and pay attention to how they communicate. The better you can understand the motivations of others, the easier it is to convey cultural competence with communication.

Figure 39

Symbol of the Day of the Dead Celebration

Note: This picture is a symbol of the Day of the Dead celebration, a traditional Mexican holiday. This image was obtained from Microsoft Word, 2023.

What Are the Key Concepts from this Chapter?

- Workplace skills include technology use, information use, systems thinking, resource management, and communication skills.
- Technology use refers to how to use various technologies to create, store, retrieve and transmit data in real time. As a result, technology use informs our professional and personal lives.
- Information use refers to the process of understanding what information sources people choose and how they apply them to their lives and situations. Information is the data that people acquire through all five senses to understand the world around them.
- Systems thinking is the analysis of how systems work holistically. It requires recognizing, understanding, and integrating the parts into a functioning system.
- Resource management is the practice of allocating resources for the greatest organizational value. It requires planning, scheduling, allocation, and transparency.

- Communication is a complex exchange of information that is influenced by multiple factors.
- Effective communication has been proven to improve patient satisfaction and adherence to care. These leads to improved care quality and positive treatment outcomes (Afriyie, 2020).
- Cultural diversity is another factor that influences communication. Cultural diversity accounts for a person's and their parents' country of birth, ancestry, languages spoken, religious affiliation, customs, and belief systems (Brooks et al., 2019).

Summary

This chapter explored the workplace category of employability skills. Workplace skills encompass technology and information use, systems thinking, resource management, and communication. These skills have the most significant influence on a company's success. Companies that fail to use their resources effectively lose money and market share. Communication is the most important of these skills, especially for healthcare providers. While all these skills seem like relatively simple concepts, these are the areas that graduates struggle with the most. The next chapter examines how healthcare students and graduates are perceived by those already working in the field.

References

Afriyie, D. (2020). Effective communication between nurses and patients: An evolutionary concept analysis. *British Journal of Community Nursing*, *25*(9), 438–445. https://doi.org/10.12968/bjcn.2020.25.9.438

Brooks, L. A., Manias, E., & Bloomer, M. J. (2019). Culturally sensitive communication in healthcare: A concept analysis. *Collegian*, *26*(3), 383–391. https://doi.org/10.1016/j.colegn.2018.09.007

Clark, K., & Hoffman, A. (2019). Educating healthcare students: Strategies to teach systems thinking to prepare new healthcare graduates. *Journal of Professional Nursing*, *35*(3), 195–200. https://doi.org/10.1016/j.profnurs.2018.12.006

del Río-Lanza, A.-B., Suárez-Vázquez, A., Suárez-Álvarez, L., & Iglesias-Argüelles, V. (2020). Mobile health (mhealth): Facilitators and barriers of the intention of use in patients with chronic illnesses. *Journal of Communication in Healthcare*, *13*(2), 138–146. https://doi.org/10.1080/17538068.2020.1777513

Encyclopedia of Communication and Information. (Retrieved February 22, 2023). "Use of Information." Encyclopedia.com. https://www.encyclopedia.com/media/encyclopedias-almanacs-transcripts-and-maps/use-information.

Hansen, B. (2022, May 31). *What is resource management and why is it important?* Wrike. https://www.wrike.com/blog/what-is-resource-management/

Hwang, J., & Park, H. (2017). Nurses' systems thinking competency, medical error reporting, and the occurrence of adverse events: A cross-sectional study. *Contemporary Nurse: A Journal for the Australian Nursing Profession*, *53*(6), 622-632. https://doi.org/10.1080/10376178.2017.1409081

Mainga, W., Daniel, R. M., & Alamil, L. (2022). Perceptions of employability skills of undergraduate business students in a developing country: An exploratory study.

Higher Learning Research Communications, *12*(1), 28–63.
Phillips, S. A., Ali, M., Modrich, C., Oke, S., Elokda, A., Laddu, D., & Bond, S. (2019). Advances in health technology use and implementation in the era of healthy living: Implications for precision medicine. *Progress in Cardiovascular Diseases*, *62*(1), 44–49. https://doi.org/10.1016/j.pcad.2018.12.007
Suojanen, K., Woodall, K., Hammonds, J. R., Monie, D., Scribani, M., Krupa, N., Jenkins, P., Weil, H., & Frye, J. J. (2018). Teaching future doctors to communicate: A communication intervention for medical students in their clinical year. *Journal of Communication in Healthcare*, *11*(4), 263–277. https://doi.org/10.1080/17538068.2018.1507082
Terry, L. (2020). Understanding and applying personality types in healthcare communication. *Nursing Standard (Royal College of Nursing (Great Britain): 1987*, *35*(7), 27-34. https://doi.org/10.7748/ns.2020.e11509

Chapter 7: Perceptions of Today's Healthcare Students and Graduates

Introduction

The employability competencies deemed most lacking in today's healthcare students and graduates include impaired safety, poor clinical reasoning, lack of professionalism, poor self-awareness, and impaired interpersonal and communication skills. These deficiencies are consistently lacking among all types of healthcare providers across the globe. Caruana & Damilakis (2021) explained that employability skills are difficult to teach, which could be why they are lacking among students.

Terminal Learning Objectives

By the end of this chapter, the reader will better understand how today's healthcare students and graduates are perceived by the clinical educators who supervise these students during their clinical experiences and the employers who seek to hire them.

Enabling Learning Objectives

By the end of this chapter, the reader will be able to:

- Categorize the perceptions about today's healthcare students and graduates.
- Speculate as to why these deficits might exist.
- Explain the generational impact of employability skills deficits.
- Describe who is in healthcare education.
- Interpret the perceptions of clinical educators for allied healthcare students.
- Describe a student performing below expectations (SPBE).
- Break down the types of safety issues displayed by SPBE.
- Describe the poor clinical reasoning skills displayed by SPBE.
- Categorize what is lack of professionalism.
- Break down the common deficits with interpersonal and communication skills displayed by SPBE.
- Describe the perceptions of clinical educators for non-allied healthcare professions.
- Apprise the implications of SPBE.

Instructor Notes

- *You will notice the headers in this textbook are in the form of a question. Students should be prompted to state the question and where to locate it to ensure they master the concepts.*
- *For synchronous and asynchronous teaching, have students describe the impact the perceptions of clinical educators and employers has on their academic goals. This can be completed as a discussion, essay, or video log (Vlog).*

What Are the Perceptions of Today's Healthcare Students and Graduates?

Deluliis & Saylor (2021) explain who they are determined that the workforce will be comprised of 50% Generation Y over the next two years. Generation Y is comprised of people born between the early 1980s and the late 1990s. The National Association of Colleges and Employers (NACE) class of 2019 survey identified significant disparities in key areas of employment. Graduate students felt they are competent with employability skills, while employers saw gaps in professionalism and work ethic. While almost 95% of students considered themselves not lacking in professionalism, employers described graduates as "entitled and overly confident" (Deluliis & Saylor, 2021).

The World Economic Forum (2018) identified that the top ten skills employers demanded by 2020 were predominately employability skills, followed by technical skills. Nirmala & Dsouza (2022) studied a variety of factors to determine their impact on employability skills development. They concluded that employability skills are not dependent on demographical variables or gender. They explained that employability competency is dependent upon the student's attributes, the university's teaching and learning strategies, and employers' expectations. Consistent among all the research of the stakeholders is that proper communication learned through higher education is the most valued employability skill.

Figure 40

Healthcare Provider Explaining Something to a Student

Note: This healthcare provider is explaining something to a student. This image was obtained from Microsoft Word, 2023.

The clinical educators supervising the healthcare students during their clinical experiences have noted deficits related to impaired safety awareness and difficulty with clinical reasoning. There is an increasing number of allied healthcare students who during clinical experiences display deficits with employability skills (Continisio et al., 2021; So et al., 2019; Wells et al., 2021). Clinical educators have complained of issues with professionalism and poor self-awareness. The deficits which have the greatest impact on the clinical experience are interpersonal and communication skills. All these skills are imperative to provide patient-centered care.

Why Might These Deficits Exist?

These deficits are partly the result of the additional coursework at the doctoral level. This paradigm shift has resulted in fewer teaching strategies focused on the development of employability skills, and more time dedicated to the technical skills of healthcare providers (Metgud & D'Silva, 2021). This has been the case in many healthcare professions. Healthcare students have reported feeling increased stress and anxiety, especially during didactic education. factors that have impacted healthcare education include the increase in class or cohort size, which decreases the amount of one-on-one time dedicated to each student.

Does Generation Have an Impact on the Presence of Employability Skills Deficits?

Through the application of generational theory, Whitney et al. (2021) described who they are sought to understand the development of professional communication.

Professional communication is defined as the relay of information in a variety of formats(e.g., written, oral, digital) in a workplace context. Generational Theory states that cohorts are defined by the sociocultural environment acquired through a set of shared experiences. This occurs over approximately 20 years.

Figure 41

Three Generations of Women

Note: Three generations of women. This image was obtained from Microsoft Word, 2023.

Whitney et al. (2021) researched the development of professional communication of the Y Generation. This is the generation that comprises much of the healthcare student population. Due to the influences of popular culture, Generation Y graduates desire a casual approach to working along with a strong need for positive feedback. The Y generation has been described as having difficulty accepting and processing constructive feedback. Generation Y graduates communicate more casually when speaking or writing. This fits with their desire for a casual work environment and is influenced by the prolific use coupled with the influence of technology and social media. The use of text language has contributed to poor grammar and spelling in professional communication.

The Generation Y graduate is accustomed to having immediate access to information. This has resulted in an increased expectation for clarity and explanations, and these expectations have trickled into the workplace. Generation Y graduates do not respond well to micromanagement, yet they expect detailed instructions. Graduates from this generation expect to remain in contact in their personal lives via technology throughout their working days. This need for connection exists regardless of the work setting or who is in their presence (Whitney et al., 2021).

Most healthcare students are between 23-26 years old. This places them in the Generation Y or Z age group. Generation Z are people born between 1997 and 2012. Students in the Y generation tend to have high expectations in terms of salary and flexibility in the work environment (Chaudhari et al., 2021who are they). Students in the Y generation desire a work schedule that promotes a healthy work-life balance. The Y generation seeks less stress and a lighter workload. Students in this demographic also expect more leave time than the generation before them. They want their emotions, feelings, and social experiences to be valued by their organization. Students from the Z generation are the least likely to have worked when they were younger (Schroth, 2019). The Z generation students have more incidences of depression and anxiety. These students also gravitate toward technology and social media, social justice movements, and awareness of cultural safety (Chaudhari, 2021).

Logically speaking, if a large section of the current workforce does not include members of the Y or Z generation, then it's reasonable to assume that generational differences could be contributing to the mismatch of actual and expected performance. Although, generation is not exclusively to blame. The COVID-19 pandemic also influences many of today's graduates.

Instructor Notes

- *For synchronous and asynchronous teaching, have students explain whether they feel it is important to adapt to other generations. This can be a discussion, essay, or Vlog. A rubric for this assignment is included in Appendix H.*

The COVID-19 pandemic also impacted many aspects of healthcare. The pandemic impacted how healthcare services and education were delivered. In the clinical setting, many elective surgeries were postponed allowing for the triage of patients. In the didactic portion of education, universities transitioned to the use of more virtual classes to meet social distancing requirements. Clinical educators consistently felt that students who received limited face-to-face instruction were not as ready for clinical experiences as compared to those students who received routine face-to-face instruction (Neely, 2022).

This brings us back to the perceptions of the clinical educators and employers who work with today's healthcare students and graduates. Before we look more in depth into those perceptions, we will break down who is who in healthcare education. This begins with the difference among providers.

Who's Who in Healthcare Education?

Healthcare providers include licensed professionals providing services geared toward health and wellness. Doctors, nurses, and physical therapists are ~~all~~ healthcare providers. Allied health professions are separate from medical and nursing professions (Association of Schools Advancing Health Professions [ASAHP], 2022). These include physical and occupational therapists and speech-language pathologists.

The trajectory among healthcare professions is for students to graduate from an accredited program, pass a competency examination, and obtain licensure for practice. Educational healthcare programs include a didactic and a clinical experience component. The didactic curriculum is focused on knowledge and skill-based competencies. The clinical experience curriculum focuses on a diversity of clinical experiences, within a variety of settings, across the continuum of care and lifespan. During the clinical experiences, students are engaged in hands-on learning and focusedreflection as they apply their newly acquired knowledge and skills. This is also the time when students' competency with employability skills has the greatest impact on their overall success.

Figure 42

Students Learning from Their Clinical Instructor

Note: Healthcare students learning from their instructor. This image was obtained from Microsoft Word, 2023.

Clinical experiences are an integral part of healthcare education. Clinical experiences provide students with the opportunity to apply their knowledge and clinical skills under the direct supervision of a licensed clinician. The clinical experiences provide students with the opportunity to interact with and treat real patients. Each clinical setting has its unique culture and structure. Some settings require healthcare students to interact with an interdisciplinary team, as they work in unison for the benefit of the patient. Factors such as the acuity level of the patient's condition and the pace of the environment contribute to the student's ability to demonstrate employability skills.

Assessment of student performance during clinical experiences relies heavily on the recommendations and ratings of clinical educators (So et al., 2019). The healthcare program refers to clinical educators as the university's faculty. Clinical educators are responsible for approximately 20% of the overall educational experience. As such, student performance during clinical experiences is directly linked to matriculation.

Instructor Notes

- *For synchronous and asynchronous teaching, have students explain why they chose an allied healthcare profession over a medical program. This can be a discussion, essay, or Vlog.*

What Are the Perceptions of Clinical Educators for Allied Healthcare Students?

The four areas in which students display the greatest deficiency during their clinical experiences are the inability to perform a clinical assessment or treatment safely; the inability to manage a specified caseload; a lack of critical thinking skills, and the inabilityto demonstrate professionalism when interacting with patients, families, the clinical educator, or other members of the healthcare team (So et al., 2019). The five factors that affect behavioral performance are: behavioral intention; knowledge and skills; saliency; environmental constraints, and experience and habit. Developed by Ajzen & Fishbein in 1980, the Theory of Planned Behavior states that the main determinant of behavior is intention, which is influenced by a person's attitude toward behavior, subjective norms, and perceived behavioral control. (Khani Jeihooni et al., 2022).

Wolff-Burke (2005) also identified four themes that clinical educators have observed in Doctor of Physical Therapy students during their clinical experiences. These include poor communication skills, lack of professionalism, having a bad attitude, and lack of interest. Choi & Change (2023) determined that poor communication occurs when the meaning intended by the sender is not understood by the receiver. When this happens in the clinical setting it can compromise patient safety. Sah (2022) described professionalism as the quality of acting with integrity without bias or for personal gain. Attitudes are formed through a combination of internal personal factors and external, environmental factors that merge into a self-identity. Jamshidi et al. (2016) determined that students' behavior in the clinical setting could negatively impact patient progression and affect the clinician's professional performance. Students who reported feeling discriminated against by full-time staff said this perception contributed to their behavior.

Figure 43

Clinical Instructor Showing Healthcare Students How to Document

Note: This clinical instructor is showing students how to document in the computer. This image was obtained from Microsoft Word, 2023.

Another deficit identified by Wolff-Burke (2005) is healthcare students not accepting responsibility for their learning. Dupre et al. (2020) studied this through the lens of Bloom's Taxonomy and determined that willingness to accept responsibility for one's actions and errors, including remediation, is reflective of the highest domain of learning, i.e., "internalizing". The competencies of accountability, professional behaviors, communication, and cultural competence were determined to have the greatest impact on patient safety (Dupre et al., 2020).

Jensen et al. (2022) emphasized the need to strengthen the relationship between didactic and clinical education. This was in response to the perceptions of the clinical educators regarding students' performance during their clinical experiences. They expressed that healthcare students lack adequate preparation for their employability skills. Several themes were identified: safety issues, poor clinical reasoning, lack of professionalism, deficits in interpersonal and communication skills, and poor self-awareness. Before these concepts are explored further, it is important to note that safety and poor clinical reasoning are directly impacted by the employability skills of communication and information use. Professionalism is derived from the employability skill of systems thinking. Interpersonal skills, communication and self-awareness originate from the employability skills of communication, resource management, information use, and systems thinking (U.S. Department of Education, n.d.).

What Qualifies as a Student Performing Below Expectations (SPBE)?

Students performing below expectations are students who are unable to safely perform an assessment or treatment, unable to maintain a caseload appropriate to their level of education and training, lack critical thinking skills, and/or lack professionalism in their interactions (Haines & Chin-I, 2021; So et al., 2019). The number of students performing below expectations is increasing (Continisio et al., 2021; Silberman et al., 2018;). So et al. (2019) explained that clinical educators have identified several factors related to these students. The concerns are about safety, clinical reasoning, and lack of professionalism. In addition, they identified issues with interpersonal and communication skills, and an overall lack of self-awareness by students.

Instructor Notes

- *In a synchronous or asynchronous discussion, have students explain how learning of the perceptions of the clinical educators and employers makes them feel. They should note their immediate response, and their response after some time to reflect. A rubric is provided in Appendix I.*

What Are the Types of Safety Issues Displayed by SPBE?

Safety issues are commonly the result of poor interpersonal and communication skills. Poor communication contributes to compromised patient safety, patient mortality, and medical errors. Students struggle with developing a therapeutic alliance with the patient due to their insufficient social interaction skills and the inability to communicate effectively with patients. Inability to ascertain pertinent information about or from the patient results in actions that place patient safety at risk (Babatunde et al., 2017; Engelsrud et al., 2019).

How To Describe the Poor Clinical Reasoning Skills Displayed by SPBE?

Clinical reasoning is a complex cognitive process of using one's discipline-specific knowledge to collect and analyze patient information to identify the root of the problem and determine the best way to improve patient outcomes (Hosseinzadeh et al, 2022). Gilliland & Wainwright (2020) explained how poor clinical reasoning is due to deficient interpersonal and communication skills. This is because students struggle to develop an intuitive flow of social interaction with the patient. Without this flow, students fail to grasp pertinent cues from the patient necessary for effective clinical reasoning. Students performing below expectations are inefficient at collecting and interpreting information during the patient's assessment and examination. The process usually is less organized and less effective. Students have difficulty putting all information together to conduct efficient clinical reasoning, which in turn impairs the student's ability to develop a thorough plan of care for the patient (Gilliland & Wainwright, 2020; Huhn et al., 2018).

What Is Considered a Lack of Professionalism?

Wolff-Burke (2005) explained that professionalism issues tend to stem from attitudes, values, beliefs, and overall immaturity, rather than a lack of knowledge or technical skills. Unacceptable student professional behavior includes a lack of initiative, wanting answers without putting forth any effort, and failing to complete assignments assigned by the clinical educator to remediate unprofessional behavior. Clinical educators described students as displaying a lack of interest in the patient population and/or setting and having "an attitude". This was the term used to describe students who behaved in an arrogant, abrasive, or authoritative manner.

Figure 44

This Person's Facial Expression Conveys an Attitude

Note: This professional is displaying an attitude through her facial expression. This image was obtained from Microsoft Word, 2023.

Clinical educators expressed frustration with students who have poor work ethics, poor commitment to learning, not following policies, and displaying a "know-it-all" behavior, which was deemed very inappropriate. Other unprofessional issues displayed by students include dressing inappropriately for the clinical setting, being dishonest, not maintaining patient confidentiality, and poor time management. Finally, crying on the job indicated a lack of balance between one's personal and professional life (Wolff-Burke, 2005). Crying on the job is a sign of poor emotion management, which is the ability to recognize, monitor, and steer one's reactions to interact appropriately with the current situation (Lei, 2022).

What Are the Common Deficits with Interpersonal and Communication Skills Displayed by SPBE?

Healthcare professionals require both hands-on and employability skills. Hands-on skills are the abilities that a person needs to perform the psychomotor aspects of their job. Employability skills consist of the traits necessary to work well with others and fit into any work environment. Employability skills encompass many behaviors such as emotional intelligence, communication, self-awareness, cultural competency, and compassion to deliver high-quality, patient-centered care. Healthcare companies most desire employability skills, specifically communication abilities, in their employees (Messum et al., 2011). Healthcare providers need to possess proficient communication skills to build a trusting relationship with patients for the effective evaluation and treatment phases of care.

While all healthcare providers must possess effective communication skills, the style of this communication varies depending on their roles. In acute care facilities, such as a hospital, communication between doctors and patients tends to be brief and direct. This style of communication is often dictated by the setting and time constraints. Communication with allied health professionals is much more extensive. This is because allied professionals often spend 30-60 minutes with each patient session, compared to the 5 or 10-minute interactions with the doctor or nurse.

Figure 45

Healthcare Provider Communicating with a Patient

Note: This healthcare provider is communicating with a patient. This image was obtained from Unsplash.com, 2023.

Allied healthcare providers rely on effective communication skills to gather pertinent information from the patient and to make clinical decisions about the patient's care. Allied healthcare providers are trained to perform motivational interviewing when interacting with patients. Motivational interviewing is a talk-based therapy that uses a patient-centered approach to build patient confidence and readiness to change (Patel et al., 2022).

Silberman et al. (2018) determined that 44.7% of DPT students during their clinical experiences displayed deficits in their employability skills, especially communication. Deficiencies with employability skills are not isolated to physical therapy students.

Issues have been reported with occupational therapy students and nursing students (Fogel & Lamash, 2021; Wells et al., 2021). Fogel & Lamash (2021) explained that the most critical employability skill for occupational therapy students is communication.

Communication and clinical reasoning skills are essential for providing quality patient-centered care. When students have deficits in their communication skills, they are more likely to conduct a less thorough examination and grasp pertinent cues from the patient, which impacts their safe patient handling and mobility (Afriyie, 2020; Gilliland & Wainwright, 2020). Nemec et al. (2017) determined that effective communication is dependent upon the allied healthcare student's proficiency with active listening and reflective responding.

Figure 46

Healthcare Student Conducting a Less Thorough Examination

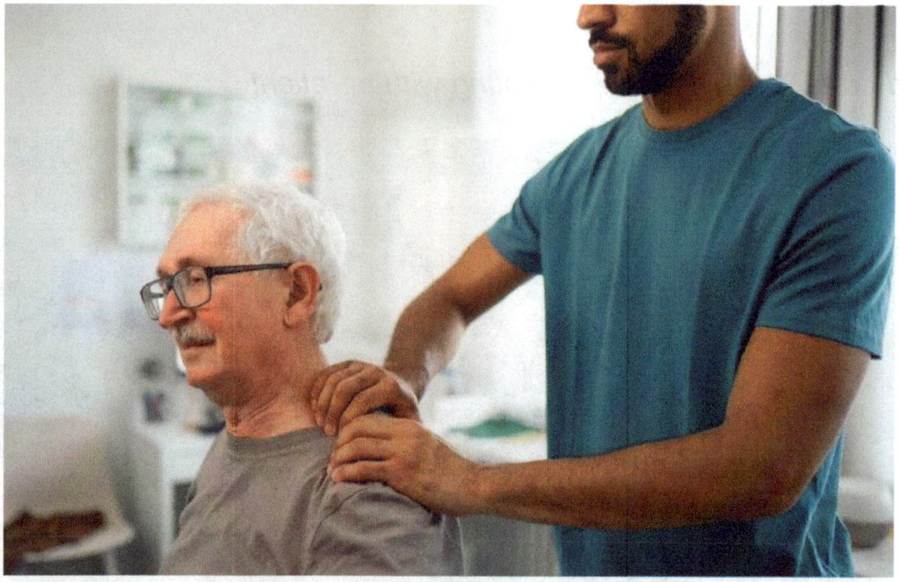

Note: This healthcare student is conducting a less thorough examination. This image was obtained from Microsoft Word, 2023.

Motivational interviewing is a very useful communication skill for making positive changes in patient behaviors because motivational interviewing empowers the patient and builds self-efficacy (Arnett et al., 2022). Effective communication in allied healthcare professions has a positive impact on gaining patient compliance with treatment interventions. This is because when the patient thoroughly understands the benefits of a treatment intervention, they are more inclined to comply with the protocol, as instructed.

Communication is the employability skill that has the greatest impact on patient care. Today the healthcare environment is very complex. This complexity is the result of a more diverse patient population and the increased time constraints within the work environment. Combined with the increasing complexity of the work environment and the shift toward patient-centered care, a communication deficiency hinders human interactions (Ciulea et al., 2021). Ineffective communication leads to medical errors and impaired safety during patient care and is a factor in 70% of adverse events (Guttman et al., 2021). Adverse events are the result of errors or failures in the delivery of healthcare services that cause the patient permanent harm or even death (Hunter & Rhodus, 2022).

Timmerberg et al. (2019) found that for a successful clinical experience, clinical educators considered competency with employability skills more important than didactic knowledge or hands-on abilities. Clinical educators have reported that the employability skills most lacking in allied healthcare students are interpersonal and communication skills, emotional management, teamwork, problem-solving, poor clinical reasoning, a lack of self-awareness, and willingness to accept responsibility when receiving feedback (Continisio et al., 2021; Falco & Monaghan, 2018; So et al., 2019). Collectively, these deficiencies impact the student's ability to provide a safe patient encounter and to work effectively as a part of a collaborative team.

Communication impacts several aspects of interpersonal relationships. Sharma (2021) explained that communication skills impact the relationship with the patient. This is because effective communication skills are essential to help the patient understand their diagnosis, treatment, and rehabilitation (Sharma, 2021). Wells et al. (2021) identified that new allied healthcare graduates are perceived to have low levels of confidence and underdeveloped communication and interpersonal skills, which impacts their ability to develop rapport with patients.

Figure 47

Healthcare Provider Communicating with a Patient During an Examination

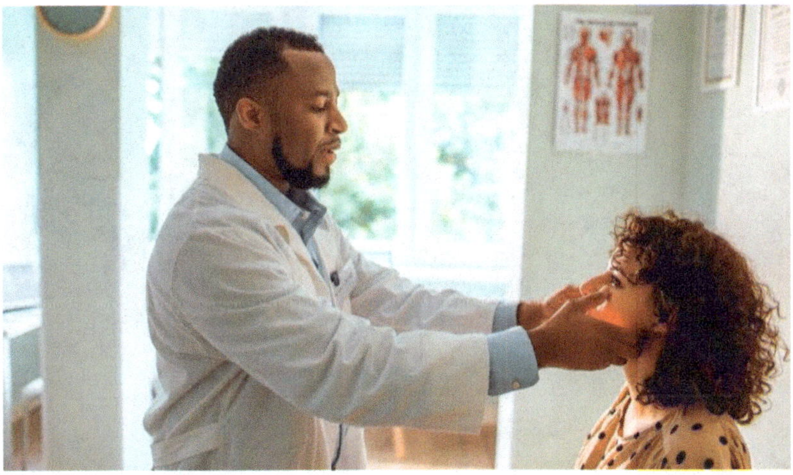

Note: This healthcare provider is communicating with a patient during an examination. This image was obtained from Microsoft Word, 2023.

Sharma (2021) explained that effective communication is a difficult skill to learn and takes a long time to become proficient. That is because effective communication is a culmination of thinking, self-control, body language, and a positive self-concept. These qualities are crucial to navigating difficult situations, novel tasks, and taking calculated risks. Self-control enables a person to control their impulses, emotions, and attention.

These are necessary to resolve conflict and make decisions. A person's body language reflects a person's thoughts. A positive self-concept helps a person handle difficult situations.

Instructor Notes

- *For synchronous face-to-face teaching, divide students into pairs. This activity is called Blind Drawing. The purpose of this activity is to build communication skills. Provide one person in the pair one piece of blank copy paper (i.e., without lines). Give the other student in the pair one of the pictures from Appendix J. The student with the blank paper is to draw the shape on the picture using only verbalinstructions from the other student in the pair. The student with the picture shouldnot share the actual picture of the shape until the exercise is completed. Give students up to two minutes to complete the task.*

Cultural differences can have a significant impact on effective communication. Cultural differences can be related to pragmatics, language barriers, emotions, and struggles related to the setting. Using inappropriate language and/or making inappropriate gestures is a common source of poor communication. Wolff-Burke (2005) described students performing below expectations as asking inappropriate questions to the clinical educator in front of the patient. Criticizing the clinical educator is extremely inappropriate.

Figure 48

Family Enjoying a Cultural Celebration

Note: This family is enjoying a cultural celebration. This image was obtained from Microsoft Word, 2023.

Clinical educators have reported that students are more passive and noncollaborative when it comes to communication. This includes ignoring signs of physical or emotional distress by patients, which have tremendous potential to negatively impact patient care and safety. These types of behaviors make it challenging for the clinical educator and student to have productive and effective communication, which limits the learning potential (Wolff-Burke, 2005). Bernhardsson et al. (2017) stressed that when students are unaware of patient preferences related to treatment strategies, they can become disengaged in the therapeutic process. Patient outcomes will be affected, and compliance with participation can diminish.

Nonverbal communication can pose challenges. Clinical educators have expressed frustration with students who appear disinterested or display a flat affect. When a student is unable to express themselves effectively, this can be interpreted as being unwilling to take an active role in the learning process or not taking responsibility for their actions (Wolff-Burke, 2005).

Ineffective communication negatively impacts the healthcare team's ability to make decisions and problem-solve clinical situations (Falco & Monaghan, 2018; Timmerberg et al., 2019; Wolff-Burke, 2005). Communication influences teamwork, work experience, and management demands in response to issues. Picard et al. (2022) studied communication among healthcare teams in the operating room. They determined that ineffective communication led to adverse events more than 30% of the time, which impacted patient outcomes and team morale.

Figure 49

Healthcare Provider Displaying Ineffective Communication

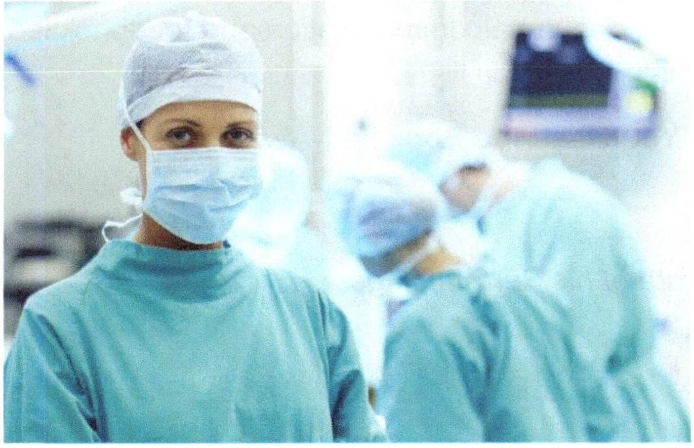

Note: This healthcare provider is displaying ineffective communication by appearing not to be engaged. This image was obtained from Microsoft Word, 2023.

Jetha et al. (2021) explained how workplaces are social environments. When coworkers communicate effectively, this helps to establish trust among the team, which improves the delivery of patient care. Communication also impacts the style of management. Soekardi et al. (2020) found that a management style that embraces open communication directly improves work performance and job satisfaction. The reverse was also true; leaders who failed to communicate effectively produced a culture of misinformation and dissatisfaction.

The ability to provide a safe patient encounter is dependent upon the student's ability to develop a therapeutic alliance with the patient. In 2013, the American Nurses Association (ANA) published standards for safe patient handling and mobility (Kanaskie & Snyder, 2018). These standards are designed to prevent or minimize injuries for the patient, the healthcare provider, and the student.

Babatunde et al. (2017) found that building a therapeutic alliance with a patient is established through collaboration and communication. A therapeutic alliance develops, at least in part, based on how the provider's communication is received and experienced by the patient (Bright & Reeves, 2022). A therapeutic alliance is reliant upon collaboration between the client and the therapist to accomplish the mutually agreed therapy (Bishop et a., 2021). This unique personal bond of collaboration and communication directly impacts the student's ability to provide a safe patient care experience (Babatunde et al., 2017; Falco & Monaghan, 2018).

Communication and interpersonal skills have been impacted by advancements in technology. Gonçalves-Bradley (n.d.) explained how the widespread use of communication technologies has enabled patients to view their medical records online, to ask pertinent questions to a specialist. The accessibility of communication has improved due to the increased availability of formats to deliver information. Because technology improves access to healthcare services, it broadens the diversity of the patient population. This increases the demand for healthcare providers, especially thosein the allied fields, to be well-versed in social determinants of health and cultural diversity to ascertain the intent of the communication. This also applies to nonverbal communication. Ruben et al. (2021) determined that the practice of decoding nonverbalcommunication and feedback leads to the development of interpersonal skills.

How Would You Describe Poor Self-Awareness?

Figure 50

A Dog Unaware of his Surroundings

Note: The towel prevents this dog from seeing his surroundings. This image was obtained from Microsoft Word, 2023.

Huhn et al. (2018) explained that clinical educators report consistently encouraging students to perform self-reflection. Students are prompted to think back on an experience to understand the rationale behind it and the consequences of their actions. Self-reflection has been identified as a strategy to transform a clinician from novice to expert (Buccieri et al., 2013). Students often display a limit in their ability to assess their performance and shortcomings accurately (Huhn et al., 2018).

Dupre et al. (2020) examined reflection as it relates to the multiple levels within Bloom's Taxonomy. They determined that reflection and accepting responsibility for one's actions and errors are within the highest domain of learning. This could be a potential reason that students display poor self-awareness.

de Schepper et al. (2021) identified significant concerns regarding graduates' abilities to reflect critically. They studied the three dimensions of critical reflection that include: experimenting, asking for feedback, and career awareness. They explained the benefits of strengthening these key employability skills. Experimenting allows a person to try new ways of thinking, working, and being open-minded. Asking for feedback promotes personal development and fitting into organizational norms and values. It also strengthens social interactions. Career awareness is knowing one's strengths and weaknesses and leveraging the resources of the organization to develop those skills. Developing critical reflection aids in raising self-awareness, which promotes teamwork and advances organizational culture.

What Are the Perceptions of Clinical Educators for Non-Allied Healthcare Professions?

Deficiencies in employability skills are not isolated to the field of physical therapy or the United States. Caruana & Damilakis (2021) conducted a strengths-weaknesses-opportunities-threats (SWOT) analysis and concluded that medical physics students in Europe displayed significant weaknesses in their employability skills.

Nursing students in Jakarta, Indonesia have also been considered novices regarding their competence with employability skills (Ernawati & Bratajaya, 2021). Studies show that a lack of competence with employability skills impacted nurses' ability to handle their emotions and adapt to different situations. Nursing graduates in Africa have limited knowledge of the employability skills required to provide quality patient care. While they were competent with their clinical skills, they lacked confidence and displayed high levels of stress in emergencies (Ashipala & Shatimwene, 2021).

Kaitelidou et al. (2017) studied nurses, healthcare assistants, and social workers in Greece, France, Italy, and Cyprus to determine training needs. They compared the healthcare worker's reporting of self-competency with the perceptions of their patients. The healthcare workers assessed themselves as skilled in their employability skills, while the patients rated them as moderately competent. Patients described healthcare workers as insufficiently skilled in managing patients' feelings of isolation and loneliness, communicating effectively, and managing their emotional reactions.

Figure 51

Healthcare Student Giving a Patient an Injection

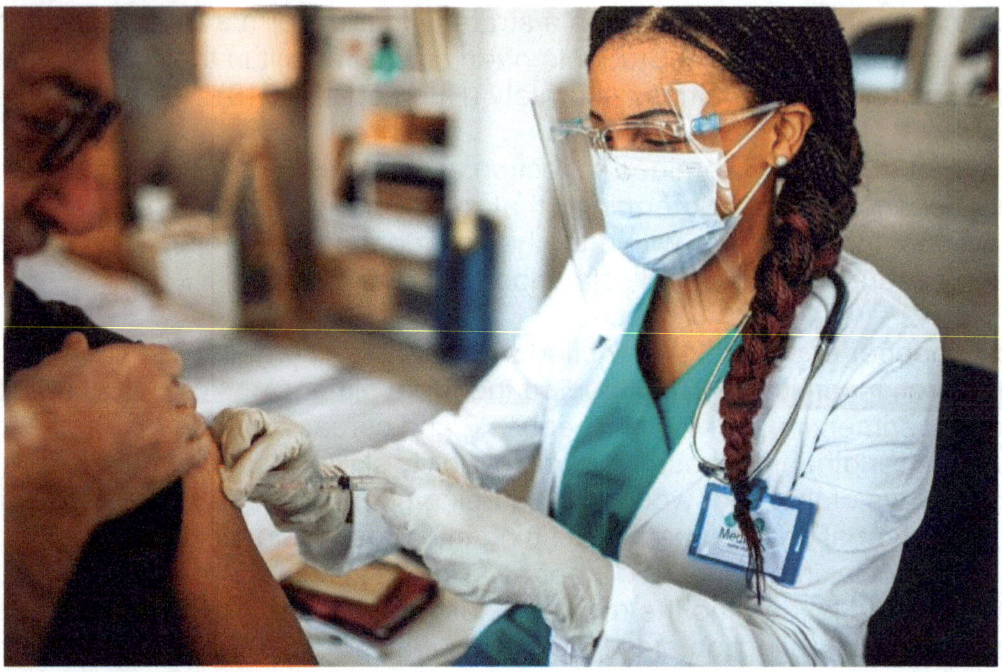

Note: This healthcare student is giving a patient an injection. This image was obtained from Microsoft Word, 2023.

The greatest deficit in employability skills appears to be related to communication. Gilligan et al. (2020) also identified the need for more training on effective communication among medical students in Australia. Maznieda et al. (2022) identified breakdowns in communication that impacted the ability of the emergency management crews in Malaysia to respond effectively during a crisis.

Effective communication skills are not part of most ophthalmic postgraduate curricula (Bhagat et al., 2019). This lack of training has resulted in patient distrust and dissatisfaction and patient complaints. It also contributed to conflicts and compromised healthcare delivery and difficulties with the development of management competence within the professional practice (Ashipala & Shatimwene, 2021; Uhm et al., 2019). Communication competence is imperative to safe, patient-centered care (Laari & Dube, 2017).

Unfortunately, it is not just patients that suffer from a lack of competency with employability skills. Semaan et al. (2021) studied burnout among healthcare workers. They discovered that nurses had a higher level of burnout than dentists, radiologists, midwives, nutritionists, psychotherapists, and speech therapists. They determined that job satisfaction was negatively associated with burnout and that a higher level of burnout is associated with lower employability skills. This indicates that employability skills training could boost job satisfaction and reduce levels of burnout.

What Are the Implications of SPBE?

So et al. (2019) explained that clinical educators were found to be more likely to recommend a failing grade for a student if there was a series of repeated incidents, rather than an isolated incident. Recommending a failing grade for a student is difficult emotionally and procedurally. Many clinical educators worry that their documentation of the student's behavior might be insufficient to justify the failing recommendation.

SPBE is a time-consuming process that can generate feelings of failure, guilt, and lowered self-confidence in the clinical educator. This causes them increased stress due to the extra time demands required to observe, mentor, provide feedback, and document student performance, especially related to patient safety. Many clinical educators have reported working longer hours when students are not performing well, which then impacts their personal lives.

In addition, if students become defensive when the clinical educators provide feedback, this becomes emotionally draining. Finally, some clinical educators reported feelings of empathy when considering their recommendations because the clinical educators feared the negative effect that failing a student on an internship could have on a student's personal and professional trajectory, along with the extra expense associated with repeating the internship.

Personal and professional integrity had the greatest influence on whether a clinical educator reported the students as performing below expectations to the academic~~,~~ and clinical faculty (So et al., 2019). Clinical educators are more likely to report an issue with a student when the academic faculty has shown support and a willingness to remediate the behavior(s). Clinical educators have expressed that a lack of faculty support creates a reluctance to reporting students performing below expectations. This perceived lack of support by the university and pressure by the university to pass the student despite their inappropriate behavior leads to graduates whose academic performance is substandard. Other factors considered by the clinical educators include the specific aspects of student performance and the availability of strategies and resources.

What Are the Key Concepts from this Chapter?

- The top ten skills employers demanded are employability skills more than technical skills.
- Employability skills are not dependent on demographical variables or gender.
- Employability skills are a competency dependent upon the student's attributes.
- A large section of the current workforce does not include members of the Y or Z generation. This contributes to the mismatch between actual and expected performance.
- Allied health professions are those separate from medical and nursing such as physical and occupational therapists, and speech-language pathologists.
- Clinical educators have observed the following problems with students during their clinical experiences.
    - Poor communication skills
    - Lack of professionalism

- Poor attitude
- Lack of interest
- Not accepting responsibility for learning
- Safety issues
- Poor clinical reasoning
- Deficits in interpersonal skills
- Poor self-awareness

- Students performing below expectations are students who are:
  - Unable to perform an assessment or treatment safely
  - Unable to maintain a caseload appropriate to their level of education and training
  - Unable to think critically
  - Lacking professionalism in their interactions
- The five factors that affected behavioral performance are:
  - Behavioral intention
  - Knowledge and skills
  - Saliency
  - Environmental constraints
  - Experience and habit
- Safety issues are frequently the result of poor interpersonal and communication skills.
- Clinical reasoning is a complex cognitive process of using one's discipline-specific knowledge to collect and analyze patient information to identify the root of a problem and determine the best way to improve patient outcomes (Hosseinzadeh et al., 2022).
- Gilliland & Wainwright (2020) explained how poor clinical reasoning is due to deficient interpersonal and communication skills.
- Lack of professional behaviors displayed by students include:
  - A lack of initiative
  - Wanting answers without putting forth sufficient effort
  - Failing to complete assignments
  - Having an "negative attitude" which includes displaying a lack of interest, arrogance, abrasiveness, or an authoritative manner
  - Poor work ethics
  - Poor commitment to learning
  - Not following policies
  - Displaying a "know-it-all" behavior
  - Dressing inappropriately for the clinical setting
  - Being dishonest
  - Not maintaining patient confidentiality
  - Poor time management
  - Lack of balance between one's personal and professional life
  - Crying on the job or poor emotion management
- Motivational interviewing is a talk-based therapy that uses a patient-centered approach to build patient confidence and readiness to change (Patel et al., 2022).
- The employability skill that has the greatest impact on patient care is a deficiencyin communication skills.

- Ineffective communication leads to medical errors and impaired safety during patient care and is a factor in 70% of adverse events (Guttman et al., 2021).
- Communication is a culmination of thinking, self-control, body language, and a positive self-concept.
- Cultural differences can be related to pragmatics, language barriers, emotions, and struggles with the setting itself.
- Communication influences teamwork, work experience, and management demands in response to issues.
- Self-reflection has been identified as a strategy that transforms the clinician from novice to expert (Buccieri et al., 2013).
- Students often display a limit in their ability to assess their performance and shortcomings accurately (Huhn et al., 2018).
- The three dimensions of critical reflection include experimenting, asking for feedback, and career awareness.

Summary

This chapter examined the perceptions of the clinical educators who supervise healthcare students during their clinical experiences and employers of healthcare graduates. Consistent feedback was received from around the globe. While healthcare graduates feel they embody the qualities of a professional, the consensus of the workforce disagrees. This means educators need to do a better job of preparing today's healthcare students for the work environment. The next chapter covers the best ways to teach and learn employability skills.

References

Afriyie, D. (2020). Effective communication between nurses and patients: An evolutionary concept analysis. *British Journal of Community Nursing*, *25*(9), 438–445. https://doi.org/10.12968/bjcn.2020.25.9.438

Arnett, M. C., Evans, M. D., & Stull, C. L. (2022). Brief Motivational Interviewing: Evaluation of a skills-based education program. *Journal of Dental Hygiene*, *96*(4), 46–56.

Ashipala, D. O., & Shatimwene, G. P. (2021). Perceptions of employability skills of newly qualified nursing graduates from the University of Namibia. *Africa Journal of Nursing & Midwifery*, *23*(1), 1–17. https://doi.org/10.25159/2520-5293/8017

Association of Schools Advancing Health Professions. (2015, October 27). What is allied health? https://www.asahp.org/what-is

Babatunde, F., MacDermid, J., & MacIntyre, N. (2017). Characteristics of therapeutic alliance in musculoskeletal physiotherapy and occupational therapy practice: A scoping review of the literature. *BMC Health Services Research*, *17*(1). https://link.gale.com/apps/doc/A511285835/AONE?u=lirn55718&sid=ebsco&xid=fb76adf9

Bernhardsson, S., Larsson, M. E. H., Johansson, K., & Öberg, B. (2017). "In the physio we trust": A qualitative study on patients' preferences for physiotherapy. *Physiotherapy Theory & Practice*, *33*(7), 535–549. https://doi.org/10.1080/09593985.2017.1328720

Bhagat, P. B., Prajapati, K. M., Bhatt, R. B., Prajapati, V. K., Dureja, R. & Tank, G. P.

(2019). Development and introduction of a communication skills module for postgraduate students of ophthalmology. *Indian Journal of Ophthalmology, 67*(11), 1810–1815. https://doi.org/10.4103/ijo.IJO_366_19

Bishop, M., Kayes, N., & McPherson, K. (2021). Understanding the therapeutic alliance in stroke rehabilitation. *Disability and Rehabilitation: An International, Multidisciplinary Journal*, *43*(8):1074-1083. doi:10.1080/09638288.2019.1651909

Bright, F. A. S., & Reeves, B. (2022). Creating therapeutic relationships through communication: A qualitative metasynthesis from the perspectives of people with communication impairment after stroke. *Disability & Rehabilitation, 44*(12), 2670–2682. https://doi.org/10.1080/09638288.2020.1849419

Buccieri, K. M., Pivko, S. E., & Olzenak, D. L. (2013). Development of an expert clinical instructor: A theoretical model for clinical teaching in physical therapy. *Journal of Physical Therapy Education (American Physical Therapy Association, Education Section)*, *27*(1), 48–57.

Caruana, C. J., & Damilakis, J. (2022). Being an excellent scientist is not enough to succeed! Soft skills for medical physicists. *European Journal of Radiology*, 155. https://doi.org/10.1016/j.ejrad.2021.110108

Chaudhari, S., Yadav, R., & Rai, S. (2021). Work values & job attitudes: A study of Gen Y in public sector. *Indian Journal of Industrial Relations*, *57*(1), 142.

Choi, Y.-R., & Chang, S. O. (2023). Exploring interprofessional communication during nursing home emergencies using the SBAR framework. *Journal of Interprofessional Care*, *37*(1), 83–90. https://doi.org/10.1080/13561820.2021.1985985

Ciulea, L. E., Ban, A. R., Papp, E. G., & Szabo-Csifo, B. (2021). The importance of soft skills in fitness-specific activities. *Romanian Journal of Physical Therapy*, *27*(47), 25–33.

Continisio, G. I., Serra, N., Guillari, A., Simeone, S., Lucchese, R., Gargiulo, G., Toscano, S., Capo, M., Capuano, A., Sarracino, F., Esposito, M. R., & Rea, T. (2021). Evaluation of soft skills among Italian healthcare rehabilitators: A cross-sectional study. *Journal of Public Health Research*, *10*(4), 65–71. https://doi.org/10.4081/jphr.2021.2002

Deluliis, E. D., & Saylor, E. (2021). Bridging the gap: Three strategies to optimize professional relationships with generation Y and Z. *Open Journal of Occupational Therapy*, *9*(1), 1L. https://doi.org/10.15453/2168-6408.1748

de Schepper, J., Sotiriadou, P., & Hill, B. (2021). The role of critical reflection as an employability skill in sport management. *European Sport Management Quarterly*, *21*(2), 280–301.

Dupre, A.-M., McAuley, J. A., & Wetherbee, E. (2020). Objectives to assess student readiness for first, full-time clinical education experiences in physical therapist education. *Journal of Physical Therapy Education (Lippincott Williams & Wilkins)*, *34*(3), 242–251.

Engelsrud, G., Øien, I., & Nordtug, B. (2019). Being present with the patient--A critical investigation of bodily sensitivity and presence in the field of physiotherapy. *Physiotherapy Theory & Practice*, *35*(10), 908–918. https://doi.org/10.1080/09593985.2018.1460431

Ernawati, E. & Bratajaya, C. N. A. (2021). Senior nurses' perceptions of essential soft skills for novice nurses in a private hospital in Jakarta, Indonesia: A phenomenological study. *Belitung Nursing Journal*, *7*(4), 320–328.

https://doi.org/10.33546/bnj.1549
Falco, K., & Monaghan, H. M. (2018). Soft skills: The foundation for effective SPHM program leadership: A national survey. *International Journal of Safe Patient Handling & Mobility (SPHM)*, *8*(2), 76–90.
Fogel, Y., & Lamash, L. (2021). Role perception of occupational therapists in education systems: Self-efficacy and employability skills. *Occupational Therapy International*, 1–7. https://doi.org/10.1155/2021/5531224
Gilliland, S. & Wainwright, S. F. (2020). Perspectives and practice: Physical therapist students' clinical reasoning. *Journal of Physical Therapy Education*, *34*(2), 150-159. doi: 10.1097/JTE.0000000000000129.
Gonçalves-Bradley, D. C. (n.d.). Mobile technologies to support healthcare provider to healthcare provider communication and management of care. *Cochrane Database of Systematic Reviews, 8.*
Guttman, O. T., Lazzara, E. H., Keebler, J. R., Webster, K. L. W., Gisick, L. M., & Baker, A. L. (2021). Dissecting communication barriers in healthcare: A path to enhancing communication resiliency, reliability, and patient safety. *Journal of Patient Safety*, *17*(8), e1465–e1471. https://doi.org/10.1097/PTS.0000000000000541
Haines, J., Arnold, M., & Chin-I, C. (2021). Safe patient handling and mobility principles in Doctor of Physical Therapy students: Intentions for future practice. *International Journal of Safe Patient Handling & Mobility (SPHM)*, *11*(2), 61–75.
Hosseinzadeh, A., Sahab-Negah, S., Nili, S., Aliyari, R., Goli, S., Fereidouni, M., Alami, A., Shati, M., Ahmadnezhad, E., Mehravaran, S., Fateh, M., Khajeha, H., Emamian, Z., Behmanesh, E., Mahdavi, S., Enayatrad, M., Mangolian shahrbabaki, P., Ansari-Moghaddam, A., Heidarzadeh, A., & Shahraki-Sanavi, F. (2022). COVID-19 cases, hospitalizations, and deaths after vaccination: A cohort event monitoring study, Islamic Republic of Iran. *Bulletin of the World Health Organization*, *100*(8), 474–483. https://doi.org/10.2471/BLT.22.288073
Huhn, K., Black, L., Christensen, N., Furze, J., Vendrely, A., & Wainwright, S. (2018). Clinical reasoning: Survey of teaching methods and assessment in entry-level physical therapist clinical education. *Journal of Physical Therapy Education (Lippincott Williams & Wilkins)*, *32*(3), 241–247. https://doi.org/10.1097/JTE.0000000000000043
Hunter, E. G., & Rhodus, E. (2022). Interventions within the scope of occupational therapy to address preventable adverse events in inpatient and home health postacute care settings: A systematic review. *AJOT: American Journal of Occupational Therapy*, *76*(1). https://doi.org/10.5014/ajot.2022.047589
Jamshidi, N., Molazem, Z. Sharif, F., Torabizadeh, C., Najafi Kalyani, M. (2016, June 5). The challenges of nursing students in the clinical learning environment: A qualitative study. *The Scientific World Journal*, *16.* Doi:https://doi.org/10.1155/2016/1846178.
Jensen, G. M., Jette, D. U., Timmerberg, J. F., Chesbro, S. B., Dole, R. L., Kapasi, Z., & Lotshaw, A. (2022). Competency-based education in physical therapy: Developing a framework for education research. *Journal of Physical Therapy Education (Lippincott Williams & Wilkins)*, *36*(4), 334–340. https://doi.org/10.1097/JTE.0000000000000254
Jetha, A., Le Pouésard, M., Mustard, C., Backman, C., & Gignac, M. A. M. (2021). Getting the message right: Evidence-based insights to improve organizational return-to-work communication practices. *Journal of Occupational Rehabilitation*,

31(3), 652–663.
Kaitelidou, D., Baret, C., Konstantakopoulou, O., Zafiropoulou, M., Theodorou, M., Siskou, O., Kalafati, M., Chatzopoulou, M., Karra, V., Delloro, G., Patiraki, E., Lemonidou, C., & Sourtzi, P. (2017). Competencies of formal care takers regarding basic clinical and soft skills in the provision of outpatient services and patients' perspective: The two sides of the same coin. *Value in Health*, *20*(9), A692
Kanaskie, M. L., & Snyder, C. (2018). Nurses and nursing assistants' decision-making regarding use of safe patient handling and mobility technology: A qualitative study. *Applied Nursing Research*, 39, 141. https://doi.org/10.1016/j.apnr.2017.11.006
Khani Jeihooni, A., Layeghiasl, M., Yari, A., & Rakhshani, T. (2022). The effect of educational intervention based on the theory of planned behavior on improving physical and nutrition status of obese and overweight women. *BMC Women's Health*, 22(1), 1–9. https://doi.org/10.1186/s12905-022-01593-5
Laari, L. & Dube, B.M. (2017). Nursing students' perceptions of soft skills training in Ghana. *Curationis*, *40*(1), e1–e5. https://doi.org/10.4102/curationis.v40i1.1677
Maznieda, M., Dalila, R., Rosnah, S., Rohaida, I., Rosmanajihah, M. L., Mizanurfakhri, G., & Nurhanie, M. (2022). The soft skills emergency management that matters at the hardest time: A phenomenology study of healthcare worker's experiences during Kelantan flood 2014. *International Journal of Disaster Risk Reduction*, 75. https://doi.org/10.1016/j.ijdrr.2022.102916
Messum, D., Wilkes, L., & Jackson, D. (2011). Employability skills: Essential requirements in health manager vacancy advertisements. *Asia Pacific Journal of Health Management*, *6*(2), 22–28.
Metgud, S., & D'Silva, P. (2021). Soft skills in physical therapy profession: Need of the hour. *Indian Journal of Physical Therapy and Research*, *3*(2), 69.
Neely, L., Pabian, P., Darby, A., Tintor, M., Vatansever, S. & Stock, M. (2022). Examining clinical readiness and performance of students on clinical education experiences: Is there an influence from virtual learning? *Journal of Physical Therapy Education, Publish Ahead of Print*, doi: 10.1097/JTE.0000000000000243.
Nemec, P. B., Spagnolo, A. C., & Soydan, A. S. (2017). Can you hear me now? Teaching listening skills. *Psychiatric Rehabilitation Journal*, *40*(4), 415–417. https://doi.org/10.1037/prj0000287
Nirmala, C., & Dsouza, S. J. (2022). A critical evaluation of employability skills of postgraduates and its impact on their job prospects. *SDMIMD Journal of Management*, 13, 1–14. https://doi.org/10.18311/sdmimd/2022/29623
Patel, K., Auton, M. F., Watkins, C. L., Sutton, C. J., Benedetto, V., Hackett, M. L., Holland, E.-J., & Lightbody, C. E. (2022). Delivering motivational interviewing early post stroke: Standardization of the intervention. *Disability and Rehabilitation*, *44*(14), 3453–3458. https://doi.org/10.1080/09638288.2020.1864035
Picard, J., Evain, J.-N., Douron, C., Maussion, É., Stihle, X., Manhes, P., Romegoux, P., Baron, A., Chapuis, C., Vermorel, C., Garel, B., Faucheron, J.-L., Bouzat, P., Bosson, J.-L., & Albaladejo, P. (2022). Impact of a large interprofessional simulation-based training course on communication, teamwork, and safety culture in the operating theatre: A mixed-methods interventional study.

Anaesthesia Critical Care & Pain Medicine, *41*(1). https://doi.org/10.1016/j.accpm.2021.100991

Ruben, M. A., Stosic, M. D., Correale, J., & Blanch-Hartigan, D. (2021). Is technology enhancing or hindering interpersonal communication? A framework and preliminary results to examine the relationship between technology use and nonverbal decoding skill. *Frontiers in Psychology*, 11. https://doi.org/10.3389/fpsyg.2020.611670

Sah, S. (2022). The professionalism paradox: A sense of professionalism increases vulnerability to conflicts of interest. *Academy of Management Perspectives*, *36*(3), 896–918. https://doi.org/10.5465/amp.2021.0033

Schroth, H. (2019). Are you ready for Gen Z in the workplace? *California Management Review, 61*(3), 5–18. https://doi.org/10.1177/0008125619841006

Semaan, M.S., Bassil, J.P.A., & Salameh, P. (2021). Effect of soft skills and emotional intelligence of health-care professionals on burnout: A Lebanese cross-sectional study / Effekte von Soft Skills und emotionaler Intelligenz auf Burnout von Fachkräften im Gesundheitswesen: eine Querschnittsstudie aus dem Libanon. *International Journal of Health Professions*, *8*(1), 112–124. https://doi.org/10.2478/ijhp-2021-0011

Sharma, S. (2021). Medical profession and soft skills. *Journal of Ayurveda*, *15*(3), 153.

Silberman, N., LaFay, V., Lyons Hansen, R., & Fay, P. (2018). Physical therapist student difficulty in clinical education settings: Incidence and outcomes. *Journal of Physical Therapy Education (Lippincott Williams & Wilkins)*, *32*(2), 175–182.

So, O. W., Shaw, R., O'Rourke, L., Woldegabriel, J. T., Wade, B., Quesnel, M., & Mori, B. (2019). Clinical instructors' experiences working with and assessing students who perform below expectations in physical therapy clinical internships. *Physiotherapy Canada*, *71*(4), 391–399. https://doi.org/10.3138/ptc-2018-0081

Soekardi, A., Indrawati, R. & Erni, N. (2020). The influence of communication skill toward employee performance in radiology installation unit of hospital. *Менеджмент Та Підприємництво: Тренди Розвитку*, *4*(14), 31–42. https://doi.org/10.26661/2522-1566/2020-4/14-03

Struessel, T. S., Sleddens, N. M., & Jones, K. J. (2022). Quality improvement content in physical therapist education: A scoping review. *PTJ: Physical Therapy & Rehabilitation Journal*, *102*(7), 1+. https://link.gale.com/apps/doc/A716792076/SCIC?u=lirn55718&sid=ebsco&xid=b0e8bde4

Timmerberg, J. F., Dole, R., Silberman, N., Goffar, S. L., Mathur, D., Miller, A., Murray, L., Pelletier, D., Simpson, M. S., Stolfi, A., Thompson, A., & Utzman, R. (2019). Physical therapist student readiness for entrance into the first full-time clinical experience: A Delphi study. *Physical Therapy*, *99*(2), 131–146.

Uhm, J.-Y., Ko, Y., & Kim, S. (2019). Implementation of an SBAR communication program based on experiential learning theory in a pediatric nursing practicum: A quasi-experimental study. *Nurse Education Today*, 80, 78–84. https://doi.org/10.1016/j.nedt.2019.05.034

US Department of Education. (n.d.) *Employability skills*. Perkins Collaborative Resource Network. https://cte.ed.gov/initiatives/employability-skills-framework

Wells, C., Olson, R., Bialocerkowski, A., Carroll, S., Chipchase, L., Reubenson, A., Scarvell, J. M., & Kent, F. (2021). Work readiness of new graduate physical therapists for private practice in Australia: Academic faculty, employer, and

graduate perspectives. *Physical Therapy, 101*(6), pzab078. https://doi.org/10.1093/ptj/pzab078
Whitney, R. E., Morris, M. L., & Harney, J. (2021). Perspectives on the professional communication profile and needs of emerging occupational therapists of the millennial generation: A comparison study. *Open Journal of Occupational Therapy (OJOT), 9*(1), 1–16. https://doi.org/10.15453/2168-6408.1673
Wolff-Burke, M. (2005). Clinical instructors' descriptions of physical therapist student professional behaviors. *Journal of Physical Therapy Education (American Physical Therapy Association, Education Section), 19*(1), 67–76. https://doi.org/10.1097/00001416-200501000-00009
World Economic Forum. (2020, October 21). *These are the top 10 job skills of tomorrow – and how long it takes to learn them*. World Economic Forum: https://www.weforum.org/agenda/2020/10/top-10-work-skills-of-tomorrow-how-long-it-takes-to-learn-them/

Chapter 8: Teaching and Learning Employability Skills

Introduction

Today, healthcare providers are increasingly required to adapt their skills to an ever-changing workplace and complex healthcare environments. These environments emphasize accountability and cost containment, which can be challenging for new graduates. An effective way to develop the personal skills, self-belief, and confidence to handle complex environments is through experiential learning. This is because experiential learning enhances self-promotion for the chosen profession and makes it a proven approach to teaching students from ‘Generation Y’ (Thew et al., 2018).

Figure 52

Happy Smiles at Graduation

Note: These students show the joy of graduation. This image was obtained from Microsoft Word, 2023.

Terminal Learning Objectives

By the end of this chapter, the reader will be able to apply the concepts of Kolb’s Theory of Experiential Learning to teach and learn employability skills.

Enabling Learning Objectives

By the end of this chapter, the reader will be able to:

- Explain Kolb’s Experiential Learning Theory.
- Compare the benefits of Kolb’s Theory of Experiential Learning.
- Assess Kolb’s Theory in practice.
- Appraise using experiential learning to teach employability skills.

Instructor Notes

- *You will notice the headers in this textbook are in the form of a question. Students should be prompted to make a note of the question and write their own answer to ensure they master the concepts.*

What Is Kolb's Experiential Learning Theory?

David Kolb published his learning styles model in 1984, from which he developed his learning style inventory. A learning style represents a person's preferred way to learn. Kolb's experiential learning theory is based on a four-stage cycle of learning, which encompasses four separate learning styles. Much of Kolb's theory focuses on the learner's internal cognitive processes (Uhm et al., 2019).

Kolb's Theory of Experiential Learning is based on research in psychology, philosophy, and physiology (Bradbury et al., 2021). Psychology refers to how the human mind affects a person's behavior in each context (Kruger et al., 2023). Philosophy is the study of an individual or group's beliefs and attitudes (Corcoran & Cook, 2023). Physiology is the study of how a living organism or bodily part functions (Heinrich et al., 2023).

What Is the Cycle of Kolb's Theory of Experiential Learning?

Figure 53

Cyclical Depiction of Kolb's Theory of Experiential Learning

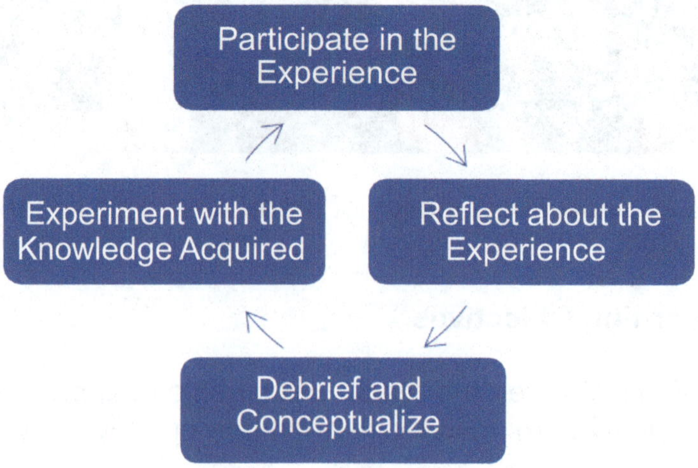

Note: A cyclical depiction of Kolb's Theory of Experiential Learning.

This theory describes the cycle of learning. It begins with the learner participating in an experience, followed by reflection on their feelings and observations of that experience. The student then participates in a debriefing and conceptualization of the experience. The final stage involves experimenting with the knowledge acquired from the experience (Ginsburg & Bain, 2017).

A common practice in healthcare education is simulation or role-playing activities to mimic a patient scenario. A fellow student, the instructor, or an actor plays the role of the patient, while the student healthcare provider practices their skills. Role-playing is a teaching strategy that is likely to have a greater impact than more traditional forms of didactic education because it allows learners to experience relevant situations in a nonthreatening environment.

Fewster-Thuente & Batteson (2018) explained that Kolb's theoretical framework provides a robust and accepted educational approach to applying the knowledge learned through role-playing and simulation. It allows students the opportunity to practice skills as they are acquired. Participating in an experiential learning experience changes the cognitive and metacognitive processes. It provides a scaffolding for enhancing and building upon knowledge previously obtained while improving self-reflection.

Learning from experience originated in the 1800s. Its history is rooted in the philosophical debates between rationalists and empiricists. Rationalists argued that knowledge is gained through reason and the information acquired through one's senses is unreliable. In contrast, empiricists claimed that knowledge is gained through empirical sense impressions. They explained that any abstract concepts that cannot be directly experienced cannot be known.

John Dewey expanded on the relationship between experience and learning in his book, Experience and Education in 1938. He explained that experiences are considered educational if they enhance the development of skills and/or morality. According to Dewey, an experience that provides a benefit to the community aids in the development of curiosity and initiative. It creates a sense of purpose in the individual (Vadeboncoeur, n.d.).

Kolb's theory encompasses the concepts of adult development, and individual learning styles (Bradbury et al., 2021). Employability skills cannot be obtained by using a standardized approach to teaching. The use of experiential learning through simulation and role-playing provides the perfect environment to develop these abilities. Furthermore, this theory was designed as a practical application to teaching concepts related to education and work (Bradbury et al., 2021).

Instructor Notes

- *For synchronous and asynchronous teaching, ask students to describe how they feel about experiential learning. This can be accomplished via a discussion, essay, or Vlog. The goal is to enhance reflection and facilitate acceptance of the process of experiential learning. A rubric is provided in Appendix G.*

What Are the Benefits of Kolb's Theory of Experiential Learning?

Without exposure to a variety of clinical scenarios, students would enter the healthcare field lacking confidence and skills. Experiential learning via simulation benefits the healthcare profession by providing the experiences students need to develop their skills (Clinard, 2022). Simulated learning experiences have the potential to dramatically enhance the educational process. The greatest potential positive impact includes the development of patient-centered care with high-risk and low-incidence populations (Clinard, 2022).

Experiential learning and role play using a variety of scenarios allows healthcare students to picture themselves as future healthcare providers. This learning format has been shown to enhance the attitude of healthcare students through experimentation. The structure provides targeted practice and feedback that provides students the opportunity to improve skills and integrate newly obtained knowledge. Experiential learning has been documented to be an effective strategy to develop communication skills (Clinard, 2022).

Figure 54

Healthcare Student Practicing Interviewing Skills

Note: This healthcare student is practicing interviewing skills. This image was obtained from Microsoft Word, 2023.

Fewster-Thuente & Batteson (2018) explained how Kolb's theoretical framework allows students the opportunity to practice skills as they are acquired. Participation in an experiential learning experience develops cognitive and metacognitive processes. Experiential training focused on the development of employability skills has been shown to achieve better outcomes in the core clinical competencies, didactic knowledge, hands-on skills, and patient satisfaction (Pang et al., 2021). It also provides a foundation for enhanced learning while improving self-reflection.

Experiential learning and didactic educational interventions have been shown to improve the level of empathy conveyed by healthcare students. Scholarly evidence indicated a positive correlation between employability skills and empathy. Healthcare provider empathy has been proven to improve patient adherence, satisfaction, and treatment outcomes (Ratka, 2018).

Real-life practice or experiential learning creates the perfect scenario for students to develop self-reflection as they process their emotions about the experience. Self-reflection helps clinicians develop the courage to face difficult clinical situations. It serves to strengthen interpersonal skills and helps manage stress and anxiety. Kaiafas (2021) explained that self-reflection is imperative to self-assess properly. Self-reflections enabled healthcare students to express their emotions to clinical experiences, which leads to the identification of problems and deeper self-awareness. These are key building blocks for the development of emotional intelligence.

Figure 55

Healthcare Provider Examines a Patient

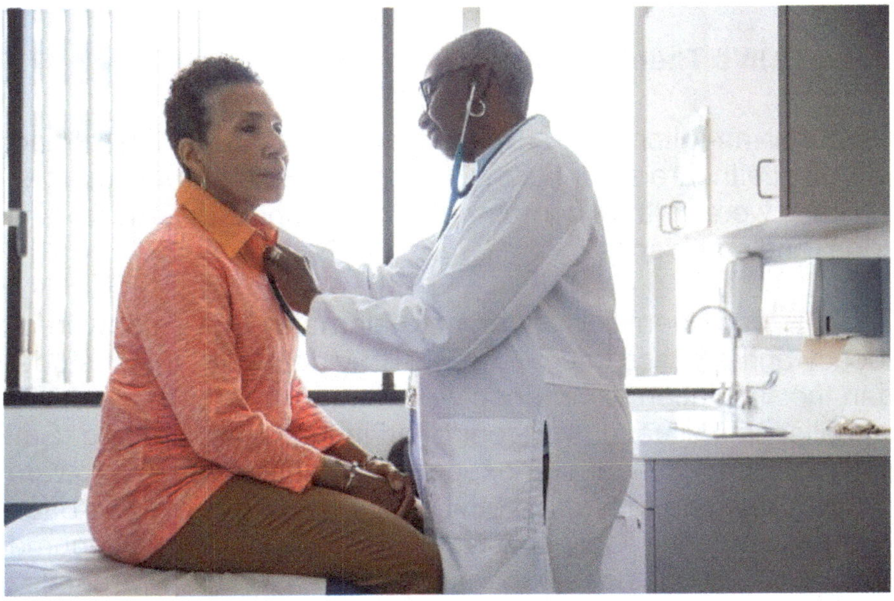

Note: A patient is examined by a healthcare provider. This image was obtained from Microsoft Word, 2023.

The advantage of experiential learning is that it requires students to reconcile their emotional responses with the simulated experience in a positive manner. This process positively contributes to the development of self-regulation, effective communication skills, and confidence (Trotter & Dunnivan-Mitchell, 2019). Self-regulation of emotional responses to situations contributes to providing effective healthcare that is delivered in an empathetic and culturally competent manner.

Instructor Notes

- *For synchronous and asynchronous teaching, ask a group of students to share an intense experience and what they learned from the experience. Then have the other students explain how that experience would have made them feel. This can be accomplished via a discussion. The goal is to enhance reflection, broaden perspective, and to facilitate experiential learning by proxy.*

Experiential learning creates an opportunity for an educator to challenge students to change their perspective and problem-solve. It broadens their view of a potential situation to see the scenario from the patient's or family member's point of view. Through this reflective process, students can practice empathy, which aids in the development of emotional intelligence (Kaiafas, 2021). Experiential learning improves situational awareness and decision-making through teamwork. Experiential learning aids in the development of leadership and stress management. It increases students' self-confidence and communication (Lluch et al., 2021).

Wain (2017) explained that reflection is a process of learning through experience. Reflection involves a systematic process of describing an experience, asking questions, generating theories or hypotheses, and then acting. The development of reflective thinking is a known benefit of experiential learning. Reflection facilitates thedevelopment of critical thinking skills and raises self-awareness.

What Does Kolb's Theory look like in Practice?

Trotter & Dunnivan-Mitchell (2019) used experiential learning to teach interprofessional healthcare students in Guatemala. Six themes emerged from the experience. These were cultural competence, communication, mentorship, empathy, self-knowledge, and confidence.

These themes were identified as the core elements that empowered the participants toward advocacy and process improvement. They determined that students who participated in the simulation experience were better able to respond to distressing and emotionally challenging situations encountered in the clinical setting (Santoso et al., 2018). Furthermore, service-learning experiences propel students toward maturation and mentorship. They help to resolve ethical and cultural dilemmas often encountered in resource-limited countries. Collectively, these stimulate the development of employability skills because these experiences increase self-awareness or knowledge, humility, and empathy (Kaiafas, 2021; Trotter & Dunnivan-Mitchell, 2019).

How Would You Teach Employability Skills Using Experiential Learning?

Employability skills are more difficult to teach than didactic knowledge and psychomotor abilities because they are dependent upon the individual characteristics and qualities of each student (Falco & Monaghan, 2018; Majid et al., 2019). For this reason, employability skills should be taught via experiential learning. This allows the students to learn through simulation and/or role-playing, both of which incorporate the individual characteristics and qualities of the learner (Ginsburg & Bain, 2017; Pensieri & La Marca, 2019).

In terms of teaching and learning employability skills, Reid et al. (2021) concluded that the best method of teaching employability skills is through experiential learning, based on Kolb's Theory. Through experiential learning, adult learners can find meaning in the activities, which enables the learner to construct authentic narratives that are important for articulating employability to prospective employers. Learners need to understand the impact these skills have on the work environment.

The best way to improve the learning experience to acquire employability skills is through authentic learning experiences, such as simulation (Sokhanvar et al., 2021). These experiences have the greatest positive impact on the development of employability skills. Simulation provides the opportunity for students to engage in and practice their communication skills. Simulation requires students to collaborate and engage in critical thinking and problem-solving to optimize the patient's functional abilities. This helps to bridge the gap between didactic knowledge and clinical practice. Because simulation is based on Kolb's Experiential Learning Theory, it provides the opportunity for students to develop their self-awareness. Experiential learning also allows students to develop confidence in their abilities.

Simulated learning experiences allow the student the opportunity to develop their critical thinking and communication skills. These simulations improve student confidence because they enable the student to go through all the motions of patient interaction in a low-risk environment. Practice, followed by debriefing and reflection, facilitates the development of interpersonal skills because it calls upon the student to react and function relative to their environment (Busch & Ma, 2023).

Park et al. (2020) determined that experiential learning is an effective method for improving competence with evidenced-based practice. Furthermore, it is useful to help healthcare students to develop empathy and enhance confidence in forming clinical questions. Research shows the sooner students encounter a simulated clinical scenario, the sooner they learn to use their critical thinking and clinical reasoning skills (de Sa Tinôco et al., 2021).

> "Education is the most powerful weapon which you can use to change the world."
> —Nelson Mandela

Within healthcare education, simulation is a very common format of experiential learning. Although simulation activities can increase a student's anxiety and stress, they have a positive impact on reducing anxiety and stress and building confidence within the clinical setting (Anticol, 2019; Dietrich et al., 2021). Studies have shown that simulation-based education is an effective manner to improve communication and teamwork skills (Fusco & Foltz-Ramos, 2018; MacLeod et al., 2022; Swift et al., 2020; Ulmer et al., 2022).

Instructor Notes

- *For synchronous and asynchronous teaching, after participation in a simulation activity, have students reflect on the experience using Kolb's Experiential Learning Reflection, provide in Appendix K.*

Figure 56

This Child Experiments with Being a Doctor

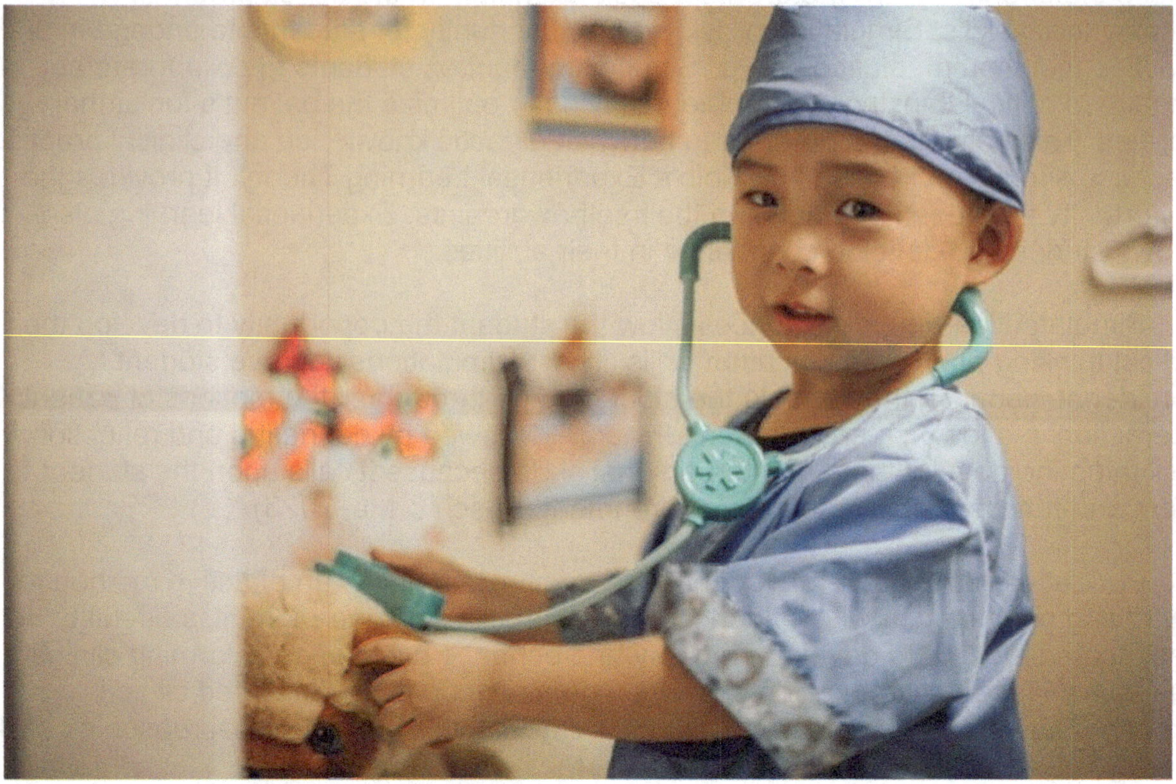

Note: This child is practicing with being a doctor by examining a teddy bear. This image was obtained from Microsoft Word, 2023.

As is the case with experiential learning, simulations, when completed properly, involve different phases. Of these, the debriefing phase is deemed the most beneficial aspect of the learning experience (Brown et al., 2018). The debriefing phase is when the student learner reflects on their actions. Students should be encouraged to be objective when they critique their performance to improve their actions for future clinical situations (Brown et al., 2018). Reflection is most important because it helps students to frame problems differently. When students broaden their perspective of the clinical situation, they can engage in a more active, empathetic, and culturally competent manner (Cheng et al., 2017; Ward et al., 2018).

By reflecting, the novice develops expertise. This is because novices tend to focus on the surface-level characteristics of a situation. It is through engagement with an expert who facilitates the simulation, students start to employ more causal forms of reasoning with the problem. Reflection is when the students articulate their clinical reasoning and what they have learned from the experience. This allows them to make connections among the concepts by reflecting other potential alternative solutions are explored. For this reason, the process of reflection helps to advance problem-solving skills (Tawfik et al., 2022).

Figure 57

Person Looking Out the Window While Reflecting

Note: This professional is looking out the window in self-reflection. This image was obtained from Microsoft Word, 2023.

Tawfik et al. (2022) determined that students commonly reduce the complexity of a problem during problem-solving. They tend to rely on their prior knowledge, which affects their problem representation. The debriefing process promotes knowledge convergence. It is the process of refining the problem and forming a new schema that helps to develop critical thinking and clinical reasoning skills. From a cognitive load perspective, learners must iteratively engage in the learning processes to clarify their final representation of the problem.

Healthcare students consistently perceive simulation to be a valuable learning experience (Costello et al., 2018). Research by Dietrich et al. (2021) determined 80% of students rated simulation as a useful and effective way to learn. This is largely because simulation allows students the opportunity to practice their clinical skills in a risk-free environment (Ayaz & Ismail, 2022). Simulation has been proven to reduce students' stress in complex and emergent situations (Dietrich et al., 2021; Swift et al., 2020). Students reported greater confidence in their ability to address the patients' needs more efficiently and accurately, thereby improving patient outcomes (Costello et al., 2018).

Experiential learning has proven effective in improving interpersonal and communication skills and clinical reasoning skills. Improved clinical reasoning and communication skills lead to improved safety awareness. Reflection facilitates improved self-awareness, which will also positively impact professionalism and teamwork. Therefore, experiential learning is an effective way to teach employability skills, specifically, the deficits most noted in healthcare students.

Using experiential learning to teach employability skills is most effective when educators display a raised awareness and purpose for the experience. The first step is to model employability skills in teaching. The second step is to help students identify their professional purpose which is their professional goals. The process of developing a professional purpose helps to measure an individual's level of commitment to aligning their values, professional aspirations, and societal outlook (Fraser et al., 2019).

Figure 58

This Professional Is Demonstrating a Growth Mindset

Note: A professional demonstrates a growth mindset. This image was obtained from Microsoft Word, 2023.

What makes experiential learning so effective is the incorporation of a mindset. A mindset helps to define the purpose of the experience thereby facilitating self-awareness. Having an action mindset guides an individual's approach to managing a complex workplace. An action mindset means having a clear vision of how the environment works and the desired outcome of the interaction. This helps students to organize the information to determine the best course of action. The mindset helps to capture the personal values and beliefs that guide an individual's reaction to events. The autonomy achieved through the experience sparks curiosity and facilitates the development of students' confidence (Fraser et al., 2019).

The experience can also be approached collaboratively. A collaboration mindset is based on the principle of using feedback from others to guide a decision. This experience aids in the validation of personal values and beliefs. It also expands a person's thinking, thereby facilitating the development of critical thinking skills and mental flexibility (Fraser et al., 2019).

A growth mindset allows a person to reflect on their purpose and to integrate the experience into their purpose. It is based on the concept of self-regulation. With the growth mindset, students are challenged to reframe failure or setbacks as opportunities for growth. Students who believe they can change the outcome of a situation by adapting their actions develop greater resilience, emotion management, and self-efficacy (Fraser et al., 2019).

What Are the Key Concepts from this Chapter?

- Kolb's experiential learning theory works on a four-stage cycle of learning:
    - The learner participates in an experience
    - The learner reflects on their feelings and observations of the experience
    - The learner participates in debriefing and conceptualizing the experience
    - The learner experiments with the knowledge acquired from the experience
- Simulated learning experiences have the potential to develop patient-centered care in a high-fidelity, low-risk simulation.
- Experiential learning positively contributes to the development of self-regulation, effective communication skills, and confidence (Trotter & Dunnivan-Mitchell, 2019).
- Experiential training that is focused on the development of employability skills has been shown to achieve better outcomes in the core clinical competencies, didactic knowledge, hands-on skills, and patient satisfaction (Pang et al., 2021).
- The advantage of experiential learning is that it requires students to reconcile their emotional responses with the simulated experience in a positive manner.
- Reflection involves a systematic process of describing an experience, asking questions, generating theories or hypotheses, and then acting.
- Reflection involves a systematic process of describing an experience, asking questions, generating theories or hypotheses, and then acting.
- Simulated learning experiences allow the students the opportunity to develop:
    - Critical thinking and clinical reasoning skills
    - Communication and interpersonal skills
    - Confidence
    - Empathy
    - Resilience
    - Teamwork skills
    - Self-awareness and reflection

Summary

This chapter covers Kolb's Experiential Learning Theory. It explains how using Kolb's Experiential Learning is an effective way to teach and learn employability skills. In healthcare education, Kolb's Experiential learning is commonly utilized via simulations. These experiences can be enhanced with a greater emphasis on employability skill acquisition. The next chapter explores the concept of assessing competency through the Dreyfus Model of Skill Acquisition.

References

Anticol, D. (2019). How does experimental learning increase skills and knowledge acquisition and retention in the non-traditional adult learner? *Adult Higher Education Alliance.* https://files.eric.ed.gov/fulltext/ED597801.pdf

Ayaz, O., & Ismail, F. W. (2022). Healthcare simulation: A key to the future of medical education-a review. *Advances in Medical Education and Practice*, 13, 301. https://doi.org/10.2147/AMEP.S353777

Bradbury, T., Schwarz, E. C., & Lenton, A. (2021). Experiential learning from an international perspective: An empirical study of the United States, Canada, Australia, and New Zealand. *International Journal of Sport Management*, *22*(1), 55–93.

Brown, D. K., Wong, A. H., & Ahmed, R. A. (2018). Evaluation of simulation debriefing methods with interprofessional learning. *Journal of Interprofessional Care*, *32*(6), 779–781. https://doi.org/10.1080/13561820.2018.1500451

Busch, C. M., & Ma, T. (2023). Speech-language pathology graduate students' perception of satisfaction, confidence, and interpersonal skill development during simulated experiences amid COVID-19. *Perspectives of the ASHA Special Interest Groups*, *8*(1), 134–150. https://doi.org/10.1044/2022_PERSP-22-00073

Cheng, A., LaDonna, K., Cristancho, S., & Ng, S. (2017). Navigating difficult conversations: The role of self-monitoring and reflection-in-action. *Medical Education*, *51*(12), 1220–1231. https://doi.org/10.1111/medu.13448

Clinard, E. S. (2022). Increasing student confidence with medically complex infants through simulation: A mixed methods investigation. *American Journal of Speech-Language Pathology*, *31*(2), 942–958. https://doi.org/10.1044/2021_AJSLP-21-00234

Corcoran, L., & Cook, K. (2023). The philosophy of Hans-Georg Gadamer: An exemplar of the complicated relationship between philosophy and nursing practice. Nursing Inquiry, 30(1), e12509. https://doi.org/10.1111/nin.12509

Costello, J. P., Olivieri, L. J., Krieger, A., Thabit, O., Marshall, M. B., Yoo, S.-J., Kim, P. C., Jonas, R. A., & Nath, D. S. (2014). Utilizing three-dimensional printing technology to assess the feasibility of high-fidelity synthetic ventricular septal defect models for simulation in medical education. *World Journal for Pediatric & Congenital Heart Surgery*, *5*(3), 421–426. https://doi.org/10.1177/2150135114528721

de Sa Tinoco, J. D., Cossi, M. S., da Conceicao Dias Fernandes, M. I., Paiva, A. C., de Oliveira Lopes, M. V., & Brandao de Carvalho Lira, A. L. (2021). Effect of educational intervention on clinical reasoning skills in nursing: A quasi-experimental study. *Nurse Education Today*, 105. https://doi.org/10.1016/j.nedt.2021.105027

Dietrich, E., Le Corre, Y., Dupin, N., Dréno, B., Cartier, I., Granry, J.-C., & Martin, L. (2021). Benefits of simulation using standardized patients for training dermatology residents in breaking bad news. *Annales de Dermatologie et de Vénéréologie*, *148*(3), 156–160. https://doi.org/10.1016/j.annder.2020.11.003

Falco, K., & Monaghan, H. M. (2018). Soft skills: The foundation for effective SPHM program leadership: A national survey. *International Journal of Safe Patient Handling & Mobility (SPHM)*, *8*(2), 76–90.

Fewster-Thuente, L., & Batteson, T. J. (2018). Kolb's experiential learning theory as a theoretical underpinning for interprofessional education. *Journal of Allied Health*, *47*(1), 3–8.

Fraser, C. J., Duignan, G., Stewart, D., & Rodrigues, A. (2019). Overt and overt: Strategies for building employability skills of vocational education graduates. *Journal of Teaching and Learning for Graduate Employability*, *10*(1), 157–172.

Fusco, N. M., & Foltz-Ramos, K. (2018). Measuring changes in pharmacy and nursing students' perceptions following an interprofessional high-fidelity simulation experience. *Journal of Interprofessional Care*, *32*(5), 648–652. https://doi.org/10.1080/13561820.2018.1496073

Ginsburg, L., & Bain, L. (2017). The evaluation of a multifaceted intervention to promote "speaking up" and strengthen interprofessional teamwork climate perceptions. *Journal of Interprofessional Care*, *31*(2), 207–217. https://doi.org/10.1080/13561820.2016.1249280

Heinrich, T., Bähring, R., Larena-Avellaneda, A., Querengässer, J., Solbrig, O., Ehmke, H., & Schwoerer, A. P. (2023). Bridging vascular physiology to vascular medicine: An integrative laboratory class. *Advances in Physiology Education*, *47*(1), 97–116. https://doi.org/10.1152/advan.00170.2022

Kaiafas, K. N. (2021). Emotional intelligence and role-modeling nursing's soft skills. *Journal of Christian Nursing: A Quarterly Publication of Nurses Christian Fellowship*, *38*(4), 240–243. https://doi.org/10.1097/CNJ.0000000000000881

Kruger, D. J., Fisher, M. L., & Salmon, C. (2023). What do evolutionary researchers believe about human psychology and behavior? *Evolution & Human Behavior*, *44*(1), 11–18. https://doi.org/10.1016/j.evolhumbehav.2022.11.002

Lluch, A. M., Lluch, C., Arregui, M., Jiménez, E., & Giner-Tarrida, L. (2021). Peer mentoring as a tool for developing soft skills in clinical practice: A 3-year study. *Dentistry Journal*, *9*(5). https://doi.org/10.3390/dj9050057

MacLeod, C. E., Brady, D. R., & Maynard, S. P. (2022). Measuring the effect of simulation experience on perceived self-efficacy for interprofessional collaboration among undergraduate nursing and social work students. *Journal of Interprofessional Care*, *36*(1), 102–110. https://doi.org/10.1080/13561820.2020.1865886

Majid, S., Eapen, C. M., Ei Mon Aung, & Oo, K. T. (2019). The importance of soft skills for employability and career development: Students and employers' perspectives. *IUP Journal of Soft Skills*, *13(*4), 7–39.

Pang, Y., Wu, Q., Bi, J., & Wang, J. (2021). Effectiveness of hierarchical, diversified soft skills training in clinical nursing training. *International Journal of Clinical Practice*, *75*(12), e14935. https://doi.org/10.1111/ijcp.14935

Park, M., Jeong, M., Lee, M., & Cullen, L. (2020). Web-based experiential learning strategies to enhance the evidence-based-practice competence of undergraduate nursing students. *Nurse Education Today*, 91. https://doi.org/10.1016/j.nedt.2020.104466

Pensieri, C. & and La Marca, A. 2019. "Virtual worlds and virtual reality. An analysis in the Healthcare education." *Formare*, *19*(1). doi:10.13128/formare-24756.

Ratka, A. (2018). Empathy and the development of affective skills. *American Journal of Pharmaceutical Education*, *82*(10), 1140–1143. https://doi.org/10.5688/ajpe7192

Santoso, R., Puspadewi, N. & Tanumiharja, T. (2018). Evaluation of the implementation of simulation-based learning in fourth year medical students of Atma Jaya Catholic University of Indonesia. *Jurnal Pendidikan Kedokteran Indonesia*, *7*(2),125–131. https://doi.org/10.22146/jpki.39103

Sokhanvar, Z., Salehi, K., & Sokhanvar, F. (2021). Advantages of authentic assessment for improving the learning experience and employability skills of higher education students: A systematic literature review. *Studies in Educational Evaluation*, 70. https://doi.org/10.1016/j.stueduc.2021.101030

Swift, M. C., Stosberg, T., Foley, A., & Brocksmith, E., (2020). Nursing Program Outcome Improves with Interprofessional Simulation. *Journal of Allied Health*, *49*(3), 157-163,163A. https://prx-usa.lirn.net/login?url=https://www.proquest.com/scholarly-journals/nursing-

program-outcome-improves-with/docview/2441571748/se-2
Tawfik, A. A., Bradford, J., Gish-Lieberman, J., & Gatewood, J. (2022). Repeated measures of cognitive and affective learning outcomes in simulation debriefing. *Journal of Physical Therapy Education (Lippincott Williams & Wilkins), 36(*2), 133–138. https://doi.org/10.1097/JTE.0000000000000233

Trotter S., & Dunnivan-Mitchell S., (2019). 'Simulation enhances soft skills among inter-professionals participating in an international service-learning experience to a resource-limited country'. *MedEdPublish*, *8*(1), 24, https://doi.org/10.15694/mep.2019.000024.1

Uhm, J.-Y., Ko, Y., & Kim, S. (2019). Implementation of an SBAR communication program based on experiential learning theory in a pediatric nursing practicum: A quasi-experimental study. *Nurse Education Today*, 80, 78–84. https://doi.org/10.1016/j.nedt.2019.05.034

Ulmer, F., Lutz, A., Müller, F., Riva, T., Bütikofer, L. & Greif, R. (2022). Communication patterns during routine patient care in a pediatric intensive care unit: The behavioral impact of in situ simulation. *Journal of Patient Safety*, *18*(2), e573-e579. doi: 10.1097/PTS.0000000000000872.

Vadeboncoeur, J. A. (2002). *Experiential education* (Vol. 2). Gale.

Ward, A., Mandrusiak, A., & Levett-Jones, T. (2018). Cultural empathy in physiotherapy students: A pre-test post-test study utilizing virtual simulation. *Physiotherapy*, *104*(4), 453–461. https://doi.org

Chapter 9: Assessing Employability Skills

Introduction

The last chapter covered how Kolb's Experiential Learning is an effective way to teach and learn employability skills. In healthcare education, this is commonly accomplished through patient care simulations. As the student moves through the learning process, their competencies must be assessed. The Dreyfus Model of Skill Acquisition provides a straightforward, simplified approach to assessing skill acquisition.

Terminal Learning Objectives

By the end of this chapter, the reader will be able to use the Dreyfus Model of Skill Acquisition to assess competency with employability skills.

Enabling Learning Objectives

By the end of this chapter, the reader will be able to:

- Appraise why one should use a competency-based assessment in healthcare
- Distinguish which competency assessment should be used to assess employability skills
- Diagram the Dreyfus Model of Skill Acquisition
- Differentiate between the benefits of using the Dreyfus Model of Skill Acquisition

Instructor Notes

- *You will notice the headers in this textbook are in the form of a question. Students should be prompted to make a note of the question and write the answer to that question in their own words to ensure they master the concepts.*

Why Use Competency-Based Assessment in Healthcare?

Healthcare organizations are constantly evolving to meet the needs of a dynamic population. This evolution includes ongoing growth of technology and the general body of knowledge. Because of complications from challenges related to the economy and healthcare disparities, organizations must strive for cost containment and value maximization (Mohammadi et al., 2020).

The concept of using competency-based assessments is derived from the Institute of Medicine's proposed set of core competencies for all health disciplines. These competencies were developed to ensure that clinicians deliver patient-centered care, based on reliable evidence, as an interdisciplinary team (Torres-Narvaez et al., 2018). Competency-based assessments focus on performance outcomes that enable healthcare providers to work as competent professionals.

This is because the performance outcomes are based on the knowledge, skills, and attitudes of the studentsor graduates (Africa, 2023).

Figure 59

Person Using a Checklist to Ensure Task Completion

Note: This person is using a checklist to ensure thoroughness and consistency in her work. This image was obtained from Microsoft Word, 2023.

Competency-based assessments are designed to ensure the learner has a predetermined level of competence with a set of defined skills. The defined set of skills required varies by the healthcare provider's specialty. The knowledge, skills, and aptitudes of healthcare students are assessed periodically to ensure progression toward competency. Direct observation during actual patient care experiences is the optimal method of competency validation. However, until a student reaches a certain level of competence, other methods to assess competency, such as simulations, case studies, or discussions, are used to ensure patient safety (Africa, 2023).

Which Competency Assessment Should Be Used to Assess Employability Skills?

There are many assessment tools to measure healthcare provider performance. These tools are evaluated to determine their validity and reliability. Validity refers to an assessment's ability to measure what is supposed to be measured (Patino & Ferreira, 2018). Reliability refers to the consistency achieved when multiple evaluators test the measure of the same subject over time Newman et al., 2021).

Unfortunately, most of these tools indirectly assess employability skills competency. These assessments have a much greater emphasis on the student's competency with a hands-on skill or their content knowledge. Routinely, these assessments will measure competency with general professionalism or communication with the pseudo patients. In addition, these assessment tools are specific to one discipline, rather than all healthcare providers. Therefore, a better alternative is to first measure each employability skill competency directly, then second, use a tool designed to measure the degree to whicha skill has been acquired.

What Is the Dreyfus Model of Skill Acquisition?

The Dreyfus Model of Skill Acquisition was developed by Stuart and Hubert Dreyfus in 1980. This model described the five levels of progression as an individual moves from the level of novice to expert (Peña, 2010). These levels of skill acquisition are like the original five levels of learning described by Bloom's Taxonomy. The Dreyfus Model was later revised to include seven levels of skill acquisition. William et al., (2017) explained that a big advantage of using a level-based approach is that it fosters individualized instruction tailored to the needs of the learner.

The Dreyfus Model of Skill Acquisition was originally used to evaluate the progression of nurses and physicians as they acquired skills within the clinical environment (Peña, 2010). Dehn et al. (2022) explained how the Dreyfus model focused on the transitions of learning. It takes into consideration three aspects of practice: the student's perspective and perception of the task, and the student's perception of the role. The student's perspective on the task described the transition from dependence on abstract principles to the application of a person's actual experience. The student's perception of the task accounted for the transition from the opinion that everything is important to the particulars of the situation. In this stage, the student learns to discern the relative importance of the individual elements. The student's perception of the role described the transition from being an outside observer to an active participant. The Dreyfus Model has an internal consistency of Cronbach $\alpha = 0.97$ making it a reliable assessment tool (William et al., 2017).

Figure 60

Pictorial Representation of the Dreyfus Model of Skill Acquisition

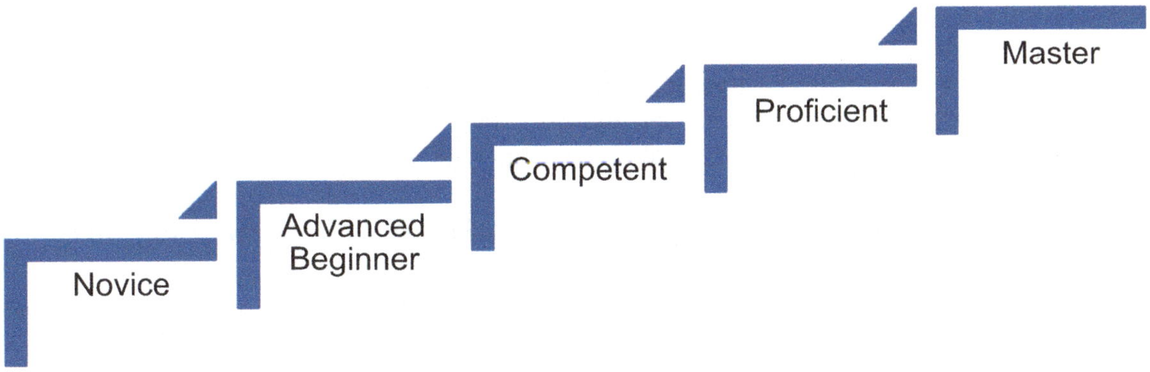

Note: This is a pictorial representation of the Dreyfus Model of Skill Acquisition.

The Dreyfus Model provides a descriptive, progressive framework, based on experiential learning. As the learner progresses through each of the five levels, the model outlines the characteristics of the learner's cognitive and professional competence, degree of skill acquisition, and ability to solve problems and act based on the knowledge acquired from prior experiences (Dehn et al., 2022).

Five Stages of Skill Acquisition (Dehn et al., 2022)

- Novice
  - Responsibility to follow the rules
  - Act on rules for specific situations
  - Feels insecure and detached as they focus on executing the task 'correctly'
    - Lacks understanding of the overall task and are unable to relate it to broader concepts
- Advanced Beginner
  - Responsibility to follow the rules
  - Acts on conditional rules
  - Feels some comfort as he or she begins to recognize and grasp concepts gained through experience
- Competent
  - Responsibility arises from decision making
  - Organizes information by relevance
  - Feels a little more engaged due to a degree of confidence as they are differentiating and prioritizing information
- Proficient
  - Responsibility increases with experience
  - Acts on pattern recognition and rules to make decisions
  - Feels confident and acts more deliberately as they can differentiate between a variety of elements with a wider perspective, acquired from experience
- Expert
  - Acknowledges responsibility to others and the environment
  - Acts on pattern recognition with little analysis required
  - Feels confident and accomplished as he or she can detach from the rule-based theory and integrate new aspects of practice

What Are the Benefits of Using the Dreyfus Model of Skill Acquisition?

The Dreyfus Model of Skill Acquisition assesses skill acquisition on multiple levels. It takes into consideration the learner's understanding of the concepts. As learners expand their comprehension of the content, they become more emotionally engaged in their learning. Emotional engagement increases as the learner integrates the knowledge they have gained through experience. The Dreyfus Model considers the learner's ability to master unpredictability and complexity. The learners gain self-reflection and awareness skills as the skills gain meaningfulness (Dehn et al., 2022).

Instructor Notes

- *The U.S. Department of Education's Employability Skills has a checklist of the components that must be incorporated into the lesson planning to ensure that all sub-competencies and addressed.*
    - *As an instructor, you can use this checklist in Appendix L to ensure you incorporate the lesson components listed below when you complete your lesson planning.*

What Are the Key Concepts from this Chapter?

- The use of competency-based assessment ensures clinicians deliver patient-centered care, based on reliable evidence, as an interdisciplinary team (Torres-Narvaez et al., 2018).
- William et al., (2017) explained that a big advantage of using a level-based approach is that it fosters individualized instruction, tailored to the needs of the learner.
- The Dreyfus model of skill acquisition describes the five levels of progression as individual moves from the level of novice to expert (Peña, 2010).
- Five Stages of Skill Acquisition (Dehn et al., 2022)
    - Novice
        - Responsibility to follow the rules
        - Acts on rules for specific situations
        - Feels insecure and detached as they focus on executing the task 'correctly'
            - Lacks understanding of the overall task and are unable to relate it to broader concepts
    - Advanced Beginner
        - Responsibility to follow the rules
        - Acts on conditional rules
        - Feels some comfort as he or she begins to recognize and grasp concepts gained through experience
    - Competent
        - Responsibility arises from active decision making
        - Organizes information by relevance
        - Feels a little more engaged due to a degree of confidence as they are differentiating and prioritizing information
    - Proficient
        - Responsibility increases with experience
        - Acts on pattern recognition and rules to make decisions
        - Feels confident and acts more deliberately as they can differentiate between a variety of elements with a wider perspective, acquired from experience
    - Expert
        - Acknowledges responsibility to others and the environment
        - Acts on pattern recognition with little analysis required
        - Feels confident and accomplished as they can completely detach from the rule-based theory and integrate new aspects of practice

- The benefits of the Dreyfus Model of Skill Acquisition include consideration of:
    - The learner's understanding of the concepts
    - The learner's comprehension of the content
    - The learner's emotional engagement in their learning
    - The learner's ability to master unpredictability and complexity
    - The learner's abilities for self-reflection and awareness
    - The learner's skills as the content becomes more meaningful.

Summary

This chapter examined the idea of using the Dreyfus Model of Skill Acquisition to assess competency with employability skills. The Dreyfus Model provides a descriptive, progressive framework, based on experiential learning, as described in Kolb's Theory of Experiential Learning. Experiential Learning has proven to be a highly effective strategy for teaching skills necessary for the delivery of healthcare services. The next chapter explores ways to apply and analyze the U.S. Department of Education's Employability Skills Framework.

References

Africa, L. (2023). Use of a competency-based framework to transition new graduate advanced practice registered nurses into practice. *Nursing Economic$*, *41*(2), 59–95.

Dehn, P., Munch Simonsen, S., & Olesen, M. L. (2022). Multidimensional factors determine skill acquisition development in guided self-determination: A qualitative study. *Scandinavian Journal of Caring Sciences*, 1. https://doi.org/10.1111/scs.13140

Kirkpatrick, K. & Mackinnon, R. (2012). Technology-enhanced learning in anaesthesia and educational theory. *Continuing Education in Anaesthesia, Critical Care & Pain*. 12. 263-267. 10.1093/bjaceaccp/mks027.

Mohammadi, F., Farahani, M., Nazarimanesh, L., Tabibi, S.J. & Riahi, L. (2020). Validity and reliability of American college of healthcare executive competencies assessment tool for the managers of healthcare networks in Zanjan Province. *Journal of Biostatistics and Epidemiology*, *6*(3). https://doi.org/10.18502/jbe.v6i3.5106

Newman, K., Martin, L. S., McLelland, V., Wang, A., Au Duong, J., Khan, S. S., Ye, B., Spasojevic, S., Iaboni, A., & Mihailidis, A. (2021). Reliability of nurses' use of a direct behavioural observation tool in the dementia context: Implications for development of predictive systems of behavioural assessment. *Perspectives: The Journal of the Canadian Gerontological Nursing Association*, 42(3), 13–21.

Patino, C. M., & Ferreira, J. C. (2018). Internal and external validity: Can you apply research study results to your patients? *Brazilian Journal of Pulmonology: Official Publication of the Brazilian Society of Pulmonology and Tisiology*, *44*(3), 183. https://doi.org/10.1590/S1806-37562018000000164

Peña, A. (2010). The Dreyfus model of clinical problem-solving skills acquisition: A critical perspective. *Medical Education Online*, *15*(0), 1–11. https://doi.org/10.3402/meo.v15i0.4846

Torres-Narvaez, M.-R., Vargas-Pinilla, O.-C., & Rodriguez-Grande, E.-I. (2018). Validity and reproducibility of a tool for assessing clinical competencies in physical therapy students. *BMC Medical Education*, 18(1). https://doi.org/10.1186/s12909-018-1377-x

Williams, B. W., Byrne, P. D., Williams, N. V., & Williams, M. V. (2017). Dreyfus and Dreyfus and indicators of behavioral performance: A study of measurement convergence. *Journal of Continuing Education in the Health Professions, 37*(1), 50–54. https://doi.org/10.1097/CEH.0000000000000138

Chapter 10: Application and Analysis of Applied Knowledge Skills

Introduction

The previous chapters covered the U.S. Department of Education's Employability Skills Framework. This was followed by an analysis of how the employability skills of today's healthcare students and graduates are being perceived by those already working in the field. Kolb's Theory of Experiential Learning was used to teach employability skills and the Dreyfus Model of Skill Acquisition to assess students' competency with employability skills. This chapter explores teaching strategies to facilitate the application and analysis of employability skills. A discussion of Bloom's Taxonomy is included to remind instructors of the bigger picture. As mentioned, applied academic knowledge skills include academic skills and critical thinking.

> "The ultimate ignorance is the rejection of something you knownothing about yet refuse to investigate."
> —Dr. Wayne Dyer

Terminal Learning Objectives

By the end of this chapter, students will be able to use strategies to facilitate the application and analysis of applied knowledge skills.

Enabling Learning Objectives

By the end of this chapter, the learner will be able to:

- Differentiate the learning and assessment levels of Bloom's Taxonomy
- Apply and analyze academic skills
- Apply and analyze their critical thinking skills

Instructor Notes

- *The headers in this textbook are in the form of a question. Learners should be prompted to make a note of the question and to write the answer in their own words to ensure they master the concepts.*

What is Bloom's Taxonomy?

Benjamin Bloom first published his taxonomy in 1956 to provide an observable and measurable way to define learning and assessment (Newton et al., 2020). The taxonomy contained three domains: Cognitive, Affective, and Psychomotor.

Within the Cognitive domain, educators design their instruction around the six classification levels: *Knowledge, Comprehension, Application, Analysis, Synthesis*, and *Evaluation*.

Figure 61

Bloom's Original Taxonomy

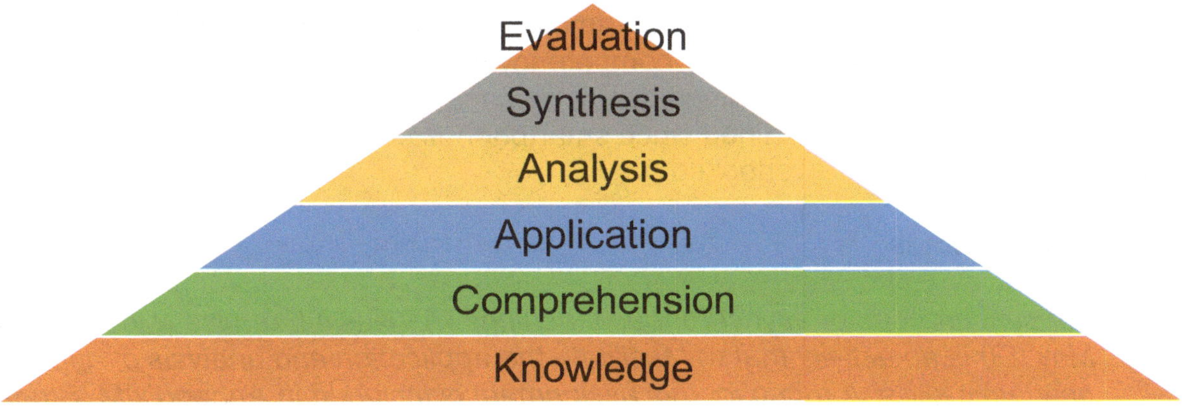

Note: The original taxonomy contained six levels of observable learning.

Bloom's Taxonomy was revised in 2001 by Anderson and Krathwohl to be more useful to educators. The Revised Bloom's Taxonomy renamed all the categories as verbs rather than nouns (The Glossary of Education Reform for Journalists, Parents, and Community Members, 2014 March 5). The verbs at the lower end of the hierarchy can be used to test factual knowledge, while the verbs at the higher end of the hierarchy are associated with higher order thinking skills (Newton et al., 2020).

Figure 62

Bloom's Revised Taxonomy

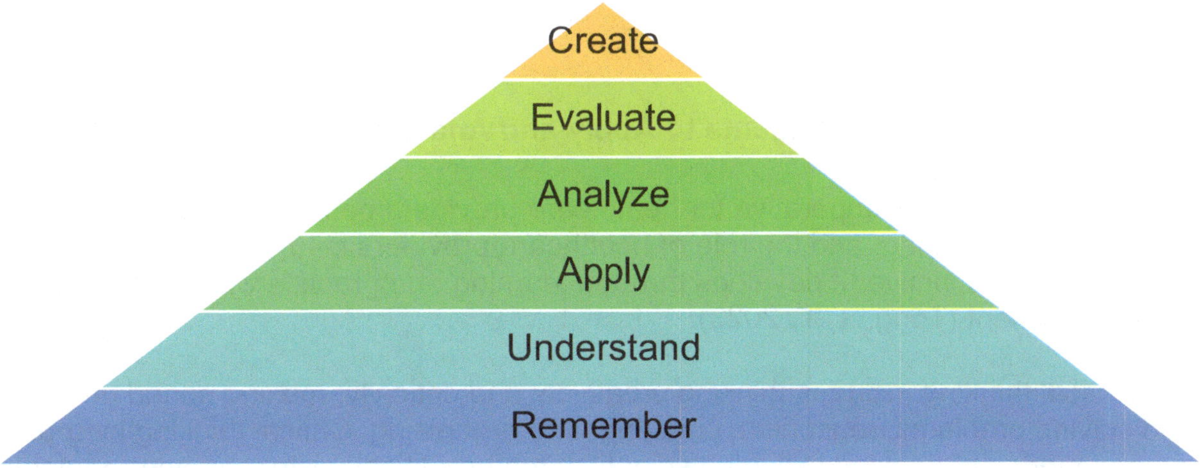

Note: Bloom's Revised Taxonomy lists verbs instead of nouns.

How Do You Teach Students to Apply and Analyze Applied Academic Skills?

Applied academic skills include reading and writing, along with math and scientific procedures and principles. While it seems that students in higher education should be proficient in these skills, this is not always the case. In today's electronic world, writing and math skills have been replaced with emojis and handheld devices. Reliance on technology has decreased students' competency with academic skills. For example, the writing skills of students has declined due to reliance on spelling and grammar checking features. Math skills have declined since smartphones contain calculators. Therefore, these skills should not be overlooked.

Instructor Notes

- *For synchronous or asynchronous teaching, The News Exercise (Metivier, 2023, May 23) is an activity that will facilitate the application and analysis of applied academic skills. A rubric for this assignment is included in Appendix M. Students should be instructed to find a current news story that includes graphs, numbers, or any representation involving numerical data. Students should be provided with the following prompts:*
    - *What are three things you learned from this article?*
    - *What are two things you found interesting and why?*
    - *What is one question you have after reading this news clip and why?*
    - *How does this news help you to understand the data?*
    - *Does the data representation make sense and why?*
    - *How do you know if the graph or table is reliable?*
    - *Is the article reliable and free from bias? (Cross, n.d.; Metivier, 2023, May 23)*

It is not uncommon for instructors to avoid assignments that require a more labor-intensive format of grading. However, assignments that require more labor-intensive grading, (e.g., essays) also facilitate the development of higher order thinking skills. Writing assignments help to improve understanding of concepts, link theory to practice, and express emotions (Miller, 2020).

How Do You Teach Students to Apply and Analyze Critical Thinking Skills?

Critical thinking is imperative for healthcare providers because it aids the development of caring, and the role of healthcare providers is to care for their patients. Caring is not instinctive. It develops through learning and practice within the confines of the environment (Tong et al., 2023).

Critical thinking includes thinking creatively and critically, making sound decisions and solving problems, reasoning, planning, and organizing. Critical thinking incorporates several modes of thinking including scientific, mathematical, historical, anthropological, economic, moral, and philosophical. Core critical thinking skills include observation interpretation, analysis, inference, evaluation, explanation, and meta-cognition (Gonçalves Nes et al., 2023).

> "Critical thinking is a desire to seek…and set in order…by acknowledging our own contexts and making a genuine effort to understand and accommodate other paradigms and problematics, weare unable to pretend that our understandings are value-free."
> – Francis Bacon

Proficient critical thinkers can analyze arguments, identify conclusions and premises, derive simple assumptions, handle irrelevance, determine the structure of an argument, and summarize the details. This requires critical thinkers to make inferences, apply logic, interpret data, and develop hypotheses. Critical thinking is a reflective process that requires continuous self-monitoring and self-correction (Gonçalves Nes et al., 2023).

Instructor Notes

- *For synchronous teaching, the Nine Dot Problem is a fun exercise that challenges a person to think outside the box. The purpose of this exercise is to demonstrate the point that deep thinking takes time. This problem is depicted in Appendix N. The solution to the problem is depicted in Appendix O.*

> "It's not that I'm so smart, it's just that I stay with problems longer."
> —Albert Einstein

Critical thinking can be difficult when a person lacks creativity. Toyama et al. (2023) explain that creativity stems from flexible, systematic, and persistent thinking, which requires the exploration of different perspectives. Studies about creativity demonstrate that people often attribute creativity to spontaneity, rather than persistence and expertise.

Instructor Notes

- *For synchronous teaching, Thirty Circles is an exercise that promotes creativity. The goal is quantity over quality. Students will be given a sheet of paper with 30 circles in Appendix P. Instruct students to draw something in as many of the 30 circles as possible in 10 minutes. Once completed, divide the class into groups to see if there are any unifying principles or designs (Birt, 2022, September 30).*

- *For synchronous or asynchronous teaching, the Dictionary Story is a great exercise to boost creativity. Students should be instructed to select a word at random from the dictionary. They are to use the word they selected, plus the word above and below the word they selected. Students should create an interesting, cohesive story from these random words. This exercise helps to improve the ability to make connections and combine ideas that don't necessarily relate (Birt, 2022, September 30).*

Sometimes creativity is impacted by mental blocks. There are several reasons why people have mental blocks. They might be:

- Defining the problem too narrowly
- Attacking the symptoms, not the problem
- Assuming there is only one answer
- Getting “hooked” on the first solution
- Getting “hooked” on a solution that almost works
- Being too distracted by irrelevant information
- Being too anxious to finish
- Defining the problem too ambiguously

> “Failure is the opportunity to begin again, only more intelligently.”
> –Henry Ford

There are several types of conceptual blocks (Williams, n.d.):

- Constancy—wanting to use a previous solution to solve all problems
- Commitment—being committed to oversimplifying things we make assumptions about, such as stereotyping. This is usually the result of information overload.
- Complacency—giving up too easily, often the result of deeper emotional blocks:
    - Fear of taking a risk
    - Dislike for uncertainty
    - Judgmental attitude
    - Lack of challenge
    - Inability to incubate
- Compression or intellectual—being too quick to solve a problem or failure to see the big picture, which is the result of being inflexible or having inadequate uses ofproblem-solving strategies
- Cultural—being limited by what the culture dictates
- Environmental—being limited by environmental constraints
- Expressive blocks—being unable to communicate ideas to others

Figure 63

Person Struggling with a Conceptual Block

Note: This person is struggling with a conceptual block. This image was obtained from Microsoft Word, 2023.

Fortunately, there are several strategies to overcome and avoid conceptual blocks (Williams, n.d.).

- Reduce stress by adjusting attitudes
- Remove or reduce the fear of failure; failure is a part of learning.
- Change the rules of the problem or the mode of the solution
- Ask provocative questions
- Use fluency or produce many solutions
- Take a mental excursion from the problem
- Break up patterns to think of the problem differently. This is often best accomplished via synectics, which is bringing people from diverse backgrounds together to share ideas.
- Use shake-up exercises to encourage risk-taking

Instructor Notes

- *For synchronous or asynchronous teaching, challenge students to develop critical thinking by having them debate certain topics. In a synchronous setting, provide students with a topic to debate and a limited amount of time to argue their position. In an asynchronous setting, have students produce a timed video arguing their position. Appendix Q contains a list of topics to debate. Inasmuch as the topics are based on opinion, there is not a set rubric for this assignment.*

What Are the Key Concepts from this Chapter?

- Benjamin Bloom first published his taxonomy in 1956 to provide an observable and measurable way to define learning and assessment (Newton et al., 2020).

- In 2001, Bloom's Taxonomy was revised to use verbs instead of nouns. Bloom's Revised Taxonomy:
    - Create
    - Evaluate
    - Analyze
    - Apply
    - Understand
    - Remember
- Writing assignments help to improve understanding of concepts, link theory to practice, and express emotions (Miller, 2020).
- Core critical thinking skills include observation, interpretation, analysis, inference, evaluation, explanation, and meta-cognition (Gonçalves Nes et al., 2023).
- Toyama et al. (2023) explain that creativity stems from flexible, systematic, and persistent thinking, which requires the exploration of different perspectives.
- There are several types of conceptual blocks (Williams, n.d.):
    - Constancy
    - Commitment
    - Complacency
    - Compression
    - Cultural
    - Environmental
    - Expressive blocks

> "It is the mark of an educated mind to be able to entertain a thought without accepting it."
> –Aristotle, Greek Philosopher

Summary

This chapter covers strategies for teaching students the application and analysis of their applied knowledge skills. These include applied academic and critical thinking skills. Developing these skills, especially critical thinking, helps students identify their professional identity and improves their self-confidence. The next chapter delves into the application of effective relationship skills.

References

Birt, J. (2022, September 30). *18 creativity exercises to improve creative thinking at work*. Indeed Career Guide. https://www.indeed.com/career-advice/career-development/creativity-exercise

Cross, K. P. (n.d.). *Teaching technique 02: 3-2-1*. The K. Patricia Cross Academy. https://kpcrossacademy.org/techniques/3-2-1/

Gonçalves Nes, A. A., Riege, F., Martini, J. G., Zlama, J., Bresolin, P., Gomes da Costa Mohallem, A., & Steindal, S. A. (2023). Brazilian undergraduate nursing students' critical thinking need to be increased: A cross-sectional study. *Brazilian Journal of Nursing*, *76*(1), 1–8. https://doi.org/10.1590/0034-7167-2022-0315

Metivier, A. (2023, May 23). *9 critical thinking exercises that actually improve your mind.* Magnetic Memory Method. https://www.magneticmemorymethod.com/critical-thinking-exercises/

Miller, J. M. (2020). Reflective practice and health sciences librarians: Engagement, benefits, and barriers. *Journal of the Medical Library Association*, *108*(1), 17–28. https://doi.org/10.5195/jmla.2020.777

Newton, P. M., Da Silva, A. & Peters, L.G. (2020). A pragmatic master list of action verbs for Bloom's Taxonomy. *Frontiers in Education,* 5. https://doi.org/10.3389/feduc.2020.00107

The Glossary of Education Reform for Journalists, Parents, and Community Members. (2014, March 5). *Bloom's Taxonomy*. Great Schools Partnership. https://www.edglossary.org/blooms-taxonomy/#:~:text=Original%20Taxonomy,Cognitive%2C%20Affective%2C%20and%20Psychomotor.

Tong, L. K., Au, M. L., Li, Y. Y., Ng, W. I., & Wang, S. C. (2023). The mediating effect of critical thinking between interest in learning and caring among nursing students: A cross-sectional study. *BMC Nursing*, *22*(1), 1–6. https://doi.org/10.1186/s12912-023-01181-4

Toyama, M., Nagamine, M., Asayama, A., Tang, L., Miwa, S., & Kainuma, R. (2023). Can persistence improve creativity? The effects of implicit beliefs about creativity on creative performance. *Psychology of Aesthetics, Creativity, and the Arts.* https://doi.org/10.1037/aca0000587.supp (Supplemental)

Williams, S. (n.d.). *Leader letter: Creative problem solving* [Website supplement to MBA 751 - Managing People in Organizations class]. Department of Management, Raj Soin College of Business, Wright State University, Dayton, Ohio. http://www.wright.edu/~scott.williams/LeaderLetter/cps.htm#Conceptual

Chapter 11: Application and Analysis of Effective Relationship Skills

Introduction

Each of us has numerous relationships. These relationships are unique to us and vary in type and relative importance. To form effective relationships, one must possess interpersonal skills complemented by personal qualities. This chapter focuses on the application and analysis of effective relationship skills.

Figure 64

Bloom's Revised Taxonomy

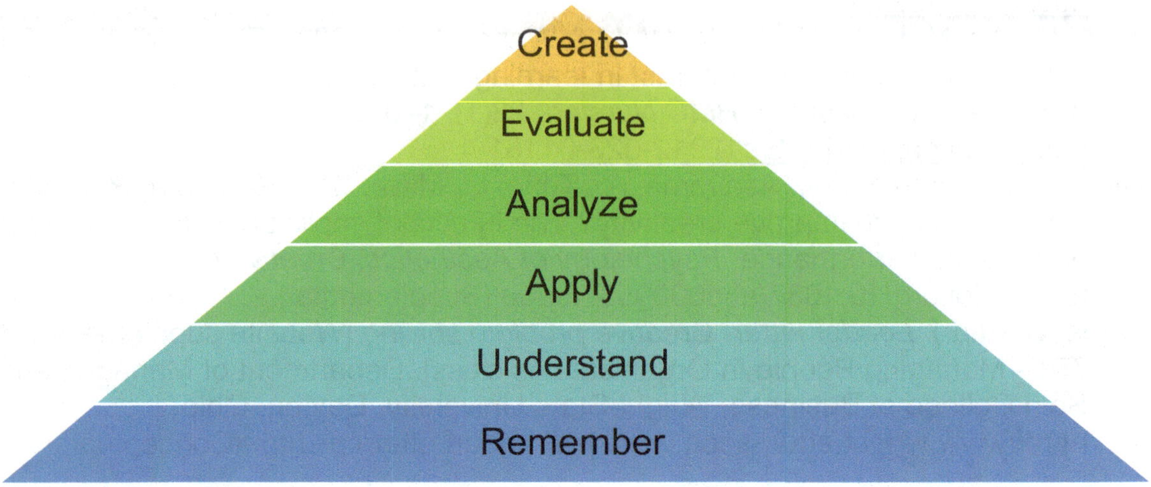

Note: Bloom's Revised Taxonomy uses verbs instead of nouns.

Terminal Learning Objectives

By the end of this chapter, learners will be able to use strategies to facilitate the application and analysis of effective relationship skills.

Enabling Learning Objectives

By the end of this chapter, the learner will be able to:
- Apply and analyze their interpersonal skills
- Apply and analyze their personal qualities

Instructor Notes

- *The headers in this textbook are in the form of a question. Learners should be prompted to note the question and write the answer to that question to ensure they master the concepts.*

"I've learned that people will forget what you said, people will forget whatyou did, but people will never forget how you made them feel."
— Maya Angelou

How Do You Teach Students to Apply and Analyze Interpersonal Skills?

Interpersonal skills encompass many abilities. These include being able to understand teamwork and how to work cooperatively. Sometimes this requires a person to step into a leadership role or to negotiate to resolve conflict. Interpersonal skills are required to respond to the needs of others and to respect individual differences.

Teamwork encompasses collaborating, delegating, and communicating the group's goals. This requires the ability to provide encouragement and assistance and to share expertise. Being an effective team member requires a person to seek and incorporate feedback and resolve conflict (Drew, 2023, May 25).

Figure 65

Pit Crew Working as a Team to Change the Tires

Note: This pit crew is working together to change the tires on the racecar. This image was obtained from Microsoft Word, 2023.

Instructor Notes

- *For synchronous or asynchronous instruction, divide students into groups and instruct them to create a one-page infographic of the best ways to sabotage a group project. This is a negative brainstorming activity. The goal of this formative assessment is for students to learn the responsibilities of being an effective team member. A rubric for this assignment is included in Appendix R. Students should be provided with these directions:*
    - *Each team member should contribute at least one way to sabotage the group project.*
    - *The team should find a cohesive way to depict their points visually.*
    - *The infographic should contain at least 10 ways to sabotage a group project.*
    - *Students should discuss and determine the ranking of the offenses from least damaging to most damaging.*
    - *The infographic should contain a legend identifying each group member's contribution*

Being able to respond to customers effectively is another interpersonal skill. Inasmuch as healthcare is a service-based industry and having the ability to respond to customers is a must for healthcare professionals. Customer service refers to the ability to aid and advise a customer. Good customer service improves customer satisfaction and retention and increases customer referrals and reviews. Good customer service creates a better working environment and competitive advantage within the industry (Indeed for Employers, n.d.).

> "Our greatest asset is the customer! Treat each customer as if they are the only one!"
> – Laurice Leitao

Tips for Handling Unhappy Customers

- Acknowledge the customer's point of view
- Don't blame others, pass the buck, or look for a scapegoat
- Listen without interrupting
- Agree without arguing
- Tell the customer you will personally handle it
- Empathize with them
- Try to establish a rapport
- Respond immediately
- Agree upon a solution or resolution
- Follow-up on the course of action
- Seek feedback from the customer to prevent future issues

Figure 66

Person Providing Customer Service

Note: This employee is providing customer service with a smile. This image was obtained from Microsoft Word, 2023.

Instructor Notes

- *For synchronous or asynchronous instruction, provide students with the list of customer services statements provided in Appendix S. Instruct students to pick one of the statements and to write an essay or produce a Vlog on the statement. Students should be instructed to provide a relevant healthcare scenario that exemplifies their statement. At least three peer-reviewed journal articles, within the past 5 years, should be cited supporting the customer service statement. A grading rubric is included in Appendix T.*

Tips for building effective communication (Birt, 2022, December 22)

- Practice effective communication
- Engage meaningfully to build relationships daily
- Focus on becoming more emotionally intelligent
- Get to know people on a personal level
- Embrace diversity and work collaboratively
- Show others you appreciate and respect them and ask for feedback
- Address conflict directly and be a problem-solver
- Follow through on commitments and be accountable for your actions
- Work collaboratively

Instructor Notes

- *For synchronous, face-to-face instruction, break students into pairs. Instruct one student to talk about whatever they want for 2 minutes straight. Instruct the other student to try not to listen. Then have the students switch roles and repeat the process. Upon completion, ask the students how the exercise made them feel when ignored. Then ask what actions each person took to demonstrate they were not listening to their partner. The goal of this exercise is to raise awareness of communication skills (Ackerman, 2017, December 29).*

Characteristics That Strengthen Work Relationships (Birt, 2022, December 22)

- Trust
- Respect
- Self-awareness
- Open communication

Trust in the workplace is more than telling the truth. Trust is about forming long-term relationships where each person is accountable for their actions and honor their commitments. Trust takes time to develop, but remarkably little time to destroy.

Respect is displayed by acting polite toward others. Respect is earned by appreciating the differences and opinions of others. Thinking before a person speaks helps a person to convey their respect for others.

Self-awareness in the workplace requires a person to know their strengths, weaknesses, and emotional triggers. This is area of growth for most students, especially as they learn how they fit within the workforce. Self-awareness improves a person's ability to recognize their boundaries and focus their efforts.

Communication brings people together or tears them apart. Open communication promotes higher quality work and stronger working relationships. It also facilitates the exchange of constructive criticism.

Tips for Building Healthy Relationships (Mental Health Foundation, n.d.)

- Get to know yourself. The more a person knows themselves, the better equipped they are express themselves clearly.
- Put in the work. Healthy relationships take time and effort.
- Set and respect boundaries. Maintaining and respecting boundaries helps to reduce stress by having clear expectations of yourself and others.
- Talk and listen with the intent to understand others. Expressing your emotions and allowing yourself to be vulnerable facilitates authentic relationships.
- Let go of control to help manage stress. Remember you can only control yourself and not the actions of others.
- Reflect on what others say and how you react and learn from the experience.

> "A great relationship is about two things. First, appreciating the similarities, and second, respecting the differences."
>
> —John Smith

Displaying strong clinical skills is often thought of as a precursor to leadership in healthcare. It happens too often that someone is great at what they do, and that person gets promoted to leadership. However, being competent at one's job does not guarantee the ability to lead a team.

Figure 67

4 Cornerstones of Leadership (Dye & Garman, 2015)

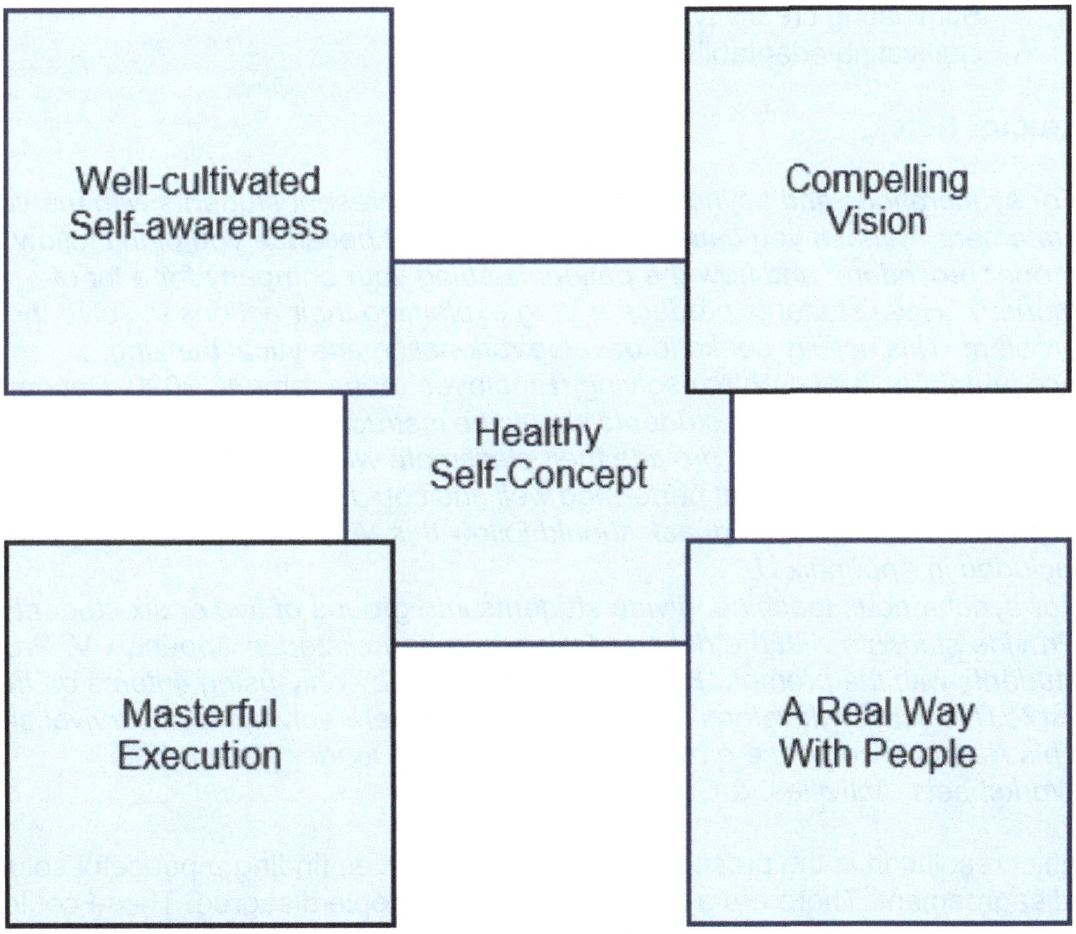

Note: Four cornerstones of effective leadership.

Sub-Competencies of Each of the Cornerstones *(Dye & Garman, 2015)*

- Well-cultivated self-awareness
  - Leading with conviction
  - Emotional intelligence
- Compelling vision
  - Developing vision
  - Communicating vision
  - Earning trust and loyalty
- A real way with people
  - Listening like you mean it
  - Giving great feedback
  - Mentoring
  - Developing high-performing teams
  - Energizing staff
- Masterful execution
  - Generating informal power—knowing how to influence an outcome
  - Building true consensus
  - Mindful decision making
  - Driving results
  - Stimulating creativity
  - Cultivating adaptability

Instructor Notes

- *For synchronous and asynchronous instruction, present students with the What If statement, "What if you caused injury to a patient because you didn't follow the proper procedure, and now the patient is suing your company for a lot of money?" Have students produce a Vlog explaining their actions to solve the problem. This activity seeks to develop rationality, analytical thinking, accountability, and problem-solving (Employee Management, 2020, December). Upon posting their Vlogs, students should be instructed to watch the Vlogs of two classmates. They should provide their classmate with constructive feedback regarding three things that performed well and could be improved upon. A written self-reflection of their feedback should follow this. A rubric for this assignment in included in Appendix U.*
- *For synchronous teaching, divide students into groups of five or six students. Provide students with the deserted island scenario listed in Appendix V. Provide students with the prompt, "How can they survive by only using 4 items on this list?" This activity develops critical thinking, problem-solving, and survival skills. This results in someone emerging as the group's leader (Teach This Worksheets, Activities, & Games, 2021).*

Conflict resolution is the process of two or more parties finding a peaceful solution to their disagreement. There are a variety of reasons people disagree. These could be for personal, financial, political, or emotional reasons. The goals of the negotiation are to find a solution, as quickly as possible, that all parties can agree upon and to improve,not strengthen the relationship between the two parties (Wolff & Nagy, n.d.).

Figure 68

These People Are Engaged in Conflict

Note: These people are engaged in conflict. This image by Afif Ramdhasuma was obtained from Unsplash.com, 2023.

Instructor Notes

- *For synchronous, face-to-face instruction, divide students into two teams. Provide each team with a secret directive regarding why they must purchase an orange owned by the farmer. Tell the students the orange is a very rare variety and the last of its kind. The first team is told that the pulp from the orange is required to produce a high-yield pharmaceutical drug. This pharmaceutical drug protects pregnant women from a deadly disease. The second team is told that the rind of the orange is required to create a nuclear component. The nuclear component is needed to avoid a reactor meltdown that threatens thousands of lives. Only one student from each team can negotiate with the farmer at a time. The students who possess strong negotiation skills should begin to collaborate with the other team instead of fighting for the last orange* (City Hunt, n.d.).

"Diversity is a mixture.
Inclusion is making the mix work."
—Andres Tapia

Instructor Notes

- *For synchronous, face-to-face instruction, have all the students stand up. Move the furniture out of the way. Instruct students to make two rows facing one another. Tell the students that you are going to recite a question from Appendix W. Instruct students to answer the questions honestly. Students should two steps toward one another if their answer to the question is 'yes'. Once everyone is finished moving, instruct the students to return to their row. Read each of the questions following the directions listed above. In conclusion, make the statement that while we are all different, we also have things in common (Vantage Circe, 2023, April 27).*

How Do You Teach Students to Apply and Analyze Personal Qualities?

Personal qualities represent the unique factors that an individual portrays to others during their interactions. These include the way a person demonstrates responsibillty, initiative, flexibility, professionalism, and integrity. An individual's expression of their personal qualities is dependent upon their sense of self-worth and their ability to accept responsibility for their professional growth.

Top 12 Personality Traits Desired by Employers (Indeed Editorial Team, 2022, August 8)

- Enthusiasm
- Conscientiousness
- Motivation
- Ambition
- Confidence
- Humility
- Honesty
- Flexibility
- Reliability
- Creativity
- Positivity
- Loyalty

Instructor Notes

- *For synchronous and synchronous instruction, provide students with the list of the top 12 personality traits desired by employers. Tell them to select three traits and write an essay or produce a Vlog about three strategies they can employ to improve those qualities within themselves. Students should explain what that trait means to them. The concepts need to be supported with at least three peer-reviewed journal articles, published within the past five years. A rubric is provided in Appendix X.*

Self-discipline means acting based on thoughts, not feelings. Self-discipline enables us to act regardless of how we feel. This is different than motivation, which is a desire to do something. Patterson (2019, August 29) identified eight strategies for improving self-discipline:

- Focus on changing your identity, not your behavior
- Remind yourself why you're being disciplined
- Embrace discomfort
- Focus on the fundamentals
- Try meditation
- Practice building new habits
- Use technology to your advantage
- Embrace imperfection

Flexibility is the ability to be easily modified or the willingness to change. Cognitive flexibility requires the ability to plan, exhibit self-control, consider multiple aspects of a problem at the same time, and control inhibitions (Cornell, 2023, May 10). Example of cognitive flexibility include these abilities:

- Perform metacognition
- Regulate stress
- Debate
- Empathize
- Think outside the box and solve problems
- Plan strategically and change directions
- Read and comprehend simultaneously
- Write creatively
- Act on formative information

Figure 69

Child Demonstrating Cognitive Flexibility

Note: This child is demonstrating cognitive flexibility to solve the puzzle. This image was obtained from Microsoft Word, 2023.

Instructor Notes

- *For synchronous and synchronous instruction, provide students with the list of the cognitive abilities listed above. Tell them to select three cognitive abilities and write an essay or produce a Vlog containing three strategies they can employ to improve those abilities within themselves. The concepts need to be supported with at least three peer-reviewed journal articles, published within the past five years. A rubric is provided in Appendix Y.*

Employers seek employees who are willing to learn. Schooley (2023, February 28) provides strategies to demonstrate a willingness to learn.

- Keep your skills up to date
- Be a good long-term investment for your company
- Be a fast learner and a team player
- Provide examples of how you are self-teaching
- Highlight your dedication to growth
- Embrace emerging technology
- Explain how your ideas have helped the bottom line
- Ask questions in the interview

Instructor Notes

- *For synchronous and asynchronous instruction, have students demonstrate their learning of a topic or lecture by using the 3-2-1 Method or a variation of it (The Teacher Tool Kit, n.d.).*
    - *3-2-1 Method*
        - *Three—Upon completion of the lecture or assignment, instruct students to record three things they learned from the lecture or assignment.*
        - *Two—Instruct students to record two things they found interesting about the content.*
        - *One—Instruct students to record one question they have about the content.*
    - *Compare and Contrast 3-2-1*
        - *Three—Instruct students to record three similarities between two concepts.*
        - *Two—Instruct students to record two differences between the concepts.*
        - *One—Instruct students to record one question they have about the content.*
    - *Reading 3-2-1*
        - *Three—Instruct students to record three of the most important ideas from the text.*
        - *Two—Instruct students to record two supporting details for each of their ideas.*
        - *One—Instruct students to record one question they have about each of the ideas.*
    - *Pyramid 3-2-1 (Appendix Z)*

    - *Three—Instruct students to record three things they learned from the experience in the bottom part of the pyramid.*
    - *Two—Instruct students to record two questions they have about the experience in the middle row of the pyramid.*
    - *One—Instruct students to describe how the information learned applies to their lives as a healthcare provider.*

> "Real integrity is doing the right thing, knowing that nobody's going to know whether you did it or not."
>
> —Oprah Winfrey

Integrity means acting in alignment with your values and doing the right thing. Doing the right thing requires moral courage. Below are four strategies to teach integrity (Ward-Seidel & Rimm-Kaufman, 2022, February 7).

- Model the appropriate behavior
- Examine the complexities of the decision
- Engage students in service-learning projects to take a stand on issues they find important
- Facilitate social-emotional skills to respond to injustice

Instructor Notes

- *For synchronous and asynchronous instruction, assign students service-learning projects (e.g., volunteering at a homeless shelter, or organizing health fairs at retirement communities). These can be completed individually or as a group. Instruct students to write a reflection about the experience. The reflection should include three factors, positive or negative, that impacted the student's experience. A rubric for this reflection is included in Appendix AA.*

Professionalism is an elusive topic. What some individuals deem as professionals, others may not. The definition of professionalism is influenced by cultural, generation, and industry differences. Below is a list of 13 strategies to demonstrate professionalism (Indeed Editorial Team, 2023, March 23).

- Valuing collaboration
- Wearing appropriate attire
- Being punctual
- Displaying a positive attitude
- Acknowledging strengths and weaknesses
- Seeking professional improvement and lifelong learning opportunities
- Always doing your best
- Doing more than what is expected

- Communicating clearly
- Separating personal from professional lives
- Preparing and planning
- Adapting to changing circumstances
- Reflecting on your actions and emotions

Task initiation requires a person to organize themselves. This means sustained attention, impulse control, and perseverance. These skills are necessary to avoid distractions, demonstrate cognitive flexibility and solve problems (Beck, 2017, September 7). There are several strategies to demonstrate initiative at work. These include being a decisive, proactive thinker. It is important to be prepared for a meeting, which includes anticipating questions and preparing answers. It helps to set realistic goals and to continually seek ways to improve policies, procedures, and systems. Other strategies for displaying initiative at work include addressing problems and sharing ideas to prevent future problems (Indeed Editorial Team, 2023, February 3).

Instructor Notes

- *For synchronous and asynchronous instruction, provide students with the positive thinking quotations in Appendix BB. Instruct students to select three positive quotes. Students should write an essay or produce a Vlog about what each quote means to them (e.g., evoke a memory that resembles their motto). There is no rubric for this assignment since it is based on opinion.*

Professional development refers to the variety of training opportunities that can help people improve their competence, skill, and effectiveness. The training opportunities are often tailored to a person's chosen profession. Professional development begins with identifying the skills and services that match the profession. Then a plan is developed and implemented (CDC, 2017). Professional development incorporates an active learning approach supported by collaboration, coaching, and feedback (Darling-Hammond, et al., 2017).

What Are the Key Concepts from this Chapter?

- Effective relationship skills are comprised of interpersonal skills and personal qualities.
    - Interpersonal skills encompass many abilities:
        - Working effectively as a team
        - Responding to the needs of others
        - Demonstrating leadership
        - Negotiating conflict
        - Respecting individual differences
    - Personal qualities are the unique attributes a person displays when interacting with others:
        - Displaying responsibility and self-discipline
        - Being flexible and able to adapt
        - Demonstrating a willingness to learn and complete tasks
        - Acting with integrity and professionalism

- Displaying a positive attitude and sense of self-worth
- Demonstrating initiative
- Being an active listener, seeking clarification when needed

Figure 70

Healthcare Provider Actively Listening to her Patient via Telehealth

Note: This healthcare provider is actively listening to her patient via a telehealth visit. This image was obtained from Microsoft Word, 2023.

Summary

This chapter examined ways to apply and analyze effective relationship skills. Several strategies were presented for developing and accessing interpersonal skills. Personal qualities were explored, including a discussion of employers' most desired personal qualities.

The next chapter covers the final category of employability workplace skills. These skills include technology and information use, systems thinking, resource management, and communication skills. This final category of employability skills is the most challenging to master because they are constantly evolving.

References

Ackerman, C. E. (2017, December 29). *Interpersonal effectiveness: 9 worksheets & examples* (+ PDF). PositivePsychology.com. https://positivepsychology.com/interpersonal-effectiveness/

Beck, C. (2017, September 7). *Executive functioning skills: How to teach task initiation.*

The OT Toolbox. https://www.theottoolbox.com/how-to-teach-task-initiation/
Birt, J. (2022, December 22). *8 strategies for building relationships effectively*. Indeed Career Guide. https://www.indeed.com/career-advice/career-development/building-relationships
Centers for Disease Control and Prevention. (2017). *Guide to Promoting Professional Development*. Atlanta, GA: Centers for Disease
Control and Prevention, U.S. Department of Health, and Human Services. https://www.cdc.gov/healthyschools/tths/17_279948-A-MPDS-Guide_WEB-508.pdf
City Hunt. (n.d.). *Conflict resolution team building activities*. https://cityhunt.com/conflict-resolution-team-building-activities/
Cornell, D. (2023, May 10). *11 cognitive flexibility examples*. The Helpful Professor. https://helpfulprofessor.com/cognitive-flexibility-examples/
Darling-Hammond, L., Hyler, M.E. & Madelyn Gardner, M. (2017). *Effective teacher professional development*. Learning Policy Institute. https://learningpolicyinstitute.org/sites/default/files/product-files/Effective_Teacher_Professional_Development_REPORT.pdf
Drew, C. (2023, May 25). *37 teamwork examples*. The Helpful Professor. https://helpfulprofessor.com/teamwork-examples/
Dye, C. F. & Garman, A. N. (2015). *Exceptional leadership: 16 critical competencies for healthcare executives* (2nd ed). Health Administration Press.
Employee Management. (2020, December). *The 12 best leadership activities to help develop your team's skill*s. Sling by Toast. https://getsling.com/blog/leadership-activities/
Furnham, A., & Robinson, C. (2022). Myths and misconceptions about personality traits and tests. *Personality and Individual Differences*, 186(Part B). https://doi.org/10.1016/j.paid.2021.111381
Herrity, J. (2023, March 29). *7 ways to improve your personal development skills.* Indeed Career Guide. https://www.indeed.com/career-advice/career-development/improve-your-personal-development-skills
Indeed Editorial Team. (2023, February 3). *9 ways to take initiative at work*. Indeed Career Guide. https://www.indeed.com/career-advice/career-development/ways-to-take-initiative-at-work
Indeed Editorial Team. (2023, March 23). *13 ways to show professionalism in teaching (and why it matters)*. Indeed Career Guide. https://www.indeed.com/career-advice/career-development/professionalism-in-teaching
Indeed Editorial Team. (2022, August 8). *What are personal qualities? 12 traits sought by employers*. Indeed Career Guide. https://www.indeed.com/career-advice/resumes-cover-letters/what-is-personal-qualities#:~:text=Personal%20qualities%20are%20the%20characteristics,of%20humor%20or%20being%20dependable.
Indeed for Employers (n.d.). *7 of the most important characteristics of great customer service*. https://www.indeed.com/hire/c/info/most-important-characteristics-of-customer-service?gclid=Cj0KCQjw1rqkBhCTARIsAAHz7K3uh5JBSy3ku8gIyrWJIRgge7HvW3hgBGhMzkEOswlc8Wovl03vYVgaAjsSEALw_wcB&aceid=&gclsrc=aw.ds
Mental Health Foundation. (n.d.). *Top tips on building and maintaining healthy relationships*. https://www.mentalhealth.org.uk/our-work/public-engagement/healthy-relationships/top-tips-building-and-maintaining-healthy-

relationships
Patterson, R. (2019, August 29). *8 techniques for building unshakable self-discipline.* College Info Geek. https://collegeinfogeek.com/self-discipline/
Schooley, S. (2023, February 28). *Career success depends on your willingness to learn.* Business News Daily. https://www.businessnewsdaily.com/9256-career boost-learning.html
Teach This Worksheets, Activities, & Games. (2021). *Teacher's notes: Island adventure.* https://www.teach-this.com/images/resources/island-adventure-2.pdf
The Teacher Tool Kit. (n.d.). *3-2-1 Method.* https://www.theteachertoolkit.com/index.php/tool/3-2-1
Vantage Circe. (2023, April 27). *20 activities of diversity and inclusion in the workplace.* https://blog.vantagecircle.com/activities-diversity-and-inclusion/
Ward-Seidel, A. R. & Rimm-Kaufman, S. E. (2022, February 7). *Four ways to help students cultivate integrity.* Greater Good Magazine, Science-based Insights for a Meaningful Life. https://greatergood.berkeley.edu/article/item/four_ways_to_help_students_cultivate_integrity
Wolff, R. & Nagy, J. (n.d.). *Section 6: Training for conflict resolution.* University of Kentucky: Community Toolbox. https://ctb.ku.edu/en/table-of-contents/implement/provide-information-enhance-skills/conflict-resolution/main#:~:text=Conflict%20resolution%20is%20a%20way,negotiation%20to%20resolve%20the%20disagreement.

Chapter 12: Application and Analysis of Workplace Skills

Introduction

Workplace skills rely on technology and information use, systems thinking, resource management, and communication skills. This final category of employability skills is challenging to master because it continuously evolves. Technology is advancing exponentially, which impacts other workplace skills. For example, technological expansion created the use of electronic health records. The transition from paper to electronic documentation changed how healthcare providers communicate and use information and resources.

Figure 71

Bloom's Revised Taxonomy

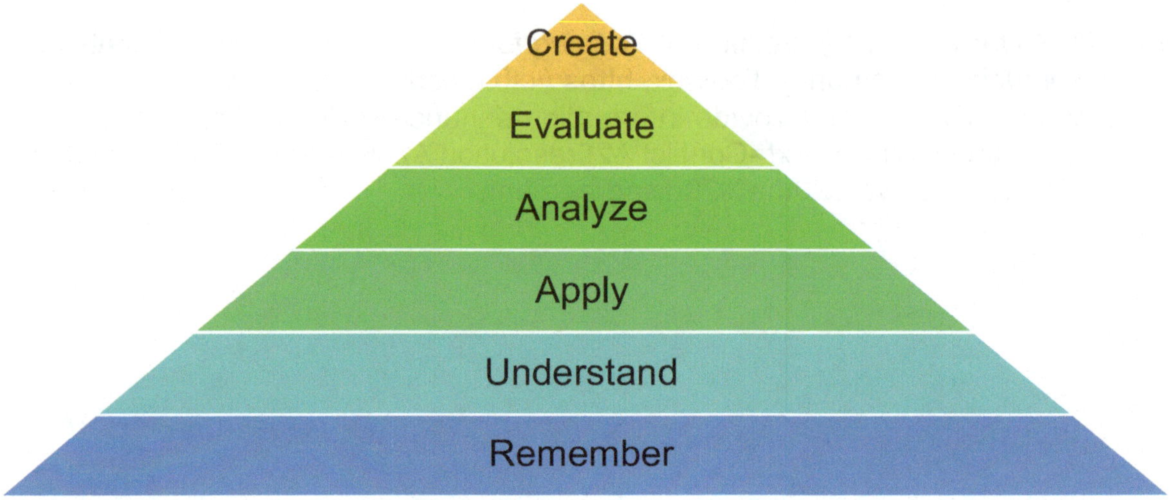

Note: Bloom's Revised Taxonomy uses verbs instead of nouns.

Terminal Learning Objectives

By the end of this chapter, the reader will be able to use strategies to facilitate the application and analysis of workplace skills.

Enabling Learning Objectives

By the end of this chapter, the learner will be able to teach students to:

- Apply and analyze their resource management skills
- Apply and analyze their information-use skills
- Apply and analyze their technology use skills
- Apply and analyze their systems thinking skills
- Apply and analyze their communication skills

Instructor Notes

- *The headers in this textbook are in the form of a question. Learners should be prompted to note the question and write the answer to ensure they master the concepts.*

How Do You Teach Students to Apply and Analyze their Resource Management Skills?

Resource management incorporates the executive functioning skills of organization, planning, allocation, and management. These skills enable professionals to prioritize tasks, follow multiple-step directions, filter distractions, and control impulses. Resource management includes managing time, money, resources, and personnel, which can require creativity.

Executive functioning skills are not innate; they must be learned. Learning begins during infancy when babies first learn to pay attention. The rate children develop executive functioning skills depends on their caregivers. Executive functioning skills are developed by establishing a routine, breaking big tasks into smaller chunks, and playing games that teach children to follow the rules and control their impulses (Center on the Developing Child, n.d.).

Figure 72

Chess Player Using Executive Functioning Skills

Note: Executive functioning skills are required to think strategically, plan, and execute the right move to win the game.

Developing executive functioning skills depends on a person's ability to plan and prioritize (Beck, 2019). When a person struggles with executive functioning, they have difficulty with task initiation and completion, attention, and organization (Beck, 2022). Examples include difficulty making decisions, inability to leave the house on time, or frequently misplacing things.

Several strategies can be used to improve resource management. The first of these involves understanding which resources are in short supply and focusing on them. It helps to agree on a common approach to prioritizing tasks across shared resources. Another strategy for resource management is to share best practices. Sharing best practices can be challenging for some people because they may be insecure about their position in the organization. There may be times when adopting a new process can improve resource use. Detailed planning facilitates resource management by forecasting needs. Increased transparency raises awareness of resource use and can reduce the need for multitasking (Townsend, n.d.).

> "Focus on being productive instead of busy."
>
> – Tim Ferris

Instructor Notes

- *For synchronous, face-to-face instruction, break students into groups. Provide each group with a puzzle of similar difficulty. Do not provide students with the big picture of the puzzle. Set a time limit. This activity offers students the experience of working together without knowing how the final product will turn out. For asynchronous instruction, the same activity could be used utilized if you took pictures of each puzzle piece (3veta, n.d.).*
- *For synchronous or asynchronous instruction, have students write their daily routine and how energized they felt throughout the day in Appendix CC. Then, ask students when they are most productive or distracted and what is the best time to take a break. This activity helps students to boost their productivity (3veta, n.d.).*
- *For synchronous or asynchronous instruction, ask students or groups of students if they had $86,400 for only one day; how would they spend the money? Students should develop an itemized list outlining their plans for every $1.00. Tell students they must spend all the money or lose it all. Then point out that there are 86,400 seconds each day, and each person determines how to use them (3veta, n.d.).*

Personnel management can be an organization's greatest asset. Personnel management is challenging because people are motivated by different things. Examining how a team works together is critical to ensure productivity and harmony. When a group is charged with a task, natural roles emerge (Mind Tools Content Team, n.d.).

- Initiator—proposes ideas or different ways to approach the task.
- Information Seeker—requests clarification relevant to the task.
- Information Giver—provides information to the group as an authority on the subject.
- Opinion Seeker—asks about group members' values, attitudes, and opinions.
- Opinion Giver—expresses their opinions about the task.

- Elaborator—builds upon the ideas of others and proposes thoughts and actions.
- Coordinator—explains the relationships between ideas.
- Orienter—clarifies the group's position by summarizing the progress to date.
- Critic—evaluates the proposals to determine if they are reasonable, evidenced-based, and manageable as a solution.
- Energizer—concentrates the group's energy for continued momentum.
- Procedural Technician—facilitates group discussion by taking care of the logistics.
- Recorder—serves as the secretary to track ideas and progress.

> "Hire character. Train skill."
> – Peter Schutz

Instructor Notes

- *For synchronous and asynchronous instruction, students should select the roles they find the most and least comfortable with when completing a group project. Instruct students to write an essay or produce a Vlog explaining their comfort level with each role. They should include examples that support their rationale for selecting each function. A rubric for this assignment is included in Appendix DD.*

Figure 73

Group of Coworkers

Note: Each group member contributes uniquely to the group's collective goal. This image was obtained from Microsoft, 2023.

Roles that Emerge in Social Settings to Facilitate Positive Group Interactions (Mind Tools Content Team, n.d.):

- Encourager—praises the group members.
- Harmonizer—seeks ways to reduce tension among group members. This is generally accomplished via a clarifying explanation or use of humor.
- Compromiser—offers to change their position for the benefit of the group.
- Expediter—regulates the flow of communication.
- Commentator—provides the group with feedback about how they are functioning.
- Follower—accepts what others decide without contribution.

> "Teamwork is the ability to work together toward a common vision. The ability to direct individual accomplishments toward organizational objectives. It is the fuel that allows common people to attain uncommon results."
> — Andrew Carnegie

Roles that Emerge and Create Dysfunction in the Group (Mind Tools Content Team, n.d.):

- Aggressor—attacks others with belittling and insulting comments.
- Blocker—opposes every idea that is put forward without providing a suggestion.
- Recognition Seeker—draws personal attention to themselves.
- Self-Confessor—uses group meetings to disclose personal feelings and issues.
- Disrupter—uses group meetings to get out of work.
- Dominator—attempts to control the group.
- Help Seeker—expresses feelings of inadequacy to seek sympathy.
- Special Interest Pleader—provides suggestions based on the thoughts and feelings of others.

How Do You Teach Students to Apply and Analyze their Information Use Skills?

Information use refers to locating, organizing, analyzing, and communicating pertinent information. Information use has evolved significantly since the innovation of the internet. The increase in the accessibility of information does not guarantee its quality. The information user must ensure the reliability of the content and its source.

Figure 74

This Person Is Seeking Information

Note: Students must be taught how to seek and use information. This image was obtained from Microsoft, 2023.

Instructor Notes

- *For synchronous and asynchronous instruction, assign case studies for presentation. These presentations could be completed as a group or individually and students should be instructed to research the factors pertinent to the patient's case. Students should identify the most appropriate source for information. The information should be presented orally, supplemented by a graphic organizer (e.g., concept map, tables). The students should be evaluated on their ability to organize and analyze the information for the class. A rubric for this assignment is included in Appendix EE.*

How Do You Teach Students to Apply and Analyze their Technology Use Skills?

Technology use refers to understanding and relying on digital technology to conduct research, create presentations, and display data. Technology has impacted healthcare in five significant ways. First came the implementation of electronic health records, which improved the quality and safety of patient care. Technology has enabled a more personalized treatment using wearable devices. This has resulted in patients who are more engaged in the healthcare process. Technology has also improved access to healthcare services via telehealth visits. Various surgical advancements have been based on technology, which has improved patient care outcomes and shortened recovery times. Finally, artificial technology and augmented reality have changed the delivery of healthcare services (Scherman, 2019, May 20).

Figure 75

Using Technology to Diagnosis the Patient

Note: An example of how technology is used in healthcare. This image was obtained from Microsoft, 2023.

Instructor Notes

- *For synchronous and asynchronous instruction, students should select one technological advancement that has impacted the delivery of healthcare. Students should be instructed to use an online discussion forum to explain how the technology is used and highlight three benefits and three disadvantages of its use. Instruct students to review and comment on the technological advancement of at least two classmates. Comments should include one 'glow,' one 'grow,' and one question they still have about the technology. The 'glow' is one aspect of the student's discussion post presented clearly. The 'grow' is one suggestion to improve the student's explanation of the technology. A rubric for this assignment is included in Appendix FF.*

How Do You Teach Students to Apply and Analyze their Systems Thinking Skills?

Systems thinking skills include understanding, using, monitoring, and improving systems. These skills enable students to understand their roles and responsibilities when collaborating. There are several benefits to teaching systems thinking. It is beneficial for explaining complex concepts because it facilitates multidimensional thinking. Systems thinking incorporates an interdisciplinary approach to problem-solving. Using a "systems" approach effectively evaluates interdependencies among the concepts (InTeGrate, n.d.).

The systems thinking method contains four steps. The first is to identify the problem or issue. This is followed by forming a hypothesis and then testing it. The final step is implementing changes and communicating an understanding of the solution. The systems thinking model requires seven critical thinking skills for each step (Richmond, n.d.).

Figure 76

Systems Thinking Steps with Critical Thinking Skills (Richmond, n.d.)

Critical Thinking Skill	Systems Thinking Step
Dynamic Thinking This involves thinking about how the problem or issue behaves over time to determine if there is a pattern.	Define the Problem or Issue
System as a Cause Thinking This involves placing the responsibility onto those who manage the policies and procedures related to the problem or issue **Forest Thinking** This involves believing that to know about the problem or issue, one must understand the relationship among all factors that contribute to the problem or issue. **Operational Thinking** This involves focusing on what is causing the problem or issue. **Closed Loop Thinking** This involves considering the causality of an ongoing process rather than a single event. Due to the ongoing process, the cause and effect affect each other over time. **Quantitative Thinking** This involves accepting that even though problems and issues can be quantified, they cannot always be measured	Develop the Hypothesis
Scientific Thinking This involves recognizing that models are working hypotheses that have limited applicability	Test the Hypothesis ↓ Implement and Communicate the Solution

Note: Systems Thinking steps with the critical thinking skills required during each step (Richmond, n.d.).

When healthcare students compartmentalize specific competencies into academic silos, they struggle to develop systems thinking. Therefore, the job of educators is to facilitate the academic training of new graduates with more focus on systems thinking because not doing so promotes healthcare education that occurs in academic silos. Therefore, the task of healthcare educators is to integrate the concept of learning through systems thinking so students can understand how their roles as providers fit into the healthcare system (Clark & Hoffman, 2019).

Systems thinking is best taught through three teaching styles: pedagogy, andragogy, and reductionism. Pedagogy is used to teach new information through a structured approach to enhance learning. Andragogy incorporates the learners' experience to solve problems. Andragogy requires learners to be more self-motivated.Reductionism is used to explain a complex phenomenon in simple terms. This combination is important because providing healthcare services requires these interconnected skills (Clark & Hoffman, 2019).

For example, when an allied healthcare provider renders services, they must incorporate a pedagogical approach to educate the patient about their condition. Then using an andragogical approach, the provider and the patient develop a plan of care focused on solving the patient's condition. Throughout this experience, the provider must also engage in reductionism to explain the patient's complex condition in layperson terminology.

"Intelligence is something we are born with.
Thinking is a skill that must be learned."
–Edward de Bono

Instructor Notes

- *For synchronous and asynchronous instruction, students should complete the dynamic self-assessment quiz in Appendix GG to determine if they think dynamically (Ozovek, 2016, February 23).*
- *Students should be provided with the disease population graph listed in Appendix HH for synchronous and asynchronous instruction. Students should be instructed to share three questions they have about the illustration. Break students into groups and instruct them to compile their questions. As a group, students should develop one or more hypotheses based on the illustration* (CDC, 2021, March 3*). The purpose of this activity is to apply dynamic thinking skills. Students should maintain the same groups for the following assignments.*
- *Using the same group of students for synchronous and asynchronous instruction, students should be provided with the guiding questions in Appendix II. Instruct students to complete all the questions. A rubric for this assignment is included in Appendix JJ. The goal of this activity is to apply the following types of thinking skills: system as a cause, forest, operational, closed loop, quantitative, and scientific.*

How Do You Teach Students to Apply and Analyze their Communication Skills?

Communication skills are an area that needs continuous improvement because people are always evolving. The world's population continues to grow more diverse. In addition, the content we are communicating continues to evolve. Therefore, listening, observing, and comprehending are imperative to ensure proper written and oral communication.

A present-day threat to effective communication is the existence of large language models, which are a type of artificial intelligence that can mimic human intelligence. These models recognize the syntax of language and can generate written responses. An example is a chatbot, which appears on some websites. These models work by feeding them vast amounts of information and prompts, which serve as programming rules (De Angelis, et al., 2023).

While large language models can be useful for improving efficiency, they can also be used to create fake articles or other misleading content. Additionally, large language models threaten effective communication by enabling the user to skip the process of creation (De Angelis, et al., 2023). Granted, efficiency can be a strong motivator, but it should not come at the cost of a person's integrity.

Figure 77

Bonding via Communication

Note: Communication can bring people together or tear them apart.

Instructor Notes

- *Students should be provided with the 30-day random acts of kindness challenge for synchronous or asynchronous instruction. This assignment can be completed as a contest among students. Students should be told to perform a random act of kindness for a stranger. The same kindness can only be repeated once in the same 30-day period. For example, the student cannot buy a different stranger a cup of coffee daily for a month. Each kindness must be different from the others. After completing each kindness, students should complete the reflection form found in Appendix KK. Simple reflections (e.g., performing the act made me feelgood) are not accepted. Students should provide thoughtful responses. The purpose of this activity is to improve students' comfort levels by communicating with kindness and empathy for others. Students are awarded one point for each kindness. Students who learn the strangers' names receive a bonus point. You can reward the student with the most points after the 30 days with the certificate listed in Appendix LL.*

Effective communication is an integral aspect of forming relationships and conveying information. Positive interactions with others have a direct impact on one's happiness. Communication helps people to connect and decrease feelings of loneliness and isolation (Theresa Raphael-Grimm, 2015).

Positive communication results from being mindful of word selection, active listening, and conveying empathy. There are several barriers to effective communication in healthcare. Barriers include time constraints, the ability to maintain professional boundaries, biases, and the clinician's emotions (Theresa Raphael-Grimm, 2015).

"Bad communication
ends a lot ofgood things.
Good communication
ends a lot ofbad things."
–Frank Viscuso

Unfortunately, communication is not always a positive experience. For example, if a provider is overly confident in their diagnostic skills, they might make a mistake due to ignoring information that questions the validity of their idea. This can damage the patient/provider relationship. Acting mindfully is an effective strategy for avoiding clinical mistakes. Furthermore, when mistakes are made, the provider must accept their wrongdoing and apologize without excuses (Theresa Raphael-Grimm, 2015).

Communication skills are enhanced by improving emotional intelligence because it positively influences the ability to convey empathy, develop relationships, and manage conflict. Emotional intelligence is the ability to be intuitively aware of the surrounding situation and the feelings of others. Emotional intelligence requires a person to understand their emotions to make decisions before reacting to a situation (Brou Fossier, 2022; Gribble et al., 2017; White & Quinn, 2023).

"People may hear your words,
but they feel your attitude."
–John C. Maxwell

Figure 78

Domains of Emotional Intelligence (White & Quinn, 2023)

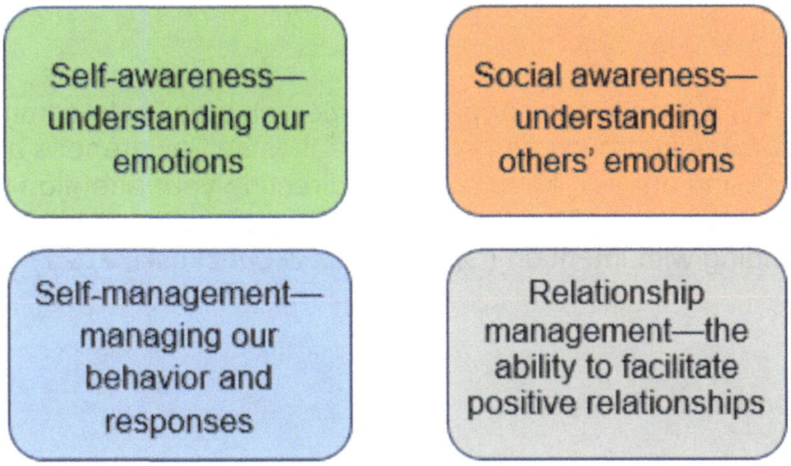

Note: The domains of emotional intelligence (White & Quinn, 2023).

There are several benefits to developing emotional intelligence skills (Brou-Fossier, 2022)

- Improves ability to accept constructive criticism which leads to a greater understanding of oneself and others
- Improves decision-making skills
- Strengthens compassion and empathy toward others
- Improves behavioral control
- Produces positive interactions
- Strengthens relationships

Instructor Notes

- *For synchronous and asynchronous instruction, engage students in a discussion about how differences in personality types among healthcare professionals influence the workplace. This discussion should occur in stages. The first prompt is for students to describe how each interdisciplinary team member collaborates for the patient's benefit. Once established, students should be instructed to discuss how different personalities affect teamwork. The discussion should conclude by instructing students to identify the potential personality differences between each professional discipline (Terry, 2020). There is no rubric for this assignment.*
- *For synchronous and asynchronous instruction, Appendix MM contains 50 different self-awareness prompts (Horey, 2019). Students should be instructed to journal on a different prompt daily for 30 days. Each journal entry should be a minimum of 500 words. A rubric for the journal reflections is included in Appendix G.*

“I am not what happened to me,
Iam who I choose to become.”
–C. G. Jung

Mindfulness has a tremendous impact on a person’s ability to communicate effectively. Mindfulness improves empathy, increases self-awareness and regulation, and reduces stress and anxiety. Mindfulness is directing your attention to each moment with curiosity and acceptance. This enables a person to switch from an automatic reaction to responding with intention (Chmielewsk & Luczynski, 2021).

Figure 79

Person Performing a Meditation

Note: Meditation is a practice that can improve mindfulness.

“Training your mind to be the present moment is thenumber one key to making healthier choices.”
–Susan Albers

There are many benefits to mindfulness. Because mindfulness is the ability to manage one’s thoughts and actions, it improves resilience. Mindfulness improves the ability to manage workflow and accept limitations which decreases stress. Studies on mindfulness show that sharing experiences helps to improve attention, mood, and self-empathy (Chmielewsk & Luczynski, 2021).

> "How we pay attention to the present moment largely determines the character of our experience, and therefore, the quality of our lives."
>
> –Sam Harris

Instructor Notes

- *For synchronous and asynchronous instruction, students should be instructed to journal their feelings from the day for five minutes. Students should set a timer and immerse themselves in journaling. This assignment should be completed every day for thirty days.*
- *For synchronous, face-to-face instruction, right before a lab practical, purposely directs the student's attention to something else, preferably something from the natural world. Bringing in a pet or looking out a window at something beautiful is a great way to redirect a person's attention. One or two minutes of sustained attention should be enough to reduce some tension. After the practical, ask students if the distraction helped to control their stress levels. This activity teaches students to manage their stress levels.*
- *Students should role-play a case conference meeting or grand rounds for synchronous, face-to-face instruction and over-emphasize different pragmatic skills from the list below. The purpose of this activity is to raise awareness of the types of behaviors that can impact effective communication.*
    - *Turn-taking*
    - *Expressing attitude/emotion*
    - *Regulating social interactions*
    - *Requesting information/action*
    - *Communicative intent*
    - *Asks questions*
    - *Physical proximity*
    - *Physical contacts*
    - *Body posture*
    - *Hand/arm movement*
    - *Facial expressions*
    - *Discourse organization*
    - *Politeness*
    - *Initiation of conversation*
    - *Topic selection*
    - *Topic maintenance*
    - *Active listening skills*
    - *Tangential speech*
    - *Interruption of others*
    - *Use of fillers*
    - *Difficulty staying on topic*
    - *Slow to respond*
    - *Distractibility*
    - *Inclusion with others*

  - *The volume of expression in certain situations*
  - *Inappropriate language in certain situations*
- *For synchronous, face-to-face instruction, students should be assigned an oral presentation of at least three minutes. The remainder of the class should be asked to stand when the presenter uses a filler (e.g., um, ah, like). The purpose of this activity is to raise awareness of students' communication skills.*
- *For synchronous instruction, students should be warned at the beginning of class they could be put on the spot. Then periodically stop and ask a student to recap what was said. The purpose of this activity is to improve active listening skills.*
- *For synchronous or asynchronous instruction, sharpen students' communication skills by learning to deliver instructions efficiently in the assignment, "in so many words" in Appendix NN (Robinson, 2022).*

Rhetoric is the art of persuasion through communication. There are three types of rhetoric. Logos is using logic and reason to convince your audience. Ethos relies on the speaker's reputation to appeal to the audience. Pathos uses an emotional connection to persuade the audience (MasterClass, 2022).

Rhetorical education engages students in diverse forms of meaning-making. A typical example of using a rhetorical education approach in healthcare is patient simulations. Rhetorical education improves empathy in healthcare students because it enables students to experience making a "personal impact" on their patient's life. When combined with reflection, this process has proven effective at developing student empathy. Rhetorical education enables the student to humanize the patient, identify with them, and understand their professional role (Campbell & Miller, 2023).

Figure 80

This Person Is Delivering a Speech

Note: This person tries to convince the audience of her cause via speech. This image was obtained from Microsoft, 2023.

The use of improvisational theatre is another form of rhetorical education. Improvisational theatre or improv is when the performance and script are spontaneously developed and played simultaneously. Improv requires a structure or format, the basis of the improvisation, and some simple rules. It also helps to have an audience. Improv is intentional, autonomous, and spontaneous (Budzyńska-Daca & Łukowska, 2023).

Instructor Notes

- *For synchronous instruction, have students improvise the spine story. This could be individually or as a group. This activity boosts students' confidence, comfort, and fluency during communication. Students should be provided three minutes to make up a story using the following prompts (Budzyńska-Daca & Łukowska, 2023):*
    - *Once upon a time…*
    - *Every day…*
    - *But one day…*
    - *Because of that…*
    - *Because of that…*
    - *Because of that…*
    - *Until finally…*
    - *And ever since then…*
- *For synchronous instruction, students should be broken into groups of five. Have each student draw a number from one to five. The number represents their social status. One is the lowest, and five is the highest. Students need to keep their numbers confidential until after the improvisation. Then select a holiday for the students to attend a fictitious holiday party. Give students five minutes to interact with the other students at the party. The goal is for students to convince others of their assigned social status. This improv helps students to improve their overall emotional resilience and communication skills (Budzyńska-Daca & Łukowska, 2023).*
- *For synchronous or asynchronous instruction, students should be assigned a three-minute speech using the prompts provided in Appendix OO. The ideal format for this assignment is a face-to-face synchronous session. Students should be allowed time to prepare and then deliver their speech. The time limit of three minutes was selected because healthcare providers are routinely called upon to make their point in a limited time. Prompts can be assigned to students or self-selected. The goal of this assignment is to facilitate the development of persuasion skills. Students should use logos, ethos, or pathos to convince the audience of their perspective. A rubric for this speech is provided in Appendix PP (Budzyńska-Daca & Łukowska, 2023).*

> "Until we can receive with an open heart, we're never really giving with an open heart. When we attach judgment to receiving help, we knowingly or unknowingly attach judgment to giving help."
> –Brene Brown

What Are the Key Concepts from this Chapter?

- Workplace skills encompass technology and information use, systems thinking, resource management, and communication skills.
- Resource management incorporates the executive functioning skills of organization, planning, allocation, and management.
- The development of executive functioning skills depends on a person's ability to plan and prioritize (Beck, 2019).
- Executive functioning skills deficits include task initiation and completion, attention, and organization (Beck, 2022).
- Resource management includes:
    - Understanding which resources are in short supply
    - Agreeing on a common approach to prioritizing tasks
    - Sharing best practices
    - Adopting new processes to improve resource use
- Management of personnel can be an organization's greatest asset.
- When a group is charged with a mission to complete, there are natural roles that emerge (Mind Tools Content Team, n.d.).
- Information use refers to locating, organizing, analyzing, and communicating pertinent information.
- Technology use refers to understanding and relying on digital technology to conduct research, create presentations, and display data.
- Technology has impacted healthcare in five significant ways.
    - Implementing electronic health records improved the quality and safety of patient care.
    - Technology enabled a more personalized treatment by using wearable devices.
    - Technology has also improved access to healthcare services via telehealth visits.
    - There have been various surgical advancements based on technology, which have improved patient care outcomes and shortened recovery times.
    - Artificial intelligence and augmented reality have changed the delivery of healthcare services (Scherman, 2019).
- Systems thinking skills include understanding, using, monitoring, and improving systems.
- System thinking is beneficial for explaining complex concepts because it facilitates multidimensional thinking.
- The systems thinking method contains four steps.
    - The first is to identify the problem or issue.
    - This is followed by forming a hypothesis.
    - Then testing the hypothesis.
    - The final step is implementing changes and communicating an understanding of the solution.
- Critical thinking skills associated with systems thinking include:
    - Dynamic thinking—involves thinking about how the problem or issue behaves over time to determine if there is a pattern.

    - System as a cause thinking—placing the responsibility onto those who manage the policies and procedures related to the problem or issue
    - Forest thinking—believing that to know about the problem or issue, one must understand the relationship among all the factors that contribute to the problem or issue.
    - Operational thinking—focusing on what is causing the problem or issue.
    - Closed-loop thinking—considering the causality an ongoing process rather than a single event.
    - Quantitative thinking—accepting that even though problems and issues can be quantified, they cannot always be measured
    - Scientific thinking—recognizing that models are working hypotheses that have limited applicability
- Systems thinking is best taught through a combination of three teaching styles:
    - Pedagogy is used to teach new information through a structured approach to enhance learning.
    - Andragogy incorporates the learners' experience to solve problems.
    - Reductionism is used to explain a complex phenomenon in simple terms.
- Barriers to effective communication in healthcare include time constraints, the ability to maintain professional boundaries, biases, and the clinician's emotions.
- Communication skills are enhanced by improving emotional intelligence becauseit positively influences the ability to convey empathy, develop relationships, and manage conflict.
- Emotional intelligence is the ability to be intuitively aware of the surrounding situation and the feelings of others.
- Domains of emotional intelligence (White & Quinn, 2023)
    - Self-awareness—understanding our emotions
    - Self-management—managing our behavior and responses
    - Social awareness—understanding others' emotions
    - Relationship management—the ability to facilitate positive relationships
- Mindfulness improves empathy, increases self-awareness and regulation, and reduces stress and anxiety.
- Mindfulness is directing one's attention to each moment with curiosity and acceptance.
- Rhetoric is the art of persuasion through communication.
- There are three types of rhetoric.
    - Logos is using logic and reason to convince an audience.
    - Ethos relies on the speaker's reputation to appeal to the audience.
    - Pathos uses an emotional connection to persuade the audience (MasterClass, 2022).

Summary

This chapter covers teaching workplace skills to healthcare students systematically using technology and information. These skills require effective communication and resource management skills. Workplace skills are continuously evolving, which requires an ongoing effort to remain competent.

This section of the textbook focused on the application and analysis of employability skills. At this level of Bloom's Taxonomy, students must be able to use their information in a variety of situations. Applying the information to multiple situations facilitates the ability to break down more complex problems into simpler components. At this stage of learning, students should be able to recognize patterns and produce evidence to support their positions.

In the final section of this textbook, students will be challenged to evaluate real-world problems and produce novel ideas to solve them. The final stages of Bloom's Taxonomy include evaluation and creation. At these levels, students must engage their skills flexibly to create new solutions to life's challenges (Ramirez, 2017).

References

Beck, C. (2022, February 14). *Adults with executive function disorder*. The OT Toolbox. https://www.theottoolbox.com/adults-executive-function-disorder

Beck, C. (2019, February 15). *Executive functioning skills: Teach planning and prioritization*. The OT Toolbox. https://www.theottoolbox.com/executive-functioning-skills-planning-prioritization/

Brou Fossier, K. (2022). Emotional intelligence. *Radiation Therapist*, *31*(1), 49–56.

Budzyńska-Daca, A. & Łukowska, A. (2023). Improvisation at rhetoric workshops as a way of teaching communication skills. *Multidisciplinary Journal of School Education*, *12*(1 (23)). https://doi.org/10.35765/mjse.2023.1223.07

Campbell, (she/her), L., & Miller, (she/her), E. L. (2023). Pedagogies of rhetorical empathy-in-action: Role playing and story sharing in healthcare education. *Rhetoric of Health & Medicine*, *6*(1), 36–63.

Center on the Developing Child. (n.d.). *What is executive function? And how does it relate to child development?* Harvard University. https://harvardcenter.wpenginepowered.com/wp-content/uploads/2019/04/ExecutiveFunctionInfographic_FINAL.pdf

Centers for Disease Control and Prevention (CDC). (2021, March 3). *Why think dynamically?* Centers for Disease Control and Prevention: Office of Policy, Performance, and Evaluation. https://www.cdc.gov/policy/polaris/tis/think-dynamically/index.html#:~:text=When%20thinking%20dynamically%2C%20you%20can,understand%20and%20communicate%20the%20issue.&text=Use%20what%20you%20know%20about,you%20don't%20have%20data.

Chmielewski, J., Los, K., & Luczynski, W. (2021). Mindfulness in healthcare professionals and medical education. *International Journal of Occupational Medicine and Environmental Health*, *34*(1), 1+. https://0b30iduo5-mp02-y-https-link-gale-com.prx-usa.lirn.net/apps/doc/A658252394/AONE?u=lirn55718&sid=ebsco&xid=21650843

Clark, K., & Hoffman, A. (2019). Educating healthcare students: Strategies to teach systems thinking to prepare new healthcare graduates. *Journal of Professional Nursing*, *35*(3), 195–200. https://doi.org/10.1016/j.profnurs.2018.12.006

De Angelis, L., Baglivo, F., Arzilli, G., Privitera, G. P., Ferragina, P., Tozzi, A. E., & Rizzo, C. (2023). ChatGPT and the rise of large language models: The new AI-driven infodemic threat in public health. *Frontiers in Public Health*, 11. https://doi.org/10.3389/fpubh.2023.1166120

Gribble, N., Ladyshewsky, R. K., & Parsons, R. (2017). Strategies for interprofessional facilitators and clinical supervisors that may enhance the emotional intelligence of therapy students. *Journal of Interprofessional Care*, *31*(5), 593–603. https://doi.org/10.1080/13561820.2017.1341867

Horey, B. (2019). Soul truth: Self-awareness card deck [Card deck]. Tarot Deck.

InTeGrate. (n.d.). *Teach systems thinking*. Carleton University: Science Education Resource Center. https://serc.carleton.edu/integrate/teaching_materials/systems.html

MasterClass. (2022, September 28). *What is rhetoric? Definition, examples, and importance*. MasterClass Articles. https://www.masterclass.com/articles/writing-101-what-is-rhetoric-learn-about-rhetorical-devices-in-writing-and-3-modes-of-persuasion-in-rhetoric#7vqmBDMJz29FJljbyaA9x1

Mind Tools Content Team. (n.d.). *Benne and Sheats' group roles*. Mind Tools. https://www.mindtools.com/a6ltrh7/benne-and-sheats-group-roles

Ozovek, J. (2016, February 23). *Dynamic thinking: The power of an outside the box mindset* [Blog post]. LinkedIn. https://www.linkedin.com/pulse/dynamic-thinking-power-outside-box-mindset-jonathan-x-ozovek-/

Ramirez, T. V. (2017). On pedagogy of personality assessment: Application of Bloom's Taxonomy of educational objectives. *Journal of Personality Assessment*, *99*(2), 146–152.

Richmond, B. (n.d.). *The "thinking" in systems thinking: How can we make it easier to master?* The Systems Thinker. https://thesystemsthinker.com/the-thinking-in-systems-thinking-how-can-we-make-it-easier-to-master/#:~:text=the%20seven%20unfold%20in%20the,quantitative%20thinking%2c%20and%20scientific%20thinking.

Robinson, A. (2022, November 30). *21 fun communication games for teams in 2023*. Teambuilding. https://teambuilding.com/blog/communication-games

Scherman, J. (2019, May 20). *5 ways technology in healthcare is transforming the way we approach medical treatment*. Rasmussen University. https://www.rasmussen.edu/degrees/health-sciences/blog/technology-in-healthcare-transformation/

Terry, L. (2020). Understanding and applying personality types in healthcare communication. *Nursing Standard (Royal College of Nursing (Great Britain): 1987)*, *35*(7), 27-34. https://doi.org/10.7748/ns.2020.e11509

Theresa Raphael-Grimm, P. C. (2015). *The art of communication in nursing and health care: An interdisciplinary approach*. Springer Publishing Company.

3veta. (n.d.). *Resource management games to boost your team's productivity* [Blog]. 3veta. https://3veta.com/blog/articles/7-resource-management-games-to-boost-your-teams-productivity/#puzzle

Townsend, S. (n.d.). *Top 12 resource management best practices*. Plan View. https://www.planview.com/resources/guide/resource-management-software/top-12-resource-management-best-practices/

White, B. A. A., & Quinn, J. F. (2023). Personal growth and emotional intelligence: Foundational skills for the leader. *Clinics in Sports Medicine*, *42*(2), 261–267.

Chapter 13: The Future of Employability Skills

Introduction

This textbook began with an introduction to the U.S. Department of Education's Employability Skills Framework. The framework consists of three subsets – applied knowledge, effective relationships, and workplace skills. Collectively, these skills enable a person to secure and maintain employment. They are outlined in the figure below.

Figure 81

Employability Skills Framework with Sub-competencies Depicted

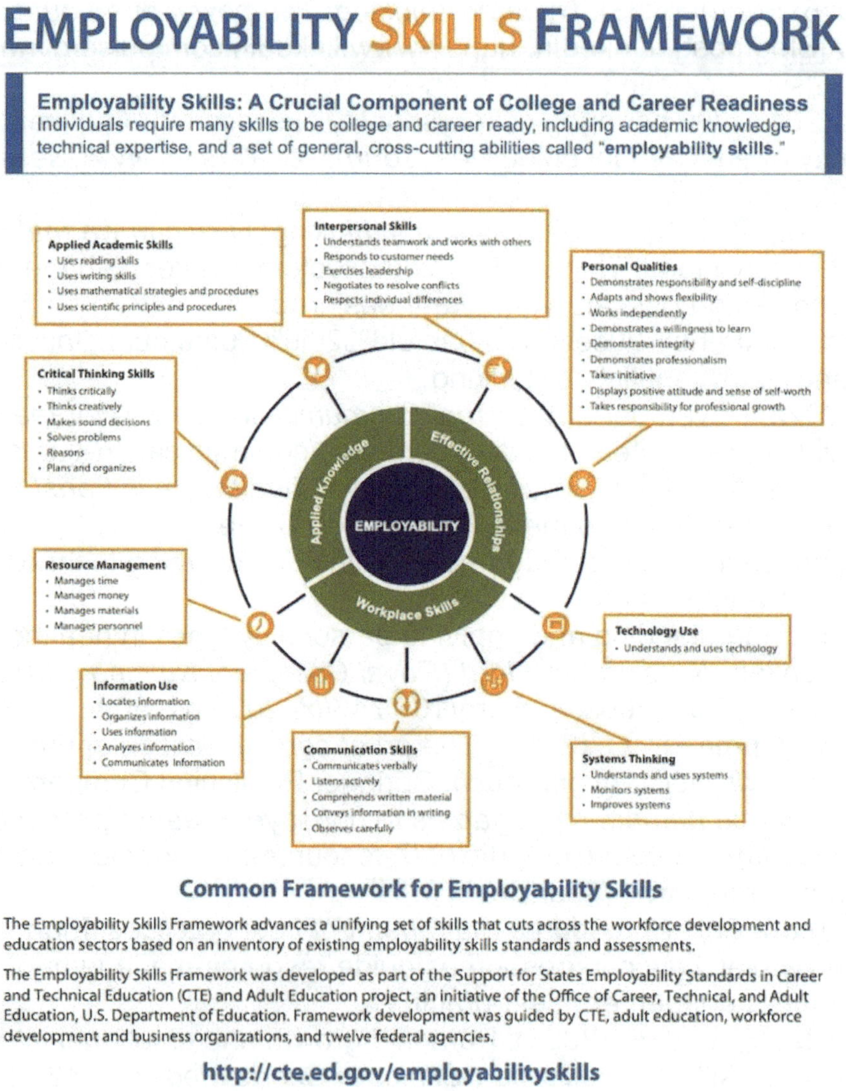

Note: This image is a visual representation of the competencies associated with employability skills. The sub-competencies are the spokes of a wheel, functioning in unison for employability. Permission was obtained to use this image on March 29, 2023,from https://cte.ed.gov/initiatives/employability-skills-framework.

Once a common understanding of employability skills was explained, the current perceptions of healthcare graduates' competence with these skills were explored. Unfortunately, healthcare students and graduates are deemed to lack competence with employability skills, according to clinical educators and employers around the globe. The research indicates the need for more emphasis on teaching and learning employability skills.

Kolb's Experiential Learning Theory explains the process preferred by adult learners. This is because adult learners possess prior experiences, which inform their actions. Kolb's Experiential Learning Theory explains how adult learners prefer to participate in an experience, which is a form of active learning. This is followed by reflection on the experience, complemented by a debriefing and conceptualizing. Finally, the adult learner applies what they have learned to novel situations.

Figure 82

Cyclical Depiction of Kolb's Theory of Experiential Learning

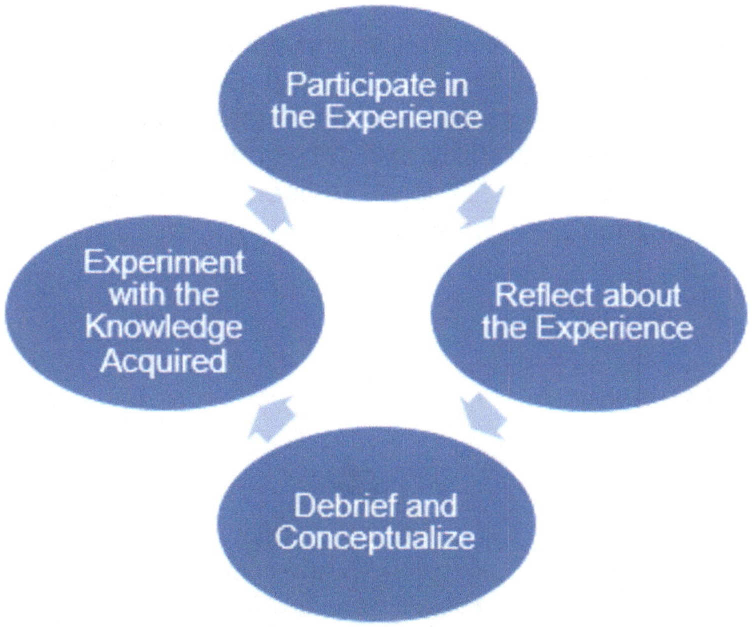

Note: A cyclical depiction of Kolb's Theory of Experiential Learning.

Before the incorporation of Kolb's Theory into the application and assessment of employability skills, the Dreyfus Model of Skill Acquisition was examined as an assessment tool. The Dreyfus Model is a simplified explanation of the learning curve associated with learning new skills. In the beginning stages of learning, the student has a limited frame of reference and relies on rules to govern their actions. As the student achieves basic competence, he or she learns by applying principles to various contexts and conditions. Competence is the first level where the student feels a sense of responsibility in the decision-making process. This is demonstrated by the figure on the next page.

Figure 83

Pictorial Representation of the Dreyfus Model of Skill Acquisition

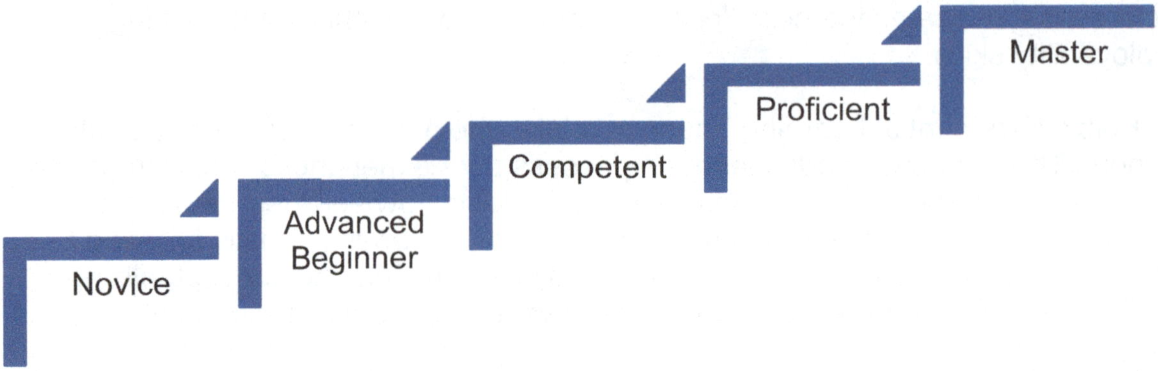

Note: This pictorial representation of the Dreyfus Model of Skill Acquisition.

The next section of the textbook focuses on the application and analysis of employability skills. According to Bloom's Taxonomy, application and analysis representthe middle levels of learning. This section is designed for students to learn through experience, grounded in Kolb's theory. A thorough analysis of employability skill sub- competencies enables the student to learn through a series of guided experiences. Bloom's revised taxonomy is revisited in this chapter at these highest levels ofevaluation and creation.

Figure 84

Bloom's Revised Taxonomy

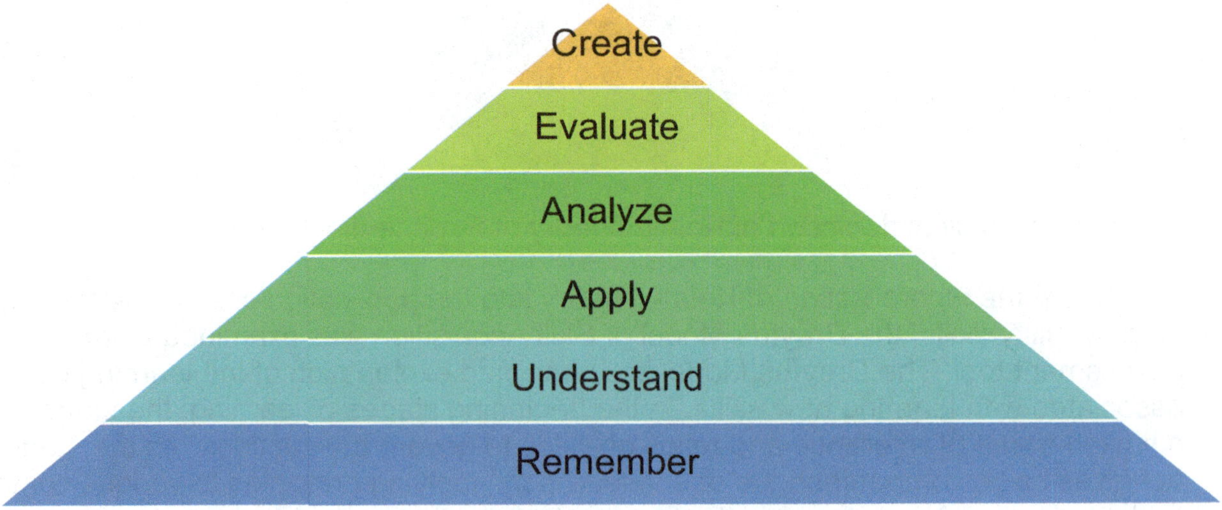

Note: Bloom's Revised Taxonomy lists verbs instead of nouns.

This final section of the textbook will focus on the synthesis and evaluation of employability skills. Synthesis and evaluation are the highest levels of Bloom's Taxonomy. At these levels, the learner relies upon acquired knowledge to evaluate decisions and synthesize original work.

Terminal Learning Objectives

By the end of this chapter, the student will be able to appraise their decisions and create original work.

Enabling Learning Objectives

By the end of this chapter, the student will be able to:

- Evaluate their employability skills.
- Create according to their employability skills.
- Interpret how Schön's model of reflective practice facilitates the transition from healthcare student to graduate.
- Adopt a strategy for lifelong learning.

Instructor Notes

- *The headers in this textbook are in the form of a question. Students should be prompted to state the question and where to locate it to ensure they master the concepts.*

How Do You Evaluate Your Employability Skills?

Evaluation is the systematic process of measuring, documenting, and communicating the effectiveness of an intervention. The three main types of evaluations include goal-based, process-based, and outcomes-based. Goal-based evaluations focus on objectives. Evaluations based on processes analyze inherent strengths and weaknesses. While outcome-based evaluations examine the results (Funding for Good, 2020).

Instructor Notes

- *For synchronous or asynchronous instruction, have students develop goals for their professional lives, and determine the best process to reach those goals and the desired outcomes. Prompts for this assignment are included in Appendix QQ.*
- *For synchronous or asynchronous instruction, have students rank their competency with employability skills, as listed in the U.S. Department of Education's Employability Skills Framework in Appendix B. Ask for a personal reflection on the three subcategories that explain why they rated themselves the way they did. A rubric for this reflection is included in Appendix G.*
- *At this point in the learning process, the hope is that the same group of students has participated collectively in the learning experiences presented in this book.*

Assuming this is the case, for synchronous and asynchronous instruction, have students select at least three of their classmates to evaluate their competency with employability skills. Students should provide an evaluation of employability skills with honest, constructive feedback with suggestions. It is important to set the tone and to model constructive feedback. An evaluation form is provided in Appendix RR. This should be followed by a video-recorded debriefing session among the students to allow for clarification questions. Students will be evaluated on their ability to provide and accept constructive feedback with clarifying questions. A rubric is included in Appendix SS.

- *For synchronous or asynchronous instruction, have students compare their employability skills self-assessment with the evaluations of the others. The student is then to develop a professional plan for the lowest three competencies according to the collective evaluations. A template is provided in Appendix TT.*
- *For synchronous or asynchronous instruction, have students determine the type of evaluation for the items listed in Appendix UU. An answer key is provided in Appendix VV.*

> "The deepest secret is that life is not a process of discovery,
> but a process of creation.
> You are not discovering yourself but creating yourself anew.
> Seek therefore, not to find out who you are,
> but seek to determine who you want to be."
> —Neale Donald Walsh

What Will You Create According to Your Employability Skills?

The quote above by Neale Donald Walsh sets the stage for the creation of a better version of you -- the student and future healthcare professional. How do you want others to perceive you? What important qualities do you possess that make you unique? What direction is your life heading? Answering questions such as these can help you decide the best way to create yourself. One thing is guaranteed, you will likely recreate yourself multiple times in your life. Ongoing self-reflection and assessment propel us to ongoing creation.

If you have not begun yet, now is the time to create your professional identity. Key features include identifying your core values and competencies. It is important to clarify your academic credentials, work experience, and achievements. You must determine why having a professional identity is important to you and what is most important (Seguna, 2020). A professional identity is the image you wish to portray to the world that aligns with your values and maximizes career opportunities. The list below outlines the necessary steps to creating your professional identity (Office of Graduate Studies, 2019).

- Assess your skills (completed above)
- Package your skills
- Be the best you can

- Avoid toxic behaviors
- Network purposefully
- Continuously develop communication skills
- Get organized, including your schedule, workspace, and tasks
- Behave and dress for the position you desire

Product packaging is the product's look and feel. Decisions on product packages derive from knowing your target audience, what your competitors are doing, and what makes you stand out. Effective packing is dependent upon knowing what your brand stands for, the design implications that comprise your brand, and highlighting your best-selling points (Lutz, n.d.).

Instructor Notes

- *For synchronous or asynchronous instruction, have students describe how each font makes them feel in Appendix WW.*
- *For synchronous or synchronous instruction, have students match the descriptive words with the images in Appendix XX. An answer key is provided in Appendix YY.*

Figure 85

This Person Is Dressed Professionally

Note: Dressed for success. This image was obtained from Microsoft Word, 2023.

The Office of Career Development (n.d.) recommends creating the following items as you transition from student to graduate. It is recommended you consider electronic and paper packaging. Resume paper can be purchased at any office store. Consider the weight, color, and other paper characteristics to deliver the desired message.

- Goals (completed above)
- Elevator pitch
- Resume

- Cover letter
- Interview
- Thank you
- Negotiation

Instructor Notes

- *For synchronous and asynchronous instruction, have students create a video-recorded elevator pitch to convey "who you are", "what you do," and "what you want to do." The pitch should not exceed 30 seconds. The pitch will be assessed based on the following criteria (Doyle, 2022). A rubric is provided in Appendix ZZ.*
    - *Must be persuasive*
    - *Emphasize skills*
    - *Be positive and flexible*
    - *Make it meaningful*
    - *Mention your goals*
    - *Speak directly to the audience*
    - *Keep it simple and focused*
    - *Provide a business card*

A resume is a living document. This means it requires continuous revisions as you grow professionally. A resume is a document that presents a person's background, skills, and accomplishments, usually for the purpose of obtaining employment. Resumes come in a variety of styles. It is important to select the style that matches your personality, that of the industry, and your experience level (Hernandez, 2023).

A chronological style resume is an excellent format for someone with ten or more years of experience. It highlights work experience and is often the preferred format. A functional style resume works well for someone with two or fewer years of experience. Reviewing a wide variety of resume templates is often helpful for identifying the best way to portray skills (Hernandez, 2023).

Resumes contain section headings that help the reader to understand what they are reading. It is not necessary to include all the headings. Regardless of which headings are included, it is best to keep the information clear and concise. Each section should be written in reverse chronological order, from most recent to oldest. The introductory section is the resume objective. This section introduces who you are and states your overall career goals. The following information is often contained in the objective (Hernandez, 2023).

- Current or desired job title
- Relevant credentials
- Objectives for the desired position
- Qualifying skills
- Relevant accomplishments

Depending on your position in life, the next section will likely be experienced. This section should contain any work and other related experiences that demonstrate your ability to excel in the desired position. Include the position title, dates, and locations of employment. A few other experiences are listed below (Hernandez, 2023).

- Volunteering and/or nonprofit experiences
- Tutoring
- Babysitting
- Manual labor (e.g., mowing lawns)
- Lifeguard duty
- Camp counseling
- Participation in a family business
- Internships

If a functional-style resume is the format of choice, a skill section is often included. A skills section should include a balance of technical and employability skills applicable to the desired position. Under each skill, list a few bulleted phrases that explain how you came to possess each qualification. Focus on the skill itself instead of the experience (Hernandez, 2023).

Education is included to justify your knowledge and technical skills. It should include your highest level of education, and the name of the degree obtained. It is customary to include the name and dates of the university attended. Optional items for the education section include your grade point average, minor or concentration, distinctions (e.g., valedictorian), and relevant coursework (Hernandez, 2023).

Other sections that could be included in a resume include extracurricular activities and membership in clubs or organizations. A list of accomplishments and certifications will add to your qualifications. The ability to speak multiple languages is a benefit for almost all positions (Hernandez, 2023).

Instructor Notes

- *For synchronous and asynchronous instruction, have students create a resume highlighting their qualifications. The resume will be assessed for visual appearance, clarity, and appropriate use of language. This includes proper grammar and spelling. A rubric is provided in Appendix AAA.*

The next step to developing your professional image is to write a cover letter. It is best to customize the cover letter the company to which you are applying. Accomplish this by researching the organization. It is important to highlight how your qualifications can help to solve the company's problems. Be sure to convey enthusiasm (Gallo, 2020).

An excellent strategy to open your cover letter is to ask a smart question that demonstrates your interest in the position. Another option is to open the letter by recapping a recent interaction. Be careful with word selection to ensure you grab the reader's attention (Gallo, 2020).

The cover letter should complement the resume. The resume provides information about your past and the cover letter is focused on the future. The cover letter should create a link between your past experiences and what you want to accomplish. Use the cover letter to explain how you will apply your skills to a different role. Be sure to highlight your transferrable skills and relevant experience. It is important not to rehash the resume, but instead add clarification and further detail (Gallo, 2020).

Two skills that are relevant to almost all jobs are adaptability and the ability to learn quickly. Try to provide examples of an accomplishment that demonstrates these skills. Emphasize your value. Use language that conveys your ability to serve the company's customers. Be clear that you want the position (Gallo, 2020).

Remember that a resume and cover letter are often the first things a company learns about you. Invest the time to make sure these documents communicate the message you want to send. A good way to achieve this is to have someone else read your documents. Ask the person what the letter is saying and if there is anything wrong with it. Just as a resume is a living document, the cover letter is as well (Gallo, 2020).

Instructor Notes

- *For synchronous and asynchronous instruction, have students create a cover letter that complements the qualifications listed on their resume. The cover letter will be assessed for visual appearance, clarity, and appropriate use of language. This includes proper grammar and spelling. A rubric is provided in Appendix BBB.*
- *For synchronous and asynchronous instruction, have students review the resume and cover letter of two other classmates. Students should provide their first impressions, along with suggestions for improvement in Appendix CCC.*
- *For synchronous and asynchronous instruction, have students review the resume and cover letter of two other classmates. Students should evaluate the resume and cover letter to indicate if they convey the ability to perform the individual employability skill competencies in Appendix DDD.*

"Interviewing someone is a very proactive process and requires taking a lot of agency into your own hands to get past people's general normal self-preservation mode."
Brandon Stanton

The next step is to secure an interview to determine whether you and the prospective employer are a good match. The interview might be in person, via telephone, or video conferencing. There are different types of interviews. These could be one-on-one, through a panel, or in a group setting. Interviewers ask a variety of questions. They could be competency-based, strength-based, or technical. Interview questions can assess your situational judgment, values, and motivators (Indeed Editorial Team, 2023).

Figure 86

This Person Is Being Interviewed

Note: This person is being interviewed. This image was obtained from Microsoft Word, 2023.

Preparation is key to interviewing well. If given the choice, select a date and time when you would interview the best. Thoroughly read the job description and requirements to be very clear on what the employer desires in their employees. Research the company, its products, services, and plans within the industry. Be prepared to answer questions about your resume (Indeed Editorial Team, 2023).

If you will be making a presentation as part of your interview, practice your timing. Prepare answers for potential questions that might be asked. Bring backup copies of everything. Consider your packaging. Prepare several questions to ask to demonstrate your enthusiasm. Dress professionally. Arrive early and make sure you know the name of the interviewer. Turn off your phone, take a deep breath to calm yourself, and take a few sips of water to ensure your throat does not dry during the interview (Indeed Editorial Team, 2023).

Use the right language and tone for a formal situation. Ask for clarification to ensure you answer the question properly. Be personable and smile. Thank the employer for their time and consideration after the interview. Reiterate your interest and ask when the employer will be making their decision (Indeed Editorial Team, 2023).

The interview is a chance for you and the potential employer to learn about one another. The potential employer will likely ask a variety of questions, some of which you can and should be prepared to answer. Below is a list of topics commonly asked by interviewers (National Career Services, n.d.).

- What do you know about the company?
- Why do you think you're a good fit?
- Why do you want to work for the company?

- What do you do in your spare time?
- What are your hobbies and interests?
- What jobs have you have had?
- What projects you led?
- Have there been times you have failed or succeeded?
- What challenging experiences have you have had?
- How have you have handled conflict?
- What are your strengths and weaknesses?
- Why did you leave your last job?

Instructor Notes

- *For synchronous and asynchronous instruction, have students write the answers to the questions above. There is no rubric for this assignment.*

When you talk about your personal qualities and interests, you should focus on the skills that are transferrable to the company. For example, playing a team sport shows that you are a team player and that you can communicate well with others. Having an interest in travel conveys an adventurous and flexible attitude (National Career Services, n.d.).

You should also be prepared to ask the potential employer questions. Ask questions about what a typical day looks like, how the company will evolve over the next few years, and what training and promotional opportunities exist. When you ask these questions think about what is important to you in an employer, but make sure you are being reasonable with your expectations (National Career Services, n.d.). After the interview, write down three things that went well, and three things you could improve for next time.

Instructor Notes

- *For synchronous and asynchronous instruction, have students select an organization or company they would like to work for. Then students will produce a video of themselves participating in an interview for that entity. Students should provide the answers to the questions above, as if they were asked by the interviewer. After answering the questions above the student should ask the prospective employer at least five questions that convey sincere interest. A rubric for this assignment is included in Appendix EEE.*

A great way to leave a positive impression after an interview is to write a thank you note. Good manners never go out of style. The person gave you their time and consideration and you want to be sure to recognize that. Gratitude is always appreciated. Start by assessing the scale of the thank you. Choose your delivery medium. Keep the message simple and concise (Harlan, 2022).

Instructor Notes

- *For synchronous and asynchronous instruction, have students create a thank you note to the interviewer. The note will be assessed for scale, medium, clarity, and appropriate grammar, spelling, and use of language. A rubric is provided in Appendix FFF.*

The last step is to finalize the transaction. If the job is not for you, simply be polite and decline the offer. If the job is for you and the terms are agreeable, then you will need to obtain the pertinent details to ensure a smooth transition to employment. However, reaching an agreement on terms will require negotiation skills (National Career Services, n.d.).

> "In business as in life, you don't get what you deserve, you get what you negotiate."
> —Chester L. Karrass

Effective negotiations involve active listening to identify the interests of both parties. It is important to use diplomacy to build and preserve relationships. Effective persuasion requires self-awareness of your needs versus wants. Negotiation skills include the ability to consider alternatives and see things from the other side's point of view. It is important to understand the consequences for both sides. Focus on mutual interests (Mylona, n.d.).

Common errors in negotiating include assuming shared values and/or similar communication preferences. Issues can arise from being too focused on big picture thinking or getting lost in the details. Other challenges include disagreement over the timeline of decision-making, not listening carefully, or trying to prove how smart or "right" you are (Mylona, n.d.).

Negotiations are most effective when they are conducted in a collaborative, honest, and empathetic manner to ensure both parties meet their objectives. The first step is to prepare. You will want to know how the organization functions and what its pain points are to position yourself effectively to fill those voids or solve problems. Write your negotiation as if it were a rhetoric speech and practice it. Negotiations are about reaching a common ground (Lares, 2022).

Preparation is key to an effective negotiation. It is helpful to write your thoughts ahead of time. You will want to answer these questions (Mylona, n.d.):

- What is the goal of your negotiation?
- What are your key issues?
- What is your position?
- What are you willing to compromise on?
- What strategy will you use to negotiate your position?
- How might the other side react to that strategy?

The next step is to probe. Ask questions and focus on active listening. Summarize and clarify what the other party said to confirm your understanding. This simple process is a concession in negation because you are giving your undivided attention and time (Lares, 2022).

The final strategy of negation is purpose. If both parties have a clear understanding of the industry and organization, there usually are no surprises in the initial offer. Making the first proposal sets the tone for action. If you are not the first to propose, use that as an opportunity to gain insight. Avoid ranges because they are vague. This calls your value into question. Be specific and justify your proposal. Using specific numbers demonstrates your efforts to be fair and equitable. Finally, do not rush to a decision. Take the time to process the proposal to ensure a thoughtful response (Lares, 2022).

Improving self-awareness and critical reflection helps graduates to assess their competence with employability skills. Employers want trustworthy employees. When a person is unable to self-reflect accurately this leads to questions about a person's trustworthiness. Employers want employees who display reliability, willingness to learn, perseverance, and initiative. These people think independently, act to solve problems independently, and actively seek ways to learn and grow their professional careers (Mainga et al., 2022).

Instructor Notes

- *For synchronous instruction, have students negotiate one of the scenarios provided in Appendix GGG. Students should prepare their talking points by answering the questions provided in Appendix HHH. Following the negotiation, students should write a reflection about the negotiation experience. A rubric is provided in Appendix G.*

How Does Schön's Model of Reflective Practice Facilitate the Transition from Healthcare Student to Graduate?

The transition from healthcare student to licensed provider can be difficult and rewarding. The new graduate must be able to demonstrate their competency confidently and autonomously. This process is supported by reflection, structure, and socialization or acclimation to the environment. Donald A. Schön (1983) developed a model for reflective practice. This model provides a framework to explain how reflection can enhance the transition to practice for healthcare graduates (Cadorette et al., 2023).

Schön's reflective practice model originally contained three types of reflection: reflection-in-action, reflection-on-action, and reflection-for-action. Reflection-in-action can be described as the ability to "think on your feet". Reflection-on-action is the process of thinking about a previous experience. Reflection-for-action is thinking about future learning (Choi & Jang, 2022).

Figure 87

This is a Pictorial Representation of Schön's Model of Reflective Practice

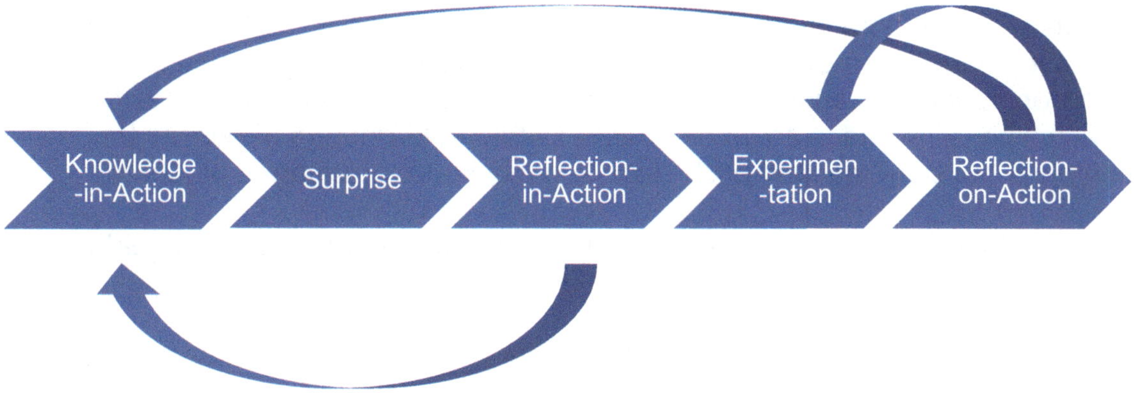

Note: This pictorial representation of Schön's Reflective Model of Practice.

For example, healthcare students begin their journey to becoming a practitioner by learning the theories and concepts related to their area of practice. For example, a healthcare student will study the body systems and structures that impact a patient's ability to maintain balance. The next step will be learning how to assess a patient's balance. This is the process of using knowledge-in-action, which leads to an outcome. As the student's skillset advances, he or she will reflect-in-action, based on their previously acquired knowledge and experience. As competence improves, students will begin to experiment with their skills. This leads to reflection-on-their actions, which leads to further experimentation, thereby adding to their knowledge base.

Healthcare graduates engage these reflection skills to inform their daily practice. As they employ their newly acquired skills, graduates continuously reflect on their actions. This aids in the development of reflection-in-action. As healthcare graduates gain confidence in their skills, they begin reflection-for-action. Over time, their healthcare career evolves to keep up with industry changes due to the advancement of technology and research. Therefore, Schön's Reflective Model of Practice accurately describes the pillars of lifelong learning (Cadorette et al., 2023).

What is Lifelong Learning?

Lifelong learning is the ongoing, voluntary pursuit of knowledge. This ongoing process is motivated by our personal and professional interests. The knowledge acquired enhances one's personal development and professional responsibility. Lifelong learning is being open to opportunities. Strategies include (McMahon, 2021):

- Viewing challenges as opportunities
- Unlearning assumptions
- Identifying personal goals

- Having confidence
- Trying new things and evaluating the results
- Mentoring others
- Becoming involved with a professional organization
- Learning something every day

Supplementary to traditional adult educational approaches, lifelong learning is a self-directed, learning-on-demand process. Given ever-changing technology and an evolving population, the augmentation of skillsets is a never-ending necessity. The speed at which the world is advancing makes lifelong learning a necessity for functioning in our personal and professional lives (Soundararajan et al., 2020).

For example, the invention of cell phones prompted middle-aged and elderly people to learnto use a new method of communication.

Lifelong learning is a pillar of healthcare education. This is because healthcare providers must maintain competence with their skills to care effectively for the population. Lifelong learning leads to improved employee competence, retention of staff, and improved self-efficacy. Healthcare providers need to feel competent in their skills to be intrinsically motivated to provide patient care (Bing et al., 2023).

Another benefit to lifelong learning is that it reduces some of the challenges with workforce supply. Workplace-based competence-enhancing activities have proven to bea sustainable way of facilitating lifelong healthcare career. Plus, competence enhancingactivities are convenient and cost-effective. They can be great ways to invest in day-to- day operations without disrupting the delivery of patient care (Bing et al., 2023).

Instructor Notes

- *For synchronous and asynchronous instruction, have students answer the prompts to the questions provided in Appendix III as outlined by James Arthur Ray in his book, Harmonic Wealth (Ray, 2008).*
- *For synchronous and asynchronous instruction, have students develop their lifelong learning plan in Appendix JJJ.*
- *For synchronous and synchronous instruction, have students participate in a discussion about the content of this textbook. Students should be provided with these questions:*
    - *What are three things you learned about yourself as you read this textbook?*
    - *What actions will you take next to refine your employability skills?*
    - *What surprised you about this textbook?*
    - *What additional information would you like to learn about regarding employability skills?*
    - *How did this textbook make you feel?*
    - *What are three messages to take away from this textbook?*

What Are the Key Concepts from this Chapter?

- Evaluation is the systematic process of measuring, documenting, and communicating the effectiveness of an intervention.
- The three main types of evaluations include goal-based, process-based, and outcomes-based.
    - Goal-based evaluations focus on objectives.
    - Process-based evaluations analyze inherent strengths and weaknesses.
    - Outcome-based evaluations examine the results.
- A professional identity is the image you wish to portray to the world that aligns with your values and maximizes career opportunities.
- Product packaging is about how the products look and feel.
- Effective packing is dependent upon knowing the pillars of your company's brand, the design elements that comprise the brand, and highlighting the best-selling points (Lutz, n.d.).
- A resume is a living document that presents a person's background, skills, and accomplishments, a key tool for obtaining employment.
- The cover letter should complement the resume. It is used to explain how you will apply your skills to a given role. It is important to highlight your transferrable skills and relevant experience and not repeat the resume. Instead, it should add clarification and further detail (Gallo, 2020).
- Adaptability and the ability to learn quickly are skills that are relevant to most jobs.
- There are several interview styles used by employers during the hiring process. These could be one-on-one, with a panel, or in a group setting. Interviewers ask a variety of questions. They could be competency-based, strength-based, technical, or personal. Interview questions can assess situational judgment, values, and motivators (Indeed Editorial Team, 2023).
- Negotiations are most effective when they are conducted in a collaborative, honest, and empathetic manner to ensure both parties meet their objectives.
- Steps to negotiation include preparation, probing, and purpose.
- Improving self-awareness and critical reflection helps graduates to assess their competence with employability skills.
- Donald A. Schön (1983) developed a model for reflective practice. This model provides a framework to explain how reflection can enhance the transition from student graduate to employment (Cadorette et al., 2023).
- Schön's reflective practice model originally contained three types of reflection: reflection-in-action, reflection-on-action, and reflection-for-action.
    - Reflection-in-action is described as the ability to "think on your feet."
    - Reflection-on-action is the process of thinking about a previous experience.
    - Reflection-for-action is thinking about future learning (Choi & Jang, 2022).
- Lifelong learning is the ongoing, voluntary pursuit of knowledge.
- Lifelong learning is motivated by personal and professional interests.
- The knowledge acquired through lifelong learning enhances one's personaldevelopment and professional responsibility.

- Lifelong learning is a pillar of healthcare because providers must maintain competence with their skills to care effectively for the population.

Summary

> "Knowing others is intelligence;
> knowing yourself is true wisdom."
> – Tao Te Ching

Gaining employment is often thought of as the final step to becoming a professional. While gaining employment is an important milestone, maintaining it requires continuous skill enhancement and reflective practice. This means continuously justifying their worth to the organization through their actions and behaviors.

Employability skills competence, especially communication, dramatically enhances the possibility of gaining employment. Employers are looking for higher-order cognitive skills, such as problem-solving, critical thinking, and creativity. These are the same skills required for clinical reasoning during patient care. Higher-order cognitive skills require the clinician to evaluate information for complex-decision-making. Employers look for a positive attitude, personal responsibility, and adaptability. It is essential candidates can work effectively and collaboratively as a team (Mainga et al., 2022).

This textbook provided a comprehensive approach to the teaching and learning of employability skills. It was carefully crafted to ensure a guided journey to achieve competence, as defined by the Dreyfus model of skill acquisition. This style of this textbook is based on Kolb's Theory of Experiential Learning. The teaching and learning prompts are designed according to Bloom's Taxonomy to ensure a methodical progression.

Author Note:

- *This author invites the readers of this textbook to provide feedback for ongoing improvement, especially regarding the activities and assignments designed to facilitate the learning process. The author can be contacted via email at LJenkins@usa.edu.*

> "Working hard for
> something we don't care
> about is called stress.
> Working hard for
> something we love is
> called passion."
> – Simon Sinek

References

Bing, J. P. C., Førsund, L. H., Hansen Stålesen, J., Vabo Nesland, B., Lindholm, I. C., & Rugsland Espegren, O. (2023). Lifelong learning in community healthcare: Testing competence after learning activities in a blended learning space. *Scandinavian Journal of Caring Sciences*. https://doi.org/10.1111/scs.13180

Cadorette, J., McCurry, M., & Danells Chin, E. (2023). Reflective transition practice model: The new graduate registered nurse. *Nursing Science Quarterly*, *36*(3), 282–291. https://doi.org/10.1177/08943184231169763

Choi, H. & Jang, S. (2022). Mediating effect of reflection types: Feedback on reflection-for-action and student perception of patient-centeredness. *Medical Education Online*, *27*(1). https://doi.org/10.1080/10872981.2022.2127166

Funding For Good. (2020, December 3). *What are evaluation methods?*

Development/Fundraising, Grant Writing. https://fundingforgood.org/what-are-evaluation-methods/#:~:text=The%20three%20main%20types%20of,%2Dbased%20and%20outcomes%2Dbased.

Doyle, A. (2022, October 11). *How to create an elevator pitch with examples*. Harvard University. https://careerservices.fas.harvard.edu/blog/2022/10/11/how-to-create-an-elevator-pitch-with-examples/

Gallo, A. (2020, December 23). *How to write a cover letter*. Harvard Business Review. https://hbr.org/2014/02/how-to-write-a-cover-letter

Harlan, J. (2022, December 29). *Day 29: An illustrated guide to saying thank you*. The New York Times. https://www.nytimes.com/2022/12/29/style/thank-you-notes-guide.html#:~:text=The%20ideal%20note%20is%20brief,you'll%20see%20the%20person.

Hernandez, G. (2023, March 23). *How to write a resume when you have no work experience*. Live Career. https://www.livecareer.com/resources/resumes/how-to/write/how-to-write-a-resume-when-you-have-no-work-experience?utm_source=google&utm_medium=sem&utm_campaign=13175117955&utm_term=&network=g&device=c&adposition=&adgroupid=121306107334&placement=&gclid=CjwKCAjwzo2mBhAUEiwAf7wjkkd6JnjaijrldlqQfCFqdETTTZSiLikdiQd9dH7zzKPyZkagRUQQ9xoCk5MQAvD_BwE

Indeed Editorial Team. (2023, April 7). *How to get an interview and secure a job offer*. https://www.indeed.com/career-advice/interviewing/how-to-get-an-interview-and-secure-a-job-offer

Lares, A. (2022, June 1). The 3 P's of great negotiations: Prepare, probe, propose.

Association for Supply Chain Management. https://www.ascm.org/ascm-insights/the-3-ps-of-great-negotiations-prepare-probe-propose/?utm_source=google&utm_medium=cpc&utm_campaign=general_nonbranded_20230515&utm_term=&gclid=Cj0KCQjwib2mBhDWARIsAPZUn_k13U1LwEA2xA5-pgVOHxHygBmzd8Qp70hSy-z0x5-osCWVHqg9G5saAuqFEALw_wcB

Lutz, C. (n.d.). *Essential elements of product packaging design explained*. Qualtrics XM. https://www.qualtrics.com/experience-management/product/product-packaging-design/

Mainga, W., Daniel, R. M., & Alamil, L. (2022). Perceptions of employability skills of undergraduate business students in a developing country: An exploratory study. *Higher Learning Research Communications, 12*(1), 28–63.

McMahon, M. F. (2021). Lifelong learning. *Journal of Trauma Nursing: The Official Journal of the Society of Trauma Nurses*, *28*(6), 339–340. https://doi.org/10.1097/JTN.0000000000000612

Mylona, E. (n.d.). *Negotiation*. https://www.upstate.edu/wims/pdf/negotiationskills.pdf

National Career Services. (n.d.). *Interview tips*. National Career Services. https://nationalcareers.service.gov.uk/careers-advice/interview-advice/interview-advice

Office of Career Development. (n.d.). *Defining your professional identity*. Chatham University. https://my.chatham.edu/documents/documentcenter/PDFDefining%20your%20professional%20identity%20one%20sheet%202017-18.pdf

Office of Graduate Studies: Graduate Connections. (2019, July 9). *Developing your professional identity*. University of Nebraska–Lincoln. https://graduate.unl.edu/connections/developing-your-professional-identity

Ray, J. A. (2008). *Harmonic wealth: The secret of attracting the life you want*. Hyperion. ISBN: 978-1-4013-2264-9

Seguna, M. F. (2020, January 18). *How to develop your professional identity*. LinkedIn. https://www.linkedin.com/pulse/how-develop-your-professional-identity-michelle-fenech-seguna/

Soundararajan, L., Rajan, P., & Priya, S. S. (2020). Competency assessment and fortitude for lifelong learning: The study among graduate students and higher educational institutions. *SAM Advanced Management Journal (07497075)*, *85*(2),

Appendix A

Tips on Forming Connections

	Deficient 0 points	Sufficient 10 points	Proficient 20 points	Points
Explains tip for making connections	Includes zero or one relevant healthcare example	Includes two relevant healthcare examples	Includes three relevant healthcare examples	
Provides three relevant healthcare examples of using the tip	Includes zero or one well-developed examples	Includes two well-developed examples	Includes three well-developed examples	
Organization	Final product is not well organized and does not reflect clear and focused thought.	Final product is somewhat organized and reflects but lacks clear and focused thought.	Final product is well organized and reflects clear and focused thought.	
Style and Language	Sentences arenot well constructed. Lacks use of high content vocabulary.	Some sentences are well constructed and have varied structure and length. Some good use of high content vocabulary.	Sentences are well constructed and have varied structure and length. Good use of high content vocabulary.	
Grammar	2-3 errors in grammar, mechanics, or spelling	2-3 errors in grammar, mechanics, or spelling	0-1 errors in grammar, mechanics, or spelling	
			Total	

Appendix B

Employability Skills Competency Self-assessment

Directions: Complete a self-assessment of your competence level with employability skills by placing a checkmark in the corresponding column.

1-Poor, 2-Below Average, 3-Average, 4-Better Than Average, 5-Excellent

	1	2	3	4	5
Applied Knowledge					
Applied academic skills					
Critical thinking skills					
Effective Relationships					
Interpersonal skills					
Personal qualities					
Workplace Skills					
Communication					
Resource management					
Information use					
Systems thinking					
Technology use					

Adapted from: U.S. Department of Education. Employability Skills Framework, Retrieved [March 29, 2023], from https://cte.ed.gov/initiatives/employability-skills-framework

Appendix C

Patient-Centered Language

Directions: Change the wording that is in the first column to patient-centered language in the second column.

Non-Patient-centered Language	Patient-centered Language
Wheelchair-bound	
Mentally impaired person	
HIV positive person	
My patient	
Blind person	
Autistic child	
Amputee	
Diabetic	
Prisoner	
Brain damage	
Depressed	
Drug offender	

Appendix D

Impacts of COVID-19 Pandemic on Healthcare Delivery

	Deficient 0 points	**Sufficient 10 points**	**Proficient 20 points**	**Points**
3 relevant healthcare examples included	Includes zero or one relevant healthcare example	Includes two relevant healthcare examples	Includes three relevant healthcare examples	
3 recent, peer-reviewed articles cited supporting examples	Includes zero or one peer-reviewed article with proper citations or two articles without proper citations	Includes two peer-reviewed articles with proper citations or three articles without proper citations	Includes three peer-reviewed articles with proper citations	
Organization	Final product is not well organized and does not reflect clear and focused thought.	Final product is somewhat organized and reflects but lacks clear and focused thought.	Final product is well organized and reflects clear and focused thought.	
Style and Language	Sentences arenot well constructed. Lacks use ofhigh content vocabular.	Some sentences are well constructed and have varied structure and length. Some gooduse of high content vocabular.	Sentences are well constructed and have varied structure and length. Good use of high content vocabulary.	
Grammar	4-5 errors in grammar, mechanics, or spelling	2-3 errors in grammar, mechanics, or spelling	0-1 errors in grammar, mechanics, or spelling	
			Total	

Appendix E

Group Project Employability Skills Rubric

Directions: This rubric can be used for group projects for students to grade each other's competency with employability skills. All members will grade each other. The instructor will average the group member feedback and provide it to the student. Students will be more inclined to be honest if the feedback is anonymous.

Descriptor	Points
Positive Attitude (1 point for each) • Displaying a 'can do' attitude • Being optimistic • Being honest • Being friendly and showing respect • Demonstrating motivation to work hard taking initiative • Ethical integrity • Self-confidence • Professionalism	0-8
Communication (1 point for each) • Being aware of how communication affects others • Asking questions • Listening actively • Showing respect in all communications, oral and written • Social skills	0-5
Teamwork (1 point for each) • Working well with others to complete tasks • Contributing to new ideas • Working well with others of different gender, culture, or beliefs • Following the directions of peers and seniors • Forming positive relationships • Developing leadership ability	0-6
Self-management (1 point for each) • Arriving at work or class on time • Wearing the right clothing and having right equipment • Noticing how personal words and actions can affect others • Showing commitment and responsibility • Being dependable • Following instructions and completing tasks • Following health and safety guidelines good work habits • Planning and organizing • Showing initiative • Emotional intelligence (self-awareness)	0-10

Willingness to Learn (1 point for each) • Being willing to learn new tasks, skills, and information • Being curious and enthusiastic about things • Looking for opportunities to improve or to help • Accepting advice and learning from feedback	0-4
Thinking Skills (e.g., problem solving and decision making) (1 point for each) • Considering all the options before deciding • Seeing problems and trying to solve them • Thinking before acting • Thinking about consequences before acting • Knowing when to seek help • Literacy and numeracy skills • Resourcefulness	0-7
Resilience (1 point for each) • Adapting to new or changing situations • Not giving up when there is a setback • Getting help when needed it • Accepting own mistakes and learning from them • Flexibility	0-5
Innovation (1 point for each) • Shows invention when applying processes • Encourages fresh thinking • Attempts new ways to solve problems • Shows creativity • Discusses alternative options Use of and confidence with technology	0-6
Entrepreneurship (1 point for each) • A persuasive manner and style • Demonstrating ways to find solutions • Discussing the effects of alternative approaches • Challenging status quo Encouraging buy-in from others to a particular perspective	0-5
Cultural Competence (1 point for each) • Acknowledges differences • Attempts to say students' names correctly • Allows for different ways of working • Acknowledges and embraces diversity • Welcoming contributions of others Invites cultural contributions	0-6
Total (Divide total points earned by 62 to determine percentage)	/62

Note: Adapted from Table 1 of Fraser, C. J., Duignan, G., Stewart, D., & Rodrigues, A. (2019). Overt and overt: Strategies for building employability skills of vocational education graduates. *Journal of Teaching and Learning for Graduate Employability,10*(1), 157–172.

Appendix F

Self-Reflection Questions

How would you describe yourself in three words and why you feel that way?
What do you feel are your greatest strengths and why?
What do you feel your greatest weaknesses are and why?
How would you describe your five most positive personality traits?
How would you describe your five most negative personality traits?
What matters most to you and why?
What accomplishment are you the proudest of and why?
How would you describe your core values and how did you develop them?
What is your greatest fear, and why do you feel that way?
What makes you extremely mad and why?
How would you describe your purpose in life and why you feel that way?
What you are most grateful for and why you feel that way?
How would you describe your level of satisfaction with your present situation in life and why you feel that way?
What motivates you, and why do you feel that way?
If you could change one thing about the world, what would it be and why?

Appendix G

Self-Reflection Rubric

	Deficient 0 points	Sufficient 12.5 points	Proficient 25 points	Points
Provides three relevant examples	Includes zero or one well-developed response	Includes two well-developed examples	Includes three well-developed examples	
Organization	Final product is not well organized and does not reflect clear and focused thought.	Final product is somewhat organized and reflects but lacks clear and focused thought.	Final product is well organized and reflects clear and focused thought.	
Style and Language	Sentences arenot well constructed. Lacks use ofhigh content vocabular.	Some sentences are well constructed and have varied structure and length. Some good use of high content vocabular.	Sentences are well constructed and have varied structure and length. Good use of high content vocabulary.	
Grammar	4-5 errors in grammar, mechanics, or spelling	2-3 errors in grammar, mechanics, or spelling	0-1 errors in grammar, mechanics, or spelling	
			Total	

Appendix H

Adjusting to the Generations of Others Rubric

	Deficient 0 points	Sufficient 10 points	Proficient 20 points	Points
Clearly presents position on adjusting to the generation of others	Does not present position on adjusting to the generations of others	Presents position on adjusting to the generations of others, but position lacks clarity	Presents clear position on adjusting to the generations of others	
Includes at least 1 recent peer-reviewedarticle to support their position	Includes zero or one peer-reviewed article with proper citations or two articles without proper citations	Includes two peer-reviewed articles with proper citations or three articles without proper citations	Includes three peer-reviewed articles with proper citations	
Include at least 3 examples of how to adjust to the generations of others	Includes zero or one unique way to adjust to the generations of others	Includes two unique ways to adjust to the generations of others	Includes three unique ways to adjust to the generations of others	
Organization	Final product is not well organizedand does not reflect clear and focused thought.	Final product is somewhat organized and reflects but lacks clear and focused thought.	Final product is well organized and reflects clear and focused thought.	
Style and Language	Sentences are notwell constructed. Lacks use of high content vocabular.	Some sentencesare well constructed and have varied structure and length. Some good use of highcontent vocabular.	Sentences are well constructed and have varied structure and length. Good use of high content vocabulary.	
Grammar	4-5 errors in grammar, mechanics, or spelling	2-3 errors in grammar, mechanics, or spelling	0-1 errors in grammar, mechanics, or spelling	
			Total	

Appendix I

Clinical Instructor Perceptions Rubric

	Deficient 0 points	Sufficient 10 points	Proficient 20 points	Points
Provides three relevant examples	Includes zero or one well-developed response	Includes two well-developed examples	Includes three well-developed examples	
Depth of Reflection	Demonstrates a poor understanding of the reflection	Demonstrates a partial understanding ofthe reflection	Demonstrates a thorough and conscious understanding of the reflection	
Organization	Final product is not well organized and does not reflect clear and focused thought.	Final product is somewhat organized and reflects but lacks clear and focused thought.	Final product is well organized and reflects clear and focused thought.	
Style and Language	Sentences arenot well constructed. Lacks use ofhigh contentvocabular.	Some sentences are well constructed and have varied structure and length. Some good use of high content vocabular.	Sentences are well constructed and have varied structure and length. Good use of high content vocabulary.	
Grammar	4-5 errors in grammar, mechanics, or spelling	2-3 errors in grammar, mechanics, or spelling	0-1 errors in grammar, mechanics, or spelling	
			Total	

Appendix J

Blind Drawing

Directions: Print this page. Cut out the pictures. Give each pair of students one blank piece of paper and one picture. The person drawing blindly should not see the picture until the activity is over. The person with the picture must verbally describe the shape to the other student. Students should be instructed to provide as much detail as possible. The goal is accuracy through effective communication.

Note: Shapes from Microsoft Word, 2023

Appendix K

Kolb's Experiential Learning Reflection

	Deficient 0 points	Sufficient 10 points	Proficient 20 points	Points
Describes the simulation experience with good detail	Does not describe the simulation experience	Describes the simulation experience with some detail	Describes the simulation experience with good detail	
Provides a reflection with at least three observations of the experience	Provides a reflection with one or zero observations of the experience	Provides a reflection with two observations of the experience	Provides a reflection with at least three observations of the experience	
Describes conceptualization of the experience with good detail	Does not describe the conceptualization of the experience	Describes conceptualization of the experience with some detail	Describes conceptualization of the experience with good detail	
Adequately explains how he or she could experiment with the information acquired to a different situation	Does not explain how he or she could experiment with the information acquired to a different situation	Explanation lacks some detailof how he or she could experiment with the information acquired to a different situation	Adequately explains how he or she could experiment with the information acquired to a different situation	
Organization, style and language, and grammar	Final product is not well organized and does not reflect clear and focused thought. Sentences are not well constructed. Lacks use of high content vocabular. 4-5 errors in grammar, mechanics, or spelling	Final product is somewhat organized and reflects but lacks clear and focused thought.Some sentencesare well constructed and have varied structure and length. Some good use of high content vocabular. 2-3 errors in grammar, mechanics, or spelling	Final product is well organized and reflects clear and focused thought. Sentences are well constructed and have varied structure and length. Good use of high content vocabulary. 0-1 errors in grammar, mechanics, or spelling	
			Total	

Appendix L

Employability Skills Lesson Components

Directions: As an instructor, you can use this checklist to ensure that you incorporate the lesson components listed below when you complete your lesson planning.

Employability Skills Lesson Components	
Applied Academic Skills Applied academic skills are evident daily in homework assignments, classwork, and Q&A exchanges during lessons.	**Reading skills** Students apply/demonstrate reading skills by interpreting written instructions/project directions and constructing responses, using print and online materials as resources, completing worksheets, and seeking clarification about what they have read.
	Writing skills Students rely on writing skills to construct lab reports, posters, and presentation materials, take notes, and compose responses to essay questions.
	Math strategies/procedures Students use computational skills appropriately and make logical choices when analyzing and differentiating among available procedures. Outside of math class, this includes creating/interpreting tables and graphs and organizing/displaying data.
	Scientific principles/procedures Students follow procedures, experiment, infer, hypothesize (even as simple as "what if we do it this way"), and construct processes to complete a task (can occur outside of math/science classes).
Critical Thinking Skills Critical thinking skills are evident in homework, group work, project-basedtasks, and presentations.	**Thinks creatively** Students create innovative and novel ideas/solutions and display divergent thinking. This can be seen in oral presentations and creative writing assignments, open-ended tasks, and project design.
	Thinks critically Students display analytical and strategic thinking. This can be seen in debating an issue, converging on an understanding, assessing a problem, and questioning (playing devil's advocate).
	Makes sound decisions Students differentiate between multiple approaches and assess options (could be linked to thinking critically).

	Solves problems Students assess problems involving the use of available resources (personnel and materials) and review multiple strategies for resolving problems (could be linked to thinking creatively).
	Reasons Students negotiate pros/cons of ideas, approaches, and solutions and analyze options using "if-then" rationale.
	Plans/organizes Students plan steps, procedures, and/or approaches for addressing tasks. This occurs naturally in most assignments, ranging from solving one problem to completing a long-term project.
Interpersonal Skills Interpersonal skills are almost always displayed when students work in pairs or teams to complete short-term or long-term tasks.	**Understands teamwork and works with others** Students participate in cooperative groups or with a partner, contribute fairly to the task, and show respect to others.
	Responds to customer needs Students help fellow students understand tasks, find resources, and fulfill assigned roles (think of fellow students as customers).
	Exercises leadership Students participate as team leaders or effective team members in project assignments and organize work to meet project goals and team roles.
	Negotiates to resolve conflict Students keep team members on track, suggest alternatives, and discuss options (can be as much about agreement as conflict).
	Respects individual differences Students listen to and consider all team members' ideas, respond supportively to ideas given in class or in teams, and work well with all teammates.
Personal Qualities Personal qualities are routinely displayed in students' everyday actions in the classroom — how they participate in lessons, communicate, contribute to the learning environment, treat their fellow students, and govern themselves.	**Demonstrates responsibility and self-discipline** Students actively participate in class, asking questions, volunteering answers, completing/submitting assignments, and working well in groups.
	Adapts and shows flexibility Students adapt easily to different modes of instructionand different types of assignments.
	Works independently Students commit to time-on-task during class and begin work without fanfare.
	Demonstrates a willingness to learn Students are cooperative and noticeably engaged.

	Demonstrates integrity Students treat work assignments with respect in that work is either original or credited correctly.
	Demonstrates professionalism Students treat others and work assignments with respect. All ideas are considered, and work is either original or credited correctly.
	Takes initiative Students commit to time-on-task during class and begin work without fanfare. This is also evident duringteamwork.
	Displays a positive attitude and sense of self-worth Students contribute positively to the class.
	Takes responsibility for professional growth Students are active listeners, seeking clarification and understanding when needed.
Resource Management Resource management is often a component of project-based learning and collaborative group work but can also apply to how an individual student manages class time.	**Manages time** Students demonstrate time management when organizing and planning project activities with a team or when organizing and managing themselves and individual class assignments and homework. Time management is inherent in almost all assignments.
	Manages money Students manage money in group projects requiring allocation of limited finances and resources (i.e., designing/marketing a toy, flipping a house, or planning a trip).
	Manages resources Students manage resources in projects requiring allocation of limited finances, resources (materials), and personnel.
	Manages personnel Students gain experience managing personnel (i.e., each other) in group projects requiring allocation of limited finances, resources (materials), and role assignments. They also manage their own behavior and participation.
Information Use Information use can include retrieving information from any medium (e.g., print, TV, Internet, or in person) and can be as simple as looking up one piece of information to writing a term paper or preparing an oral presentation.	**Locates** Students use analytical strategies to determine the best medium for finding necessary information.
	Organizes Students use any graphic organizer—outline, concept map, organization chart, tables, etc. to sort information/data.
	Uses Students use classification and analytic skills to determine the necessary information (i.e., stay on target) to complete task.

	Analyzes Students assess information to determine which is relevant (does not have to be a mathematical analysis).
	Communicates Students summarize information to compose written or oral presentations, posters, reports, slides, etc. This can also be as simple as a student explaining a problem in front of the class.
Communication Skills Routinely displayed in students' everyday actions in the classroom — how they participate in lessons, contribute to the learning environment, treat their fellow students, and govern themselves.	**Communicates verbally** Students provide oral responses. Evidence ranges from impromptu short answers during a lesson to completing a formal oral presentation.
	Listens actively Students are noticeably engaged through notetaking, questioning, and responding.
	Comprehends written material Students use/demonstrate reading skills by following. written instructions/project directions, reviewing print and digital resources, completing worksheets, and asking questions about what they have read.
	Conveys information in writing Students rely on writing skills to organize lab reports, posters, presentation materials and to take notes and reply to essay questions.
	Observes carefully Students interpret verbal and nonverbal communication efforts of others.
Systems Thinking A team working in sync to accomplish an assignment can be thought of as a system.	**Understands and uses systems** Students understand their roles and assignments when collaborating as a team (system) and contribute to the organizational structure and function of the team.
	Monitors systems Students devise methods to assess team (system) progress.
	Improves systems Students negotiate mid-course corrections, adaptations to team (system) tasks if necessary.
Technology Use In the classroom and workplace, technology skills typically refer to the use of digital electronics.	**Understands and uses technology** Students often rely on various digital technologies for calculating, collecting, and displaying data, conducting research, creating presentations, and writing reports.

Note: This table provides a checklist of the competencies to be included when developing the lesson plan to ensure all employability sub-competencies are addressed.Permission was obtained to use this image on March 29, 2023 from https://cte.ed.gov/initiatives/employability-skills-framework

Appendix M

The News Exercise Rubric

	Deficient 0 points	Sufficient 5 points	Proficient 10 points	Points
3 Things Learned	Includes less than three well-developed examples from the article without proper citation(s)	Includes less than three well-developed examples from the article with proper citation(s)	Includes three well-developed examples from the article with proper citation(s)	
2 Things Interesting	Includes less than two areas of interest	Includes two areas of the article but does not explain why	Includes two areas of the article that were of interest and explains why	
Remaining Question(s)	Does not include at least one question remaining	Includes at least one question remaining, but doesnot explain why thequestion is of interest	Includes at least one question remaining and why that question is of interest	
News Helped in Under-standing the Data	Does not explain how the news helped the student to understand the data	Explains how news helped student to understand the data, but explanation lacks clarity	Thoughtfully explains how the news helped the student to understand the data	
Does the Data Make Sense	Does not explain how the data makes sense	Explains how the data make sense, but does not explain why or the explanation lacks clarity	Thoughtfully explains how the data makes sense and why	
Graph Reliability	Does not explain the reliability of the graph	Explains the reliability of the graph, but explanation lacks clarity	Thoughtfully explains the reliability of the graph	
Article Bias	Does not explain the bias of the article	Explains the bias ofthe article, but explanation lacks clarity	Thoughtfully explains the bias of the article	

Organization	Final product is not well organized and does not reflect clear and focused thought.	Final product is somewhat organized and reflects but lacks clear and focused thought.	Final product is wellorganized and reflects clear and focused thought.	
Style and Language	Sentences are not well constructed. Lacks use of high content vocabulary.	Some sentences are well constructed and have varied structure and length. Some good use of high content vocabulary.	Sentences are well constructed and have varied structure and length. Good use of high content vocabulary.	
Grammar	4-5 errors in grammar, mechanics, or spelling	2-3 errors in grammar, mechanics, or spelling	0-1 errors in grammar, mechanics, or spelling	
			Total	

Appendix N

The Nine Dot Problem

Directions: Connect all nine dots with four lines or less without picking up your pencil.

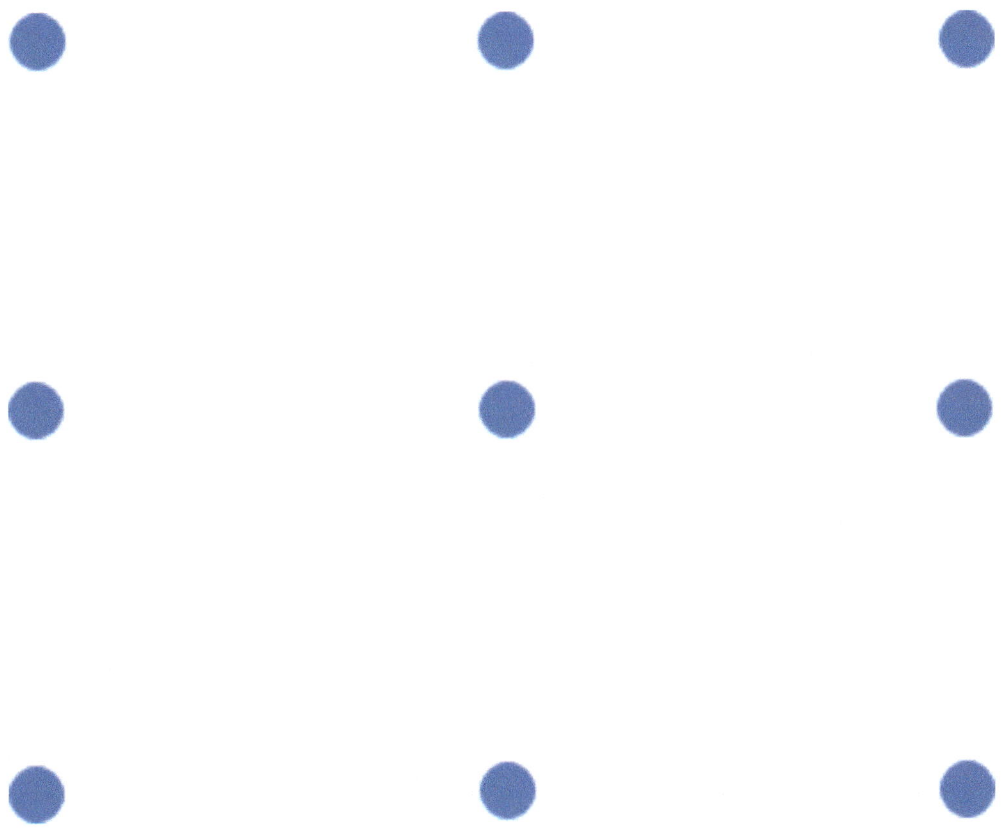

Appendix O

The Nine Dot Problem Solution

Directions: Connect all nine dots with four lines or less without picking up your pencil.

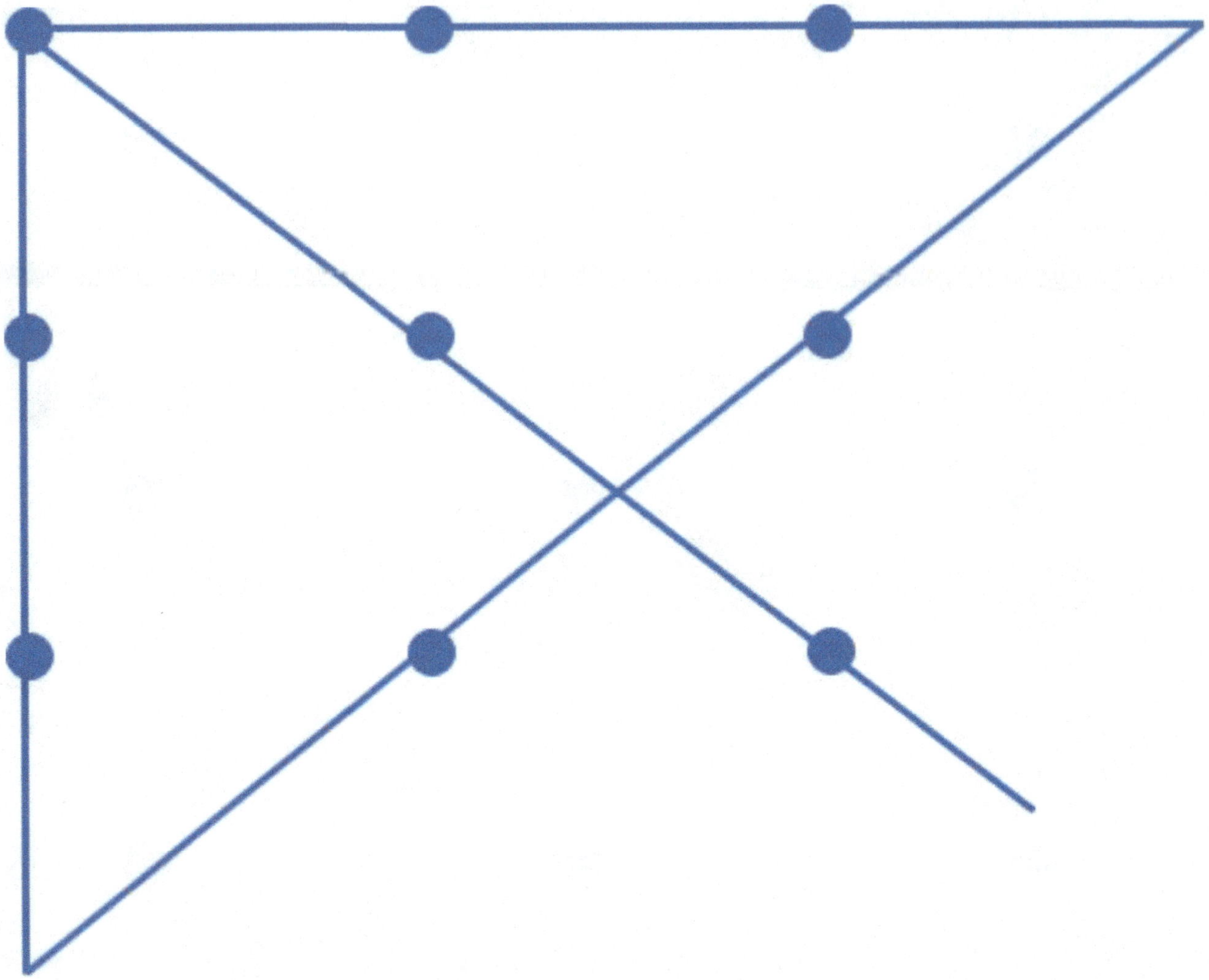

Appendix P
Thirty Circles

Appendix Q

Debate Topics

Directions: Assign students a topic to debate. Instruct students that they have two minutes to prove their position on the topic. Below is a list of topics.

1. Which is better salt or pepper?
2. What is the best color for a sedan, red or black?
3. Which is the better peanut butter type, smooth or crunchy?
4. Which is worse swimming with alligators or sharks?
5. Which are the worst to have in your house cockroaches or spiders?
6. What is the best topping for a pizza?
7. Which is better to have required uniforms in school or not?
8. Which is better chocolate or vanilla?
9. Which is the better night to go out on the town Friday or Saturday?
10. Which is better Superman or Spiderman?
11. What is the best jam or jelly to put on a peanut butter sandwich, strawberry, or grape?
12. Which is the better restaurant McDonald's or Burger King?
13. Which is it better cats or dogs?
14. Which is better for dessert cake or pie?
15. Which is the worse way to die falling into a volcano or sinking in quicksand?
16. What would be the worst way to die?
17. What is the most important room in your house?
18. If reincarnation is possible, which animal is the best one to come back as, a rhinoceros or a giraffe?
19. Which animal is smarter, cats or dogs?
20. Which is the better activity to do on a playground, swing, or slide?
21. Which emotion is stronger, love or hate?
22. Is being sensitive a strength or weakness?
23. If you had to choose one or the other, is it better to lose your memory or never be able to form new memories?
24. What is the least important subject in school?
25. Which holiday is better, Valentine's Day or Halloween?
26. Which is better love or money?
27. Which person would be better to be stuck with on a desert island, Mom, or Dad?
28. If you could be either more intelligent or more attractive, which would you choose?
29. What is the best motivator, fear, money, or love?
30. Is it better to grow up in a large or small family?
31. Is it better to display empathy or sympathy?
32. If you were to move to a country that spoke a foreign language, should you be mandated to learn the language?
33. Which has a greater impact on a child, nature, or nurture?
34. Which would make you feel more confident, taking the road more, or lesstraveled?
35. Is it better to be a passive or an aggressive person?
36. Which is better team or solo sports?

37. Which is better to receive good food with bad service or bad food with good service?
38. Which is better, being an introvert or extrovert?
39. Which would be the better sense to lose, vision or hearing?
40. Should a person's social media be considered by school admissions, potential employers, and police investigations?

Appendix R

Infographic on Ways to Sabotage a Group Project

	Deficient 0 points	Sufficient 10 points	Proficient 20 points	Points
10 ways to sabotage group project included	Includes less than five unique ways to sabotage a group project	Includes at least five, but less than ten unique ways to sabotage a group project	Includes ten unique ways to sabotage a group project	
Items are ranked in orderof least to most sabotaging	Includes less than two areas of interest	Includes two areas of the article but does not explain why	Includes two areas of the article that were of interest and explains why	
Legend indicated all members contributed	Does not include at leastone question remaining	Includes at least one question remaining, but does not explainwhy the questionis of interest	Includes at least one question remaining and why that question is of interest	
Information is presented in a visually appealing, cohesive manner	Does not explain how thenews helped the student to understand the data	Explains how news helped student to understand the data, but explanation lacks clarity	Thoughtfully explains how the news helped the student to understand the data	
Grammar	4-5 errors in grammar, mechanics, or spelling	2-3 errors in grammar, mechanics, or spelling	0-1 errors in grammar, mechanics, or spelling	
			Total	

Appendix S

Customer Service Statements

Customer Service Statements are listed in bold italics. The sentences listed below further explain each statement.

1. ***The best way to serve a customer is to listen to them…***
    a. We may fail to give the customer what they need because we simply do not know what they need. Listen, with the intent to understand and respond accordingly.
2. ***Your attitude determines the quality of service you provide…***
    a. Start positive, end positive and put positive in the middle.
3. ***It's not about right or wrong, it is about how you react when handling a problem…***
    a. Start with a smile and respond with "yes", "great", "no problem", "can do", "consider it done." The secret of customer service starts with "YES". If you own the problem, you own the customer. If you disregard the problem, you lose the customer.
4. ***Service is a feeling…***
    a. The simple secret: Don't give any feeling to others that you wouldn't want to feel ourselves.
5. ***There is no higher level of achievement than loyalty…***
    a. Loyal customers make our job easier; they tell everyone about us and refer everyone willingly.
6. ***The best way to get customer loyalty is to give loyalty…***
    a. Treat customers consistently as though they were your friend, neighbor, hero, or your mother.
7. ***The customer's perception of good or bad service is the measure of your success or failure…***
    a. Every time you communicate with a customer you have an opportunity and a choice. Create a vision of perfection centered on the customer. Paint a picture of what the perfect clinical service company would look like and then deliver it.
8. ***Customer satisfaction determines the course of our career…***
    a. Take customer complaints seriously, not personally. Thank customers for their feedback. Feedback creates opportunities to improve your overall service.
9. ***Say what mean and mean what you say…***
    a. Make sure you follow through on your responses. Failing to do what you say leads to distrust in the relationship.
10. ***Focus on consistently meeting your customer's expectations…***
    a. If you provide consistent quality service, you will earn your customer's trust and loyalty.

11. ***It's not about right or wrong, it is about how you react when handling a problem...***
    a. Start with a smile and respond with "yes", "great", "no problem", "can do", "consider it done." The secret of customer service starts with "YES". If you own the problem, you own the customer.
12. ***The purpose of customer service is to guarantee satisfaction and repeat business...***
    a. When you give more than the customer expects, you receive much more in return! Deliver customer service that is truly remarkable! Remarkable companies are memorable companies. Your high standard of service will set you apart from your competitors.
13. ***Customers are the purpose of our day...***
    a. Treat every customer contact with the intent to form a lasting, positive relationship.
    b. The customer is doing us a favor by bringing us his wants and needs and allowing us the opportunity to meet those wants and needs.
14. ***No one has ever won an argument with a customer...***
    a. While we can't please everyone all the time, we can handle each situation with professionalism and courtesy.

Appendix T

Customer Service Rubric

	Deficient 0 points	Sufficient 12.5 points	Proficient 25 points	Points
Includes a relevant healthcare example	Does not include a relevant healthcare example	Includes a relevant healthcare example, but lacks detail	Includes a relevant healthcare example with good detail	
3 recent, peer-reviewed articles cited supporting examples	Includes zero orone peer-reviewed articlewith proper citations or two articles without proper citations	Includes two peer-reviewed articles with proper citations or three articles without proper citations	Includes three peer-reviewed articles with proper citations	
Organization	Final product is not well organized and does not reflect clear and focused thought.	Final product is somewhat organized and reflects but lacks clear and focused thought.	Final product is well organized and reflects clear and focused thought.	
Style and Language	Sentences arenot well constructed. Lacks use of high content vocabular.	Some sentences are well constructed and have varied structure and length. Some good use of high content vocabular.	Sentences are well constructed and have varied structure and length. Good use of high content vocabulary.	
Grammar	4-5 errors in grammar, mechanics, or spelling	2-3 errors in grammar, mechanics, or spelling	0-1 errors in grammar, mechanics, or spelling	
			Total	

Appendix U

What If Self-Reflection Rubric

	Deficient 0 points	Sufficient 10 points	Proficient 20 points	Points
Identifies three areas for growth for two other students	Identifies one area for growth for two other students	Identifies two areas for growth for two other students	Identifies three areas for growth for two other students	
Identifies three positive behaviors for two other students	Identifies one positive behaviors for two other students	Identifies two positive behaviors for two other students	Identifies three positive behaviors for two other students	
Organization	Final product is not well organized and does not reflect clear and focused thought.	Final product is somewhat organized and reflects but lacks clear and focused thought.	Final product is well organized and reflects clear and focused thought.	
Style and Language	Sentences arenot well constructed. Lacks use of high content vocabular.	Some sentences are well constructed and have varied structure and length. Some good use of high content vocabular.	Sentences are well constructed and have varied structure and length. Good use of high content vocabulary.	
Grammar	4-5 errors in grammar, mechanics, or spelling	2-3 errors in grammar, mechanics, or spelling	0-1 errors in grammar, mechanics, or spelling	
			Total	

Appendix V

Deserted Island Activity

Scenario: You and your friends chartered a small sailboat for the day and have headed out to sea for some much-needed rest and relaxation. An unexpected storm pops up and the strong wind gusts blow the sails violently. The boom swings around suddenly and strikes your captain in the head killing him instantly. Before you and your friends can process what has happened, lightning strikes the boat, causing the boat to catch on fire.

You and your friends spot a deserted island nearby and decide to swim for shore. Knowing that you will be forced to survive on the deserted island, you must decide which four items to carry ashore to guarantee your survival. Students must explain their rationale behind each of their selected items. Below are the items your group must choose from:

- Lamp
- Sunscreen
- Toilet paper
- Pot for cooking
- First aid kit
- Hiking boots
- Axe
- Flare gun
- Insect repellant
- Lighter
- Water filter
- Hammock
- Compass
- Mirror
- Knife
- Fishing rod
- Rope
- Rifle
- Tent

Next, have the groups explain their rationale for the selected items to the rest of the class. Then, provide each group with one of the following island challenges that they must encounter once they reach the deserted island.

- The island is inhabited by nomadic tribes of hunter gathers. Some of the tribes are extremely dangerous cannibals, but some tribes are quite friendly.
- The island is home to a tribe of children, no older than eight years old, who have been shipwrecked there for over a year.
- The island is devoid of dangerous animals, but there is a very strong storm every eight hours that destroys any structures and leaves everything soaking wet.
- Remember the movie, King Kong? Well, you are on that island. Not only do you have to survive, but you must avoid King Kong, dinosaurs, and very large flying

insects.

- The island is warm during the day. However, at night the temperature on the island drops to -30 degrees Celsius and everything freezes.
- The island is full of zombies who only come out at night. They will eat you if they see you, but they are afraid of the water.
- The island is quite nice. However, it's only 50 centimeters above sea level, ad it is sinking at a rate of 1 centimeter a day. You don't have long until the whole island is going to be underwater.
- The island is perfect. There are many fruits and wild animals to eat. You found a treasure chest full of gold. However, you were spotted with the chest by pirates and now they are coming after you and the treasure.
- Welcome to snake island. The island is covered with poisonous snakes. They are everywhere. The only place which is safe is the beach. However, at high tide the beach disappears.
- The island is filled with highly evolved apes, who dominate everything. The apes are very grumpy and don't like visitors.

Award 0-3 points according to the feasibility of their survival. After each group has presented, have them roll a die. This score is added to the group's points. Groups need four or more points to survive. A score of six or more is needed to thrive on the island. A score of nine would mean that everything the group planned for worked out.

Appendix W

Two Steps Questions

1. Were you ever the class clown?
2. Are you someone who is rarely on time?
3. Do you have a tattoo?
4. Do you have a significant other?
5. Do you have brothers or sisters?
6. Have you ever had to overcome adversity?
7. Did your team win the championship?
8. Do you own an Apple product?
9. Do you drive a truck?
10. Do you have a dog?
11. Did you ever have braces?
12. Did you ever break a bone?
13. Do you have blue eyes?
14. Have you ever attended a funeral?
15. Have you ever received a speeding ticket?

Appendix X

Twelve Personality Traits Rubric

	Deficient 0 points	Sufficient 10 points	Proficient 20 points	Points
3 traits defined for the student with strategies to strengthen them	Includes zero or one trait, defined for the student, with a strategy to strengthen it	Includes two traits, defined for the student, with strategies to strengthen them	Includes three traits, defined for the student, with strategies to strengthen them	
3 recent, peer-reviewed articles cited supporting examples	Includes zero or one peer-reviewed article with proper citations or two articles without proper citations	Includes two peer-reviewed articles with proper citations or three articles without proper citations	Includes three peer-reviewed articles with proper citations	
Organization	Final product is not well organized and does not reflect clear and focused thought.	Final product is somewhat organized and reflects but lacks clear and focused thought.	Final product is well organized and reflects clear and focused thought.	
Style and Language	Sentences arenot well constructed. Lacks use of high content vocabular.	Some sentences are well constructed and have varied structure and length. Some good use of high content vocabular.	Sentences are well constructed and have varied structure and length. Good use of high content vocabulary.	
Grammar	4-5 errors in grammar, mechanics, or spelling	2-3 errors in grammar, mechanics, or spelling	0-1 errors in grammar, mechanics, or spelling	
			Total	

Appendix Y

Cognitive Flexibility Rubric

	Deficient 0 points	Sufficient 10 points	Proficient 20 points	Points
3 cognitive flexibility abilities were identified with strategies to strengthen them	Includes zero or one cognitive flexibility ability was identified with a strategy strengthen it	Includes two cognitive flexibility abilities were identified with strategies to strengthen them	Includes three cognitive flexibility abilities were identified with strategies to strengthen them	
3 recent, peer-reviewed articles cited supporting examples	Includes zero or one peer-reviewed article with proper citations or two articles without proper citations	Includes two peer-reviewed articles with proper citations or three articles without proper citations	Includes three peer-reviewed articles with proper citations	
Organization	Final product is not well organized and does not reflect clear and focused thought.	Final product is somewhat organized and reflects but lacks clear and focused thought.	Final product is well organized and reflects clear and focused thought.	
Style and Language	Sentences are not well constructed. Lacks use of high content vocabular.	Some sentences are well constructed and have varied structure and length. Some good use of high content vocabular.	Sentences are well constructed and have varied structure and length. Good use of high content vocabulary.	
Grammar	4-5 errors in grammar, mechanics, or spelling	2-3 errors in grammar, mechanics, or spelling	0-1 errors in grammar, mechanics, or spelling	
			Total	

Appendix Z

3-2-1 Pyramid

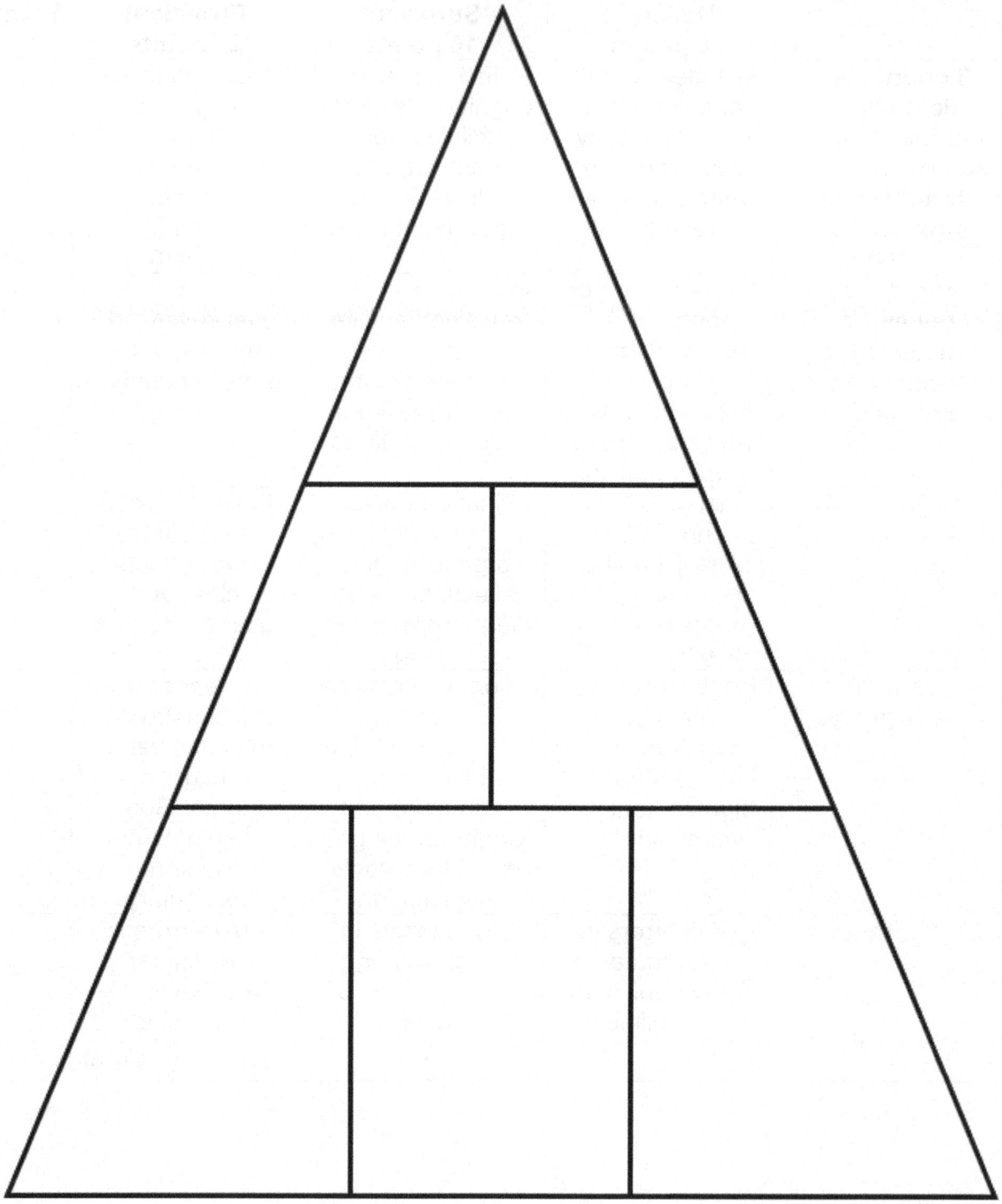

Appendix AA

Service-Learning Self-Reflection Rubric

	Deficient 0 points	Sufficient 12.5 points	Proficient 25 points	Points
Provides three factors that impacted the student's experience	Includes zero or one factor that impacted the student's experience	Includes two factors that impacted the student's experience	Includes three factors that impacted the student's experience	
Organization	Final product is not well organized and does not reflect clear and focused thought.	Final product is somewhat organized and reflects but lacks clear and focused thought.	Final product is well organized and reflects clear and focused thought.	
Style and Language	Sentences arenot well constructed. Lacks use of high content vocabular.	Some sentences are well constructed and have varied structure and length. Some good use of high content vocabular.	Sentences are well constructed and have varied structure and length. Good useof high content vocabulary.	
Grammar	4-5 errors in grammar, mechanics, or spelling	2-3 errors in grammar, mechanics, or spelling	0-1 errors in grammar, mechanics, or spelling	
			Total	

Appendix BB

Positive Thinking Quotes

1. "A positive attitude may not solve all our problems but that is the only option we have if we want to get out of problems." —Subodh Gupta
2. "If you don't like something, change it. If you can't change it, change your attitude." —Maya Angelou
3. "Optimism is the faith that leads to achievement; nothing can be done without hope." —Helen Keller
4. "Convince yourself every day that you are worthy of a good life. Let go of stress, breathe. Stay positive, all is well." —Germany Kent
5. "Positivity brings about a peace of mind which in turn relaxes your whole being." —Suman Arora
6. "To be an overachiever you have to be an over-believer." —Dabo Swinney
7. "Life is your seesaw. You may not stay balanced long, but you can aim for a high after every low." —Sanita Belgrave
8. The only time you fail is when you fall and stay down." —Stephen Richards
9. "To be a great champion you must believe you are the best. If you're not, pretend you are." —Muhammad Ali
10. "If you have a positive attitude and constantly strive to give your best effort, eventually you will overcome your immediate problems and find you are ready for greater challenges." —Pat Riley
11. "The greatest discovery of all the time is that a person can change his future by merely changing his attitude." —Marie Osmond
12. "Being what most people think is realistic is only a way of justifying negative thinking. Go for something great." —Dr. Bob Rotella
13. "Every day may not be good ... but there's something good in every day." —Alice Morse Earle
14. "You can often change your circumstances by changing your attitude."—Eleanor Roosevelt
15. "A positive attitude causes a chain reaction of positive thoughts, events, and outcomes. It is a catalyst, and it sparks extraordinary results." —Wade Boggs
16. "It isn't what you have or who you are or where you are or what you are doing that makes you happy or unhappy. It is what you think about it." —Dale Carnegie
17. "No one else makes us angry. We make ourselves angry when we surrender control of our attitude." —Jim Rohn
18. "Our attitude towards life determines life's attitude towards us." —John Mitchell
19. Everywhere you go, make positive deposits rather than negative withdrawals. You can be a people builder." —Joel Osteen
20. "Optimism is a happiness magnet. If you stay positive, good things and good people will be drawn to you." —Mary Lou Retton
21. "A positive attitude is not something that you acquire but instead is the active mental process of pointing your thoughts away from despair to that of rejoicing." —Byron R. Pulsifer
22. "Sometimes it takes a wrong turn to get you to the right place." —Mandy Hale
23. "It is good people who make good places." —Anna Sewell
24. "Excellence is not a skill. It is an attitude." —Ralph Marston

25. “Minds are like parachutes—they only function when open.” —Thomas Dewar
26. “Always bear in mind that your own resolution to succeed is more important than any other one thing.” —Abraham Lincoln
27. “The difference between ordinary and extraordinary is that little extra.” —Jimmy Johnson
28. “Make a game of finding something positive in every situation. Ninety-five percent of your emotions are determined by how you interpret events to yourself.” —Brian Tracy
29. “Keep your thoughts positive because your thoughts become your words. Keep your words positive because your words become your behavior. Keep your behavior positive because your behavior becomes your habits.” —Mahatma Gandhi
30. “Start each day by affirming peaceful, contented and happy attitudes and your days will tend to be pleasant and successful.” —Norman Vincent Peale
31. “A healthy attitude is contagious but don’t wait to catch it from others. Be a carrier.” —Unknown
32. “The struggle you’re in today is developing the strength you need tomorrow.” —Robert Tew
33. “A bad attitude is like a flat tire. You won’t get anywhere until you change it.” —Unknown
34. “Positive thinkers see possibilities, choose to pursue them, and more easily bounce back from failure. They have more energy and hope and encounter more opportunities.” —Stan Toler
35. “There is too much negativity in the world. Do your best to make sure you aren't contributing to it.” —Germany Kent

Appendix CC

Daily Routine Log

Energy Level Definitions:

- 5—I feel great.
- 4—I feel good.
- 3—I feel neither energized nor tired.
- 2—I feel tired.
- 1—I feel exhausted.

Time	Activity	Energy Level (1-5)
12:00 am – 12:59 am		
1:00 am – 1.59 am		
2:00 am – 2:59 am		
3:00 am – 3:59 am		
4:00 am – 4:59 am		
5:00 am – 5:59 am		
6:00 am – 6:59 am		
7:00 am – 7:59 am		
8:00 am – 8:59 am		
9:00 am – 9:59 am		
10:00 am – 10:59 am		
11:00 am – 11:59 am		
12:00 pm – 12:59 pm		
1:00 pm – 1:59 pm		
2:00 pm – 2:59 pm		
3:00 pm – 3:59 pm		
4:00 pm – 4:59 pm		
5:00 pm – 5:59 pm		
6:00 pm – 6:59 pm		
7:00 pm – 7:59 pm		
8:00 pm – 8:59 pm		
9:00 pm – 9:59 pm		
10:00 pm – 10:59 pm		
11:00 pm – 11:59 pm		

Appendix DD

Group Roles Rubric

	Deficient 0 points	Sufficient 12.5 points	Proficient 25 points	Points
Explains group role the student finds most comfortable with a relevant example supporting their rationale	Does not include most comfortable role or an example supporting rationale	Includes explanation of most comfortable role, but fails to provide an example supporting rationale	Includes explanation of most comfortable role with an example supporting rationale	
Explains group role the student finds least comfortable witha relevant example supporting their rationale	Does not include most comfortable role or an example supporting rationale	Includes explanation of most comfortable role, but fails to provide an example supporting rationale	Includes explanation of most comfortable role with an example supporting rationale	
Organization	Final product is not well organized and does not reflect clear and focused thought.	Final product is somewhat organized and reflects but lacks clear and focused thought.	Final product is well organized and reflects clear and focused thought.	
Style and Language	Sentences are not well constructed. Lacks use of high content vocabular.	Some sentences are well constructed and have varied structure and length. Some good use of high content vocabular.	Sentences are well constructed and have varied structure and length. Good use of high content vocabulary.	
Grammar	4-5 errors in grammar, mechanics, or spelling	2-3 errors in grammar, mechanics, or spelling	0-1 errors in grammar, mechanics, or spelling	
			Total	

Appendix EE

Information Use Rubric

	Deficient 0 points	Sufficient 10 points	Proficient 20 points	Points
Identifies 3 appropriate sources of information and cites them properly	Includes zero or one appropriate source for the information or does not include proper citations	Identifies two appropriate sources for information with proper citations	Identifies three appropriate sources for information with proper citations	
Includes an easy-to-understand, visually appealing graphic organizer of the factors impacting the case scenario	Does not include a graphic organizer	Includes a graphic organizer but is either not easy-to-understand or not visually appealing	Includes an easy-to-understand, visually appealing graphic organizer of the factors impacting the case scenario	
Organization	Final product is not well organized and does not reflect clear and focused thought.	Final product is somewhat organized and reflects but lacks clear and focused thought.	Final product is well organized and reflects clear and focused thought.	
Style and Language	Sentences are not well constructed. Lacks use of high content vocabular.	Some sentences are well constructed and have varied structure and length. Some good use of high content vocabular.	Sentences are well constructed and have varied structure and length. Good use of high content vocabulary.	
Grammar	4-5 errors in grammar, mechanics, or spelling	2-3 errors in grammar, mechanics, or spelling	0-1 errors in grammar, mechanics, or spelling	
			Total	

Appendix FF

Technology Use Rubric

	Deficient 0 points	Sufficient 10 points	Proficient 20 points	Points
Technology was explained in an easy-to-understand manner	Technology was not explained	Technology was explained, but some clarity was lacking	Technology was explained in an easy-to-understand manner	
Includes three advantages to using the technology	Includes zero or one advantage to using the technology	Includes two advantages to using the technology	Includes three advantages to using the technology	
Includes three disadvantages to using the technology	Includes zero or one disadvantage to using the technology	Includes two disadvantages to using the technology	Includes three disadvantages to using the technology	
Includes one glow, grow, and question for two fellow classmates	Does not include one glow, grow, and question for two fellow classmates	Includes one glow, grow, and question for one fellow classmate	Includes one glow, grow, and question for two fellow classmates	
Style, Language, and Grammar	Sentences are not well constructed. Lacks use of high content vocabular. 4-5 errors in grammar, mechanics, or spelling.	Some sentences are well constructed and have varied structure and length. Some good use of high content vocabular.2-3 errors in grammar, mechanics, or spelling.	Sentences are well constructed and have varied structure and length. Good use of high content vocabulary. 0-1 errors in grammar, mechanics, or spelling.	
			Total	

Appendix GG

Dynamic Thinking Self-Assessment Quiz

Directions: Answer the following questions to determine if you think dynamically.

1. Do you accept the status quo and go with the flow?
2. Do you shy away from new ideas, foods, cultures, and experiences?
3. Do you avoid taking big risks?
4. Do you avoid challenging authority, even when you do not agree?
5. Do you participate in traditions even when you do not understand them?
6. Do you almost always support the agenda positions of your chosen political party?
7. Do you usually attempt to solve problems with logic?
8. Do you concentrate on here and now?

If you answered yes to any of the questions above, you could benefit from improving your dynamic thinking skills (Ozovek, 2016, February 23).

Appendix HH

Disease Population Graph

Note: This data is not factual. It is completely fabricated for the purpose of developing systems thinking skills.

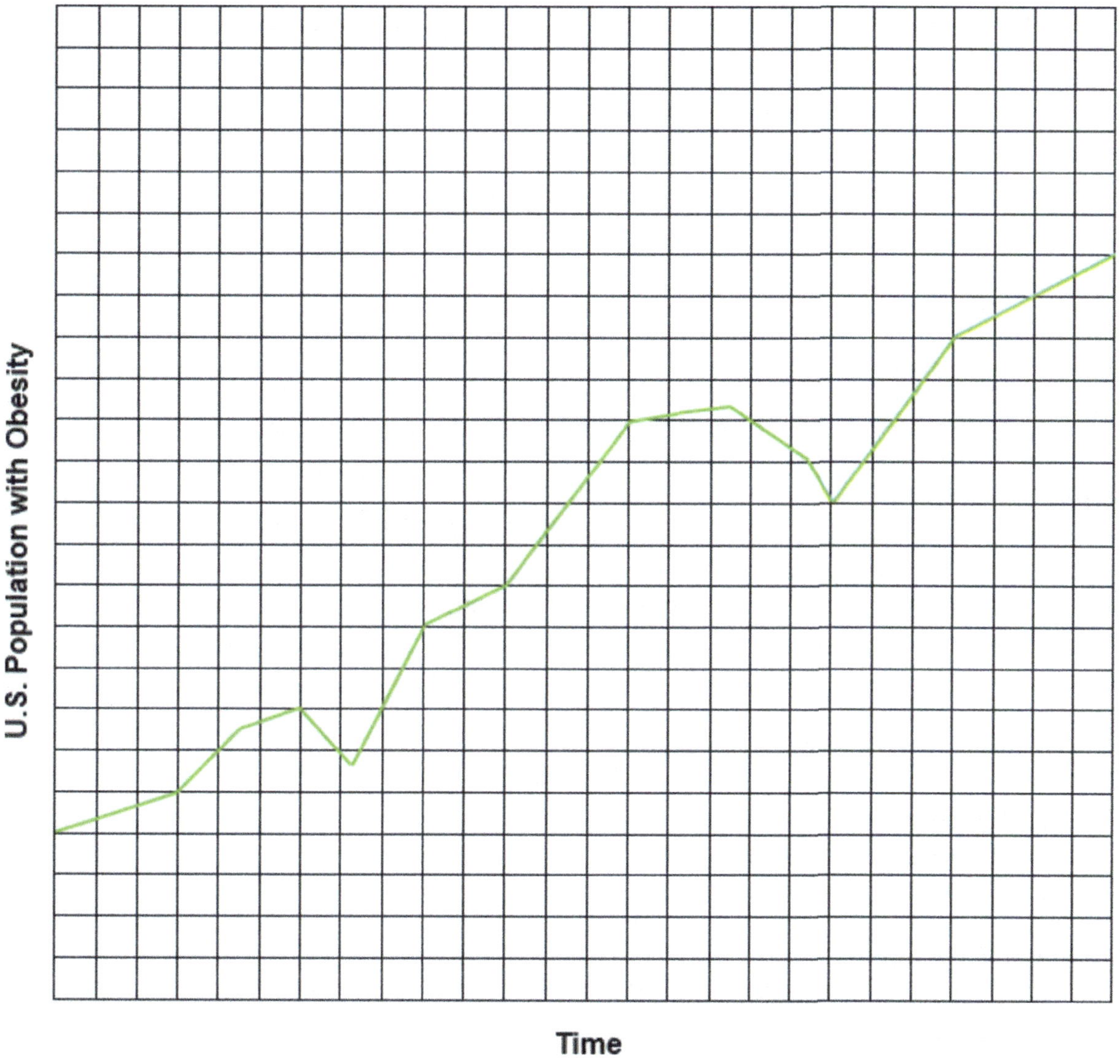

Appendix II

Systems Thinking Prompts

Directions: Complete this assignment by answering all the questions based upon the hypotheses generated by your group.

List of hypotheses generated.

H_o
H_a

H_o
H_a

H_o
H_a

System as a Cause Thinking

1. Who or what entity is responsibility for the problem?
2. Is the problem related to the related policies and procedures?

Forest Thinking

3. What are all the factors that contribute to the problem?
4. What do you know about all the factors?
5. Is there a relationship among all the factors that contribute to the problem?

Operational Thinking

6. What is causing the problem?

Closed Loop Thinking

7. Is this an ongoing process or a solitary event?
8. What is the affect over time?

Quantitative Thinking

9. Can the problem be quantified?
10. Can the problem be measured?

Scientific Thinking

11. How can the problem be tested?

Appendix JJ

Systems Thinking Rubric

	Deficient 0 points	Sufficient 12.5 points	Proficient 25 points	Points
Answers all 11 questions properly	Answers five or less questions properly	Answers at least 6 questions properly	Answers all 11 questions properly	
Organization	Final product is not well organized and does not reflect clear and focused thought.	Final product is somewhat organized and reflects but lacks clear and focused thought.	Final product is well organized and reflects clear and focused thought.	
Style and Language	Sentences are not well constructed. Lacks use of high content vocabular.	Some sentences are well constructed and have varied structure and length. Some good use of high content vocabular.	Sentences are well constructed and have varied structure and length. Good use of high content vocabulary.	
Grammar	4-5 errors in grammar, mechanics, or spelling	2-3 errors in grammar, mechanics, or spelling	0-1 errors in grammar, mechanics, or spelling	
			Total	

Appendix KK

Random Acts of Kindness Reflection

Date and time:

Location:

Act of Kindness:

Recipient's name (if obtained):

Reflection:

What was your overall mood at the time you performed the kindness?

What was the response of the recipient?

How did performing the act make you feel?

Total:

Appendix LL

Kind Person Award

This Certificate of Recognition is Awarded

to

____

for

Random Acts of Kindness

Thank you for being a kind person.

______________________ ______________________

Date *Authority*

Appendix MM

Self-Awareness Prompts (Horey, 2019)

Directions: Select a different prompt to write about every day. Journal entries should be a minimum of 500 words.

1. How can I be more flexible right now?
2. What are you trying to control?
3. Am I consistently showing up?
4. To whom am I comparing myself right now?
5. Am I afraid to be seen?
6. Do I surround myself with people who elevate me?
7. How can I deepen my trust right now?
8. What excuses am I making right now?
9. Who am I blaming right now?
10. What can I do to make a difference?
11. What is my most limiting belief?
12. Who am I ready to forgive?
13. Am I focused on what I want the most?
14. What are the dominant emotions that run my life?
15. What risk can I take today?
16. When was the last time I could not stop laughing?
17. What feeling am I resisting right now?
18. Am I allowing fear to stop my progression?
19. Do I believe I am worthy?
20. Do I know all my strengths and am I using them?
21. What am I grateful for right now?
22. Am I communicating my needs?
23. What am I afraid of?
24. What boundaries do I need to create to strengthen my relationships?
25. How create more self-love and compassion in my daily life?
26. What is lacking in my life right now?
27. How can I be more kind to myself?
28. How can I be more kind to others?
29. How can I release my inner critic?
30. Who can I serve today?
31. Do my beliefs match my dreams?
32. Do I trust myself?
33. What passion am I ready to pursue?
34. What am I most afraid of losing?
35. Am I apologizing for my truth?
36. Am I on the right path?
37. Do I trust in my own direction?
38. Who am I passing judgment on right now?
39. What am I looking for outside myself, that is already within me?
40. What would I do today if it were easy?
41. How can I surrender more in this moment?

42. Am I willing to rise to the occasion?
43. What is my body telling me right now?
44. If your body could talk, what would it say about you right now?
45. Am I ready to let go of shame?
46. How can I use my voice today?
47. Where can I create more space in my life?
48. Am I reacting from my head or my heart?
49. Am I focused on losing or gaining?
50. What am I scared of losing?

Appendix NN

In So Many Words

Directions: List the steps for making a peanut butter and jelly sandwich in exactly 25 words. Use the spaces below to enter your words. Add punctuation as needed.

Example:

1	Go	2	to	3	the	4	kitchen.	5	Then,

Steps:

1		2		3		4		5	
6		7		8		9		10	
11		12		13		14		15	
16		17		18		19		20	
21		22		23		24		25	

Directions: List the steps for making a peanut butter and jelly sandwich in exactly 15 words. Use the spaces below to enter your words. Add punctuation as needed.

Steps:

1		2		3		4		5	
6		7		8		9		10	
11		12		13		14		15	

Directions: List the steps for making a peanut butter and jelly sandwich in exactly 5 words. Use the spaces below to enter your words. Add punctuation as needed.

Steps:

1		2		3		4		5	

Appendix OO

Rhetoric Speech Prompts

Directions: Prepare a three-minute speech, utilizing one of the prompts below. The speech should employ either logos, ethos, or pathos to persuade the board to rule in favor of your proposal.

Prompts:

1. You will be attending a city council meeting as a representative of "X" social group. You must convince the city council board to approve an "investment" that willbenefit the social group.
2. You will be attending a hospital administration meeting as a representative of "X"department. You must convince the city council board to approve an "investment" that will benefit the department.
3. You will be attending a university board meeting as a representative of "X" department. You must convince the university board to approve an "investment" thatwill benefit the department.
4. You will be attending a government meeting as a representative of "X" subgroup.You must convince the government to approve a "new law" that will benefit the subgroup.
5. You are running for an elected position as a representative of "X" subgroup. Youmust convince the public to vote for you.

Appendix PP

Rhetoric Speech Rubric

Presentation Skills	Extremely Inappropriate (1 point)	Inappropriate (2 points)	Neither Appropriate or Inappropriate (2.5	Inappropriate (4 points)	Extremely Appropriate (5 points)	**Total**
Behaviors						
Confidence						
Posture						
Clear purposeful message						
Fluent						
Correct syntax						
Authoritative						
Powerful						
Appropriate body movements						
Eye contact						
Speech Content and Presentation	Bad (2.5 points)	Neither Good nor Bad (5 points)	Good (7.5 points)	Good (7.5 points)	Outstanding (10 points)	**Total**
Invention— ability to create and develop aspeech						
Composition—chose the appropriate structure for the rhetoric (i.e., logos, ethos, or pathos)						
Elocution—expressed oneself appropriately						
Memory— memorized the material needed for the speech						
Delivery— delivered the speech in a convincing way						

Note. Adapted from: U.S. Department of Education. Employability Skills Framework, Retrieved [March 29, 2023], from https://cte.ed.gov/initiatives/employability-skills- framework

Appendix QQ

Professional Plan

Directions: Develop at least one measurable, professional goal for next two, five, and ten years. Add to the goals as needed.

1. In the next two years, I will…
2. In the next five years, I will…
3. In the next ten years, I will…

Directions: Outline the necessary steps you will need to complete to accomplish your goals (e.g., obtain XYZ certification). Add to your steps as needed.

Step 1:
Step 2:
Step 3:
Step 4:
Step 5:

Directions: Describe in detail what results (e.g., obtain XYZ certification, salary, status) you must obtain to determine the effectiveness of your intervention.

Result 1:
Result 2:
Result 3:
Result 4:
Result 5:

Appendix RR

Employability Skills Competency Evaluation

Directions: Complete an assessment of a fellow classmate's competence level with employability skills by placing a checkmark in the corresponding column. Provide constructive feedback with suggestions in the applicable spaces below each sub competency.

1-Poor, 2-Below Average, 3-Average, 4-Better Than Average, 5-Excellent

Applied Knowledge					
	1	**2**	**3**	**4**	**5**
Applied academic skills					
Feedback:					
Suggestions:					
Critical thinking skills					
Feedback:					
Suggestions:					
Effective Relationships					
	1	**2**	**3**	**4**	**5**
Interpersonal skills					
Feedback:					
Suggestions:					
Personal qualities					
Feedback:					
Suggestions:					
Workplace Skills					
	1	**2**	**3**	**4**	**5**
Communication					
Feedback:					
Suggestions:					
Resource management					
Feedback:					

Suggestions:					
Information use					
Feedback:					
Suggestions:					
Systems thinking					
Feedback:					
Suggestions:					

Adapted from: U.S. Department of Education. Employability Skills Framework, Retrieved [March 29, 2023], from https://cte.ed.gov/initiatives/employability-skills-framework

Appendix SS

Constructive Feedback Debriefing Rubric

	Deficient 0 points	**Sufficient 10 points**	**Proficient 20 points**	**Points**
Provides specific constructive criticism with examples and suggestions	Provides confusing criticism with or without examples and suggestions.	Provides partially clear constructive criticism with examples and suggestions.	Provides specific constructive criticism with examples and suggestions.	
Asks well-developed clarifying questions	Asks poorly developed clarifying questions.	Asks partially developed clarifying questions.	Asks well-developed clarifying questions.	
Organization	Final product is not well organized and does not reflect clear and focused thought.	Final product is somewhat organized and reflects but lacks clear and focused thought.	Final product is well organized and reflects clear and focused thought.	
Style and Language	Sentences are not well constructed. Lacks use of high content vocabular.	Some sentences arewell constructed andhave varied structureand length. Some good use of high content vocabular.	Sentences are well constructed and have varied structure and length. Good use of high content vocabulary.	
Grammar	4-5 errors in grammar, mechanics, orspelling	2-3 errors in grammar, mechanics, or spelling	0-1 errors in grammar, mechanics, or spelling	
			Total	

Appendix TT

Professional Plan to Improve Competence

Area lacking the most competence:

Directions: Develop at least one measurable, professional goal for the next two, five, and ten years. Add to the goals as needed.

1. In the next two years, I will…
2. In the next five years, I will…
3. In the next ten years, I will…

Directions: Outline the necessary steps you will need to complete to accomplish your goals (e.g., obtain XYZ certification). Add to your steps as needed.

Step 1:
Step 2:
Step 3:
Step 4:
Step 5:

Directions: Describe in detail what results (e.g., obtain XYZ certification, salary, status) you must obtain to determine the effectiveness of your intervention.

Result 1:
Result 2:
Result 3:
Result 4:
Result 5:

Area lacking the second most competence:

Directions: Develop at least one measurable, professional goal for next two, five, and ten years. Add to the goals as needed.

1. In the next two years, I will…
2. In the next five years, I will…
3. In the next ten years, I will…

Directions: Outline the necessary steps you will need to complete to accomplish your goals (e.g., obtain XYZ certification). Add to your steps as needed.

Step 1:
Step 2:
Step 3:
Step 4:
Step 5:

Directions: Describe in detail what results (e.g., obtain XYZ certification, salary, status) you must obtain to determine the effectiveness of your intervention.

Result 1:
Result 2:
Result 3:
Result 4:
Result 5:

Area lacking the third most competence:

Directions: Develop at least one measurable, professional goal for next two, five, and ten years. Add to the goals as needed.

1. In the next two years, I will…
2. In the next five years, I will…
3. In the next ten years, I will…

Directions: Outline the necessary steps you will need to complete to accomplish your goals (e.g., obtain XYZ certification). Add to your steps as needed.

Step 1:
Step 2:
Step 3:
Step 4:
Step 5:

Directions: Describe in detail what results (e.g., obtain XYZ certification, salary, status) you must obtain to determine the effectiveness of your intervention.

Result 1:
Result 2:
Result 3:
Result 4:
Result 5:

Appendix UU

Evaluation Types

Directions: Place a checkmark in the column that indicates if the evaluation is goal-based, process-based, or outcomes-based.

	Goal-based	Process-based	Outcome-based
1. Effectiveness of the flu vaccination in controlling incidence of infection			
2. Customer loyalty			
3. Likelihood that obtaining a certification increases chances of employment			
4. Comparison of surgical approaches			
5. Reassessment of patient progress			
6. Students' ability to properly perform goniometric measurements			
7. Student satisfaction with student to teacher ratio in lab			
8. Effectiveness of recruitment strategies			
9. Ability of a vaccination to lower infection rates by75%			
10. Efficiency of mail delivery			
11. Ability to lose 10 pounds in 5 weeks			
12. Did students receive the proper type of instruction			
13. Effectiveness of training schedule			
14. Impact of a Super Bowl commercial			
15. Students' ability to demonstrate course learning outcomes			
16. Sustainability of low-income school lunch assistance program			
17. Ability to win the race			
18. Impact of low-income school lunch assistance program			
19. Accessibility of healthcare services			
20. Patient adherence to a treatment regime			

Appendix VV

Evaluation Types Answer Key

Directions: Place a checkmark in the column that indicates if the evaluation is goal-based, process-based, or outcomes-based.

	Goal-based	Process-based	Outcome-based
1. Effectiveness of the flu vaccination in controlling incidence of infection			√
2. Customer loyalty			√
3. Likelihood that obtaining a certification increases chances of employment	√		
4. Comparison of surgical approaches		√	
5. Reassessment of patient progress			√
6. Students' ability to properly perform goniometric measurements	√		
7. Student satisfaction with student to teacher ratio in lab		√	
8. Effectiveness of recruitment strategies			√
9. Ability of a vaccination to lower infection rates by 75%			√
10. Efficiency of mail delivery		√	
11. Ability to lose 10 pounds in 5 weeks	√		
12. Did students receive the proper type of instruction		√	
13. Effectiveness of training schedule			√
14. Impact of a Super Bowl commercial			√
15. Students' ability to demonstrate course learning outcomes			√
16. Sustainability of low-income school lunch assistance program		√	
17. Ability to win the race	√		
18. Impact of low-income school lunch assistance program		√	
19. Accessibility of healthcare services			√
20. Patient adherence to a treatment regime			√

Appendix WW

Branding Decisions Part 1

Directions: Describe the way each font type makes you feel.

Samantha Green	
Samantha Green	
Samantha Green	
Samantha Green	
Samantha Green	
Samantha Green	
Samantha Green	
Samantha Green	
Samantha Green	
Samantha Green	
Samantha Green	
Samantha Green	
Samantha Green	
Samantha Green	
Samantha Green	
Samantha Green	
Samantha Green	
Samantha Green	
Samantha Green	
Samantha Green	

Appendix XX

Branding Decisions Part 2

Directions: Match each descriptive word with the image.

Descriptions: Wonder, Happiness, Celebration, Complexity, Innovative, Splendor, Movement, Caring, Time, Curiosity, Unity, Progression, Amazement, Tranquility, Network, Healthy, Softness, Convention, Precision, Comforting, Wonder, Freshness, Temperature, Speed, Rhythm, Handmade

	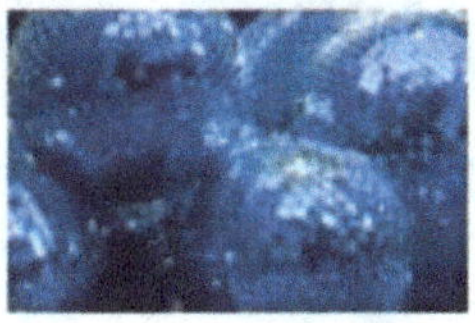			
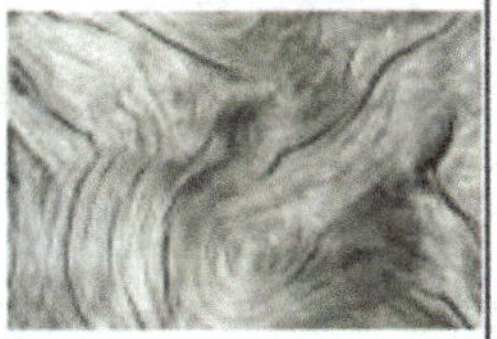			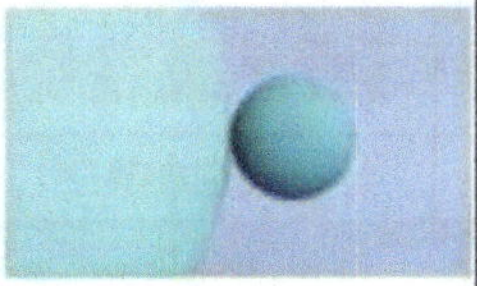	
		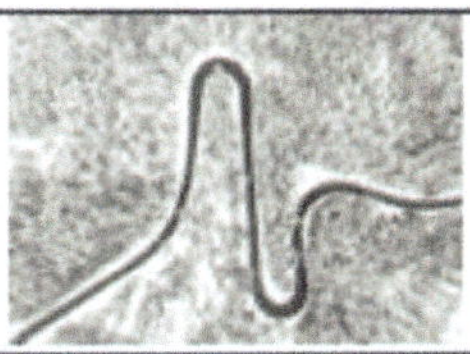		

Appendix YY

Branding Decisions Part 2 Answer Key

Directions: Match each descriptive word with the image.

Descriptions: Wonder, Happiness, Celebration, Complexity, Innovative, Splendor, Movement, Caring, Time, Curiosity, Unity, Progression, Amazement, Tranquility, Network, Healthy, Softness, Convention, Precision, Comforting, Wonder, Freshness, Temperature, Speed, Rhythm, Handmade

Splendor	Temperature	Tranquility	Speed	Softness

Healthy	Freshness	Unity	Happiness	Movement

Innovative	Celebration	Network	Convention	Caring
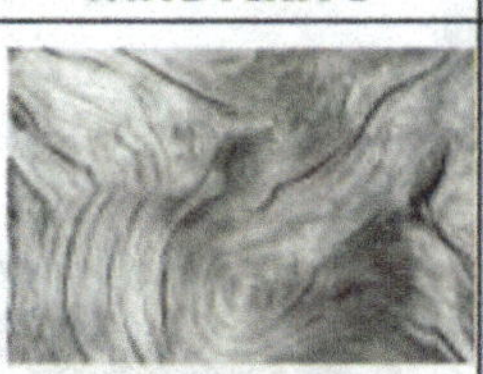			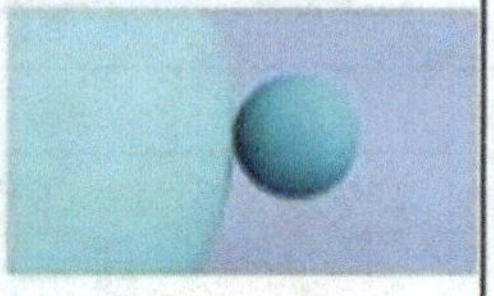	
Time	Amazement	Complexity	Precision	Comforting
		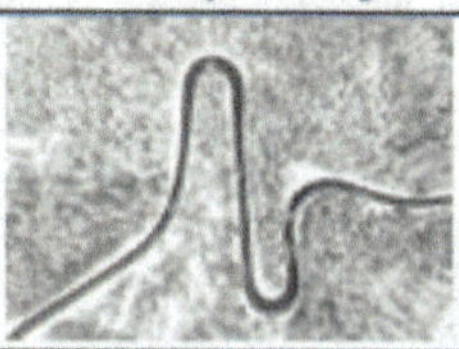	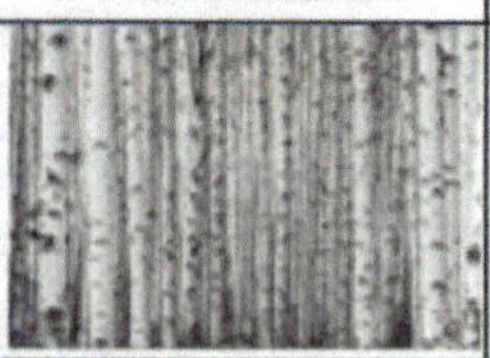	
Curiosity	Progression	Rhythm	Wonder	Handmade

Appendix ZZ

Elevator Pitch Rubric

	Deficient 0 points	Sufficient 5 points	Proficient 10 points	Points
Provides well-developed persuasive argument.	Argument lacks persuasion.	Provides partially developed persuasive argument.	Provides well developed persuasive argument.	
Emphasizes skills in a humble manner.	Does not emphasize skills.	Emphasizes skills, but not in a humble manner.	Emphasizes skills in a humble manner.	
Conveys positivity and flexibility.	Conveys negativity and inflexibility.	Lacks some positivity and flexibility.	Conveys positivity and flexibility.	
Delivers a meaningful and concise message.	Delivers a meaningful and concise message.	Delivers a meaningful message, but in a cohesive manner.	Delivers a meaningful and concise message.	
Declares professional goals.	Does not declare professional goals.	Declares professional goals, but not is a concise manner.	Declares professional goals.	
Speak directly to the audience.	Does not speak directly to the audience.	Speak directly to the audience some of the time.	Speak directly to the audience.	
Message is simple, focused, and organized.	Message is not simple and focused.	Message is somewhat simple and focused.	Final product is simple, well organized and reflects clear and focused thought.	
Provides a business card.	Does not provide a business card.		Provides a business card.	
Style and Language	Sentences are not well constructed. Lacks use of high content vocabular.	Some sentences are well constructed and have varied structure and length. Some good use of high content vocabular.	Sentences are well constructed and have varied structure and length. Good use of high content vocabulary.	
Grammar	4-5 errors in grammar.	2-3 errors in grammar.	0-1 errors in grammar.	
			Total	

Appendix AAA

Resume' Rubric

	Deficient 0 points	Sufficient 12.5 points	Proficient 25 points	Points
Visually appealing and balanced	Not visually appealing or balanced	Somewhat visually appealing and balanced	Visually appealing and balanced	
Organization	Final product is not well organized and does not reflect clear and focused thought. Sections are not listed in reverse chronological order.	Final product is somewhat organized and reflects but lacks clear and focused thought. Some sections are written in reverse chronological order.	Final product is well organized and reflects clear and focused thought. Each section is written in reverse chronological order.	
Style and Language	Not well-constructed, too wordy, with poor content vocabulary.	Somewhat well-constructed and concise with some high content vocabulary.	Well-constructed and concise with high content vocabulary.	
Grammar	4 or 5 errors in grammar, mechanics, or spelling	2-3 errors in grammar, mechanics, or spelling	0-1 errors in grammar, mechanics, or spelling	
			Total	

Appendix BBB

Cover Letter Rubric

	Deficient 0 points	Sufficient 10 points	Proficient 20 points	Points
Visually appealing and balanced	Not visually appealing or balanced	Somewhat visually appealing and balanced	Visually appealing and balanced	
Cover letter content adds clarification and detail to the resume	Cover letter rehashes content of the resume	Cover letter content adds clarification, but partially rehashes content of the resume	Cover letter content adds clarification and detail to the resume	
Organization	Final product is not well organized and does not reflect clear and focused thought.	Final product is somewhat organized and reflects but lacks clear and focused thought.	Final product is well organized and reflects clearand focused thought.	
Style and Language	Not well-constructed, too wordy, with poor content vocabulary.	Somewhat well-constructed and concise with some high content vocabulary.	Well-constructed and concise withhigh content vocabulary.	
Grammar	4 or 5 errors in grammar, mechanics, or spelling	2-3 errors in grammar, mechanics, or spelling	0-1 errors in grammar, mechanics, or spelling	
			Total	

Appendix CCC

First Impressions Feedback

Feedback for:

First Impression:

Three Positives:

1.

2.

3.

Three Areas for Improvement:

1.

Suggestion:

2.

Suggestion:

3.

Suggestion:

Appendix DDD

Employability Skills Feedback Tool

Feedback for:

Directions: Evaluate the resume and cover letter and place a checkmark in the applicable column to indicate if the resume and cover letter convey the ability to perform the skills.

Ability to convey competence	**Not at all**	**Somewhat**	**Clearly**
Applied Academic Skills			
Reading skills			
Writing skills			
Math strategies/procedures			
Scientific principles/procedures			
Critical Thinking Skills			
Think creatively			
Think critically			
Make sound decisions			
Solve problems			
Reason			
Plan and organize			
Interpersonal Skills			
Understand teamwork and work withothers			
Respond to customer needs			
Exercise leadership			
Negotiate to resolve conflict			
Respect individual differences			
Personal Qualities			
Demonstrate responsibility and self-discipline			
Adaptability and flexibility			
Work independently			
Demonstrate a willingness to learn			
Demonstrate integrity			
Demonstrate professionalism			
Take initiative			
Display a positive attitude and sense of self-worth			
Take responsibility for professionalgrowth			

Resource Management			
Manage time			
Manage money			
Manage resources			
Manage personnel			
Information Use			
Locate			
Organize			
Use			
Analyze			
Communicate			
Communication Skills			
Communicate verbally			
Listen actively			
Comprehend written material			
Convey information in writing			
Observe carefully			
Systems Thinking			
Understand and use systems			
Monitor systems			
Improve systems			
Technology Use			
Understand and use technology			

Adapted from: U.S. Department of Education. Employability Skills Framework, Retrieved [March 29, 2023], from https://cte.ed.gov/initiatives/employability-skills-framework

Appendix EEE

Interview Rubric

Presentation Skills	Extremely Inappropriate (1 point)	Inappropriate (2 points)	Neither Appropriate nor Inappropriate (3 points)	Appropriate(4 points)	Extremely Appropriate (5 points)	Total
First impression						
Appearance						
Nonverbal behavior						
Verbal communication						
Resume explanation						
Selling yourself						
Preparation						
Confidence						
Answers questions thoroughly						
Asks appropriate questions						
			Interview Grade			

Appendix FFF

Thank You Note Rubric

	Deficient 0 points	Sufficient 10 points	Proficient 20 points	Points
Expresses gratitude for the person's or people's time and consideration	Does not express gratitude for the person's or people's time and consideration	Expresses gratitude for the person's or people's time or consideration	Expresses gratitude for the person's or people's time and consideration	
Clarifies interest rogarding the position	Does not clarify interest regarding the position		Clarifies interest regarding the position	
Organization	Final product is not well organized and does not reflect clear and focused thought.	Final product is somewhat organized and reflects but lacks clear and focused thought.	Final product is well organized and reflects clear and focused thought.	
Style and Language	Not well-constructed, too wordy, with poor content vocabulary.	Somewhat well-constructed and concise with some high content vocabulary.	Well-constructed and concise with high content vocabulary.	
Grammar	4 or 5 errors in grammar, mechanics, or spelling	2-3 errors in grammar, mechanics, or spelling	0-1 errors in grammar, mechanics, or spelling	
			Total	

Appendix GGG

Negotiation Scenarios

1. The garbage pick-up in your neighborhood is scheduled very early in the morning. Because of this, neighbors, who are renting, put their garbage out the night before trash pick-up is scheduled. Your neighbor simply places the garbage bags by the side of the road. Because the bags are not placed inside a garbage cans, the raccoons will often tear into the bags, spilling garbage all over the sidewalk adjacent to your driveway. As a result, you often end up picking up their garbage when you return home from work at the end of the day. You would like for your neighbor to use the garbage can provided by the homeowner instead of placing the bags on the side of the road.
2. Your neighborhood has a community beach. During the summer months neighborhood families will routinely invite friends and family to join them at the beach for various summer recreational activities. You want to organize a neighborhood beach clean-up day and must convince your neighbors to volunteer their time.
3. Your boss gave you a deadline on a big project. You have been working on this project for almost a month. You realize at this point, that the scope of the project is much larger than initially anticipated. You must either convince your boss to postpone the deadline or convince them to allocate some extra manpower to the project.

Appendix HHH

Negotiation Rubric

	Yes/No
The problem or issue was stated without assuming shared values	
Needs of both parties were identified and no assumptions were made	
The problem or issue was restated with inclusion of needs with the appropriate amount of detail	
Synthesized the information throughout the process	
Used objective criteria to make decisions	
Possible solutions were presented	
Consensus was reached regarding the best solution	
Displayed active listening and reflection	
Focused on preserving the relationship instead of being "right"	
Redirected personal attacks onto the problem at hand	
Add 10 points for every "yes" answer to determine grade	

Appendix III

Lifelong Learning Prompts (Ray, 2008)

Directions: Answer the questions under each category.

Financial
- What is your ideal annual income?
- What is your dream net worth?
- How much do you want financial freedom?

Relational
- Do you spend quality time by yourself?
- Do you treat yourself how you want others to treat you?
- Do you allow yourself enough personal time?
- What things do you do that contribute to your happiness?
- Do you have a dream mate?
- To which clubs and associations do you belong?

Mental
- How many books and/or journals do you read a month?
- How many seminars have you attended this year?
- Are you routinely in control of your emotions?
- Do you perform reflective journaling on a routine basis?

Physical
- What is your dream weight?
- How many days to your work out?
- Do you have the physical things you want (e.g., house, car)?
- Where do you want to travel?
- What skills do you want to learn?

Spiritual
- What inspires you?
- Do you feel at peace?
- Do you have a spiritual routine that is conducive to your well-being?

Professional
- What is your dream job?
- What are your professional strengths and weaknesses?
- What do you want to accomplish professionally?
- What do you want to be known for professionally?
- Are you a mentor to someone?
- Is there a certification you desire?

Appendix JJJ

Lifelong Learning Plan

Directions: For each of the pillars listed below, develop two, five, and ten-year goals. Then outline the steps to obtaining those goals.

Financial

Goal: In the next two years, I will…

Steps:

Goal: In the next five years, I will…

Steps:

Goal: In the next ten years, I will…

Steps:

Relational

Goal: In the next two years, I will…

Steps:

Goal: In the next five years, I will…

Steps:

Goal: In the next ten years, I will…

Steps:

Mental

Goal: In the next two years, I will…

Steps:

Goal: In the next five years, I will…

Steps:

Goal: In the next ten years, I will…

Steps:

Physical

Goal: In the next two years, I will…

Steps:

Goal: In the next five years, I will…

Steps:

Goal: In the next ten years, I will…

Steps:

Spiritual

Goal: In the next two years, I will…

Steps:

Goal: In the next five years, I will…

Steps:

Goal: In the next ten years, I will…

Steps:

Professional

Goal: In the next two years, I will…

Steps:

Goal: In the next five years, I will…

Steps:

Goal: In the next ten years, I will…

Steps:

Made in United States
North Haven, CT
06 November 2026

21875925R00141